AS IT IS IN
HEAVEN

AS IT IS IN
HEAVEN

*A Biblical, Historical, and Theological Introduction
to the Traditional Church and Her Worship*

FR. PAUL A. F. CASTELLANO

As It Is in Heaven: A Biblical, Historical, and Theological Introduction to the Traditional Church and Her Worship

Published by Wheatmark®
2030 East Speedway Boulevard, Suite 106
Tucson, Arizona 85719 USA
www.wheatmark.com

ISBN: 978-1-62787-844-9 (paperback)
ISBN: 978-1-62787-845-6 (ebook)
LCCN: 2021901763

Bulk ordering discounts are available through Wheatmark, Inc. For more information, email orders@wheatmark.com or call 1-888-934-0888.

rev202101

THIS BOOK IS DEDICATED TO MY three sons, whom, though no longer with me, I know I will see again;

to the late Dr. R. C. Sproul, who influenced me theologically, intellectually, historically, philosophically, and spiritually more than I could ever adequately express;

to Prof. Dr. John M. Frame, who, more than any one professor, besides academically challenging me, lived the most Christlike life I have ever personally encountered;

to Prof. Dr. Michael S. Horton, who inspired the writing of this work many years ago by his tireless example of what it takes to diligently put forth the effort to write a book. A select few are as prolific;

and, finally, to all those, young and old, who have a thirst, desire, and longing to know the deep things of the God of the universe and trusted that there was something in this work that might help satiate that desire.

To all of you, I am forever indebted.

Soli Deo Gloria

Contents

Preface

IN 1992, I HAD THE UNIQUE privilege and experience of worshiping with Dr. John Gerstner, the late renowned Presbyterian theologian, at the Anglican church that I was attending at the time. For those who may not be familiar with him, Dr. Gerstner was a committed Presbyterian churchman. He was in town to present a two-day series of lectures on dispensationalism, having recently published a book critiquing that theological system.[1]

The Sunday following the completion of his lectures, he joined us for worship. He participated in our Anglican worship, and when it was time to come forward and receive the Eucharist, he approached the rail and knelt. This, in and of itself, is a remarkable act for a de jure Presbyterian. After he received the bread and wine, he began to tear up, and he immediately left the church. I followed him to ensure he was all right (he was in his seventies at the time and had recently had back surgery). I remained at a slight distance to allow him his privacy.

When he started to make his way back to the church, I proceeded to meet him to ask if he was OK. He met me just outside the church, and what he said has never left me. This divine-right Presbyterian looked at me, took my arm, and, referencing the Eucharist, said, "You Anglicans do it right!" It was those words, almost thirty years ago, that launched me on this journey to study biblical worship. Those of you who are Presbyterians will understand the significance of his statement. I hope that,

---

1 The title of said work is *Wrongly Dividing the Word of Truth*.

during this treatment, everyone else will come to understand its significance as well.

Now, this idea may seem a bit narrow, given that the way we understand worship in American Christianity is very fluid and open to various types of practices. However, that is the very cause for this book. As a graduate of a Reformed (predominately Presbyterian) seminary, Westminster Theological Seminary/CA, I saw that our church, St. Patrick's, attracted people who were looking for a more traditional (which I will define as we go along) form of worship; all the while, these folks were coming out of Reformed Presbyterian and, in some cases, broadly evangelical ecclesiastical backgrounds. They came to us with many questions concerning the difference in types of worship that are practiced within the Christian community of the United States. But there are two questions that were/are repeatedly asked that prompted my taking to the keyboard:

Why do Anglicans, specifically your church, worship in the manner you do? Is there scriptural evidence for this type of worship?

In answering these questions, I found an increasing number of people asking me if I have something they can read about the position I was espousing. As I explained to them, some of what I argue is unique to my understanding of worship given nearly thirty years of studying the topic, combined with pastoral ministry. Much of what I teach is culled from numerous sources that all bear on this subject (i.e., as I discuss later when addressing the issue of house worship in the early Church, important data, though not all of it, comes from archaeology and architectural evidence). Probably the most significant reason is that there is a general consensus, which I actually heard asserted from one of my professors at one particular seminary, that scripture doesn't give us a detailed prescriptive delineation of any one particular form of worship (and its attendant form of polity). We must attempt to look at the *limited* data (emphasis mine) the Bible provides, piece it together with Church history, and come to the best conclusion possible. "But," the argument follows, "unless the preponderance of evidence comes from the Bible, one cannot dogmatically assert one form of worship as superior to any other. We must be gracious and respect another's conscience even if we strongly differ with them on this issue." This is a common argument, especially within evangelicalism. However, I believe it is overstated and incorrect. I will present in this book that a scriptural case, with supporting external data, can be made for one particular form of worship—a traditional form of worship, structured and liturgical, which can be found in the Episcopal model of polity as represented in Anglican worship.

It is important to note here that the Anglican model of polity and worship is a type of Episcopal polity (and worship) but not *the only* type of Episcopal worship. Rome and Eastern Orthodoxy are the other main representatives of the Episcopal model. This is what I mean when I use the term "traditional" worship: liturgical worship in an Anglican context. Yet, even stating this, some within my own tradition will dissent. As I show, however, what I stated is that this form of worship and polity is the most biblical, and there are at least three—probably more—biblical qualities or characteristics that can be used to identify this form of worship. (As you can see, I am combining polity and worship at this juncture. They are two separate and distinct concepts, but for brevity in a more popular treatment, I am combining them.) Saying that one adheres to Episcopal polity, however, does not guarantee correct worship. So, even Anglican churches, if they fail to meet the biblical qualities or characteristics we will identify, will *disqualify* themselves as being a true church. This obviously is not without controversy, but I hope and pray that one will at least allow me to make my case before dismissing this position out of hand.

Before moving on to each particular chapter discussing these matters, I would be remiss if I did not clearly state the impetus for this work. The discussion of these topics developed initially out of questions from inquirers and subsequent members of St. Patrick's Anglican Church. During these interactions, my wife overheard me mention a connection between the Old Testament teaching on the Kingdom and Jesus's proclamation of the arrival of the Kingdom of Heaven / God in Him, His ministry, and His preaching. This was the launching point for me to connect the Kingdom of Heaven and its worship to worship in the Kingdom on Earth. Ever the researcher, my wife found several classic texts online discussing this very topic. This treatment is not going to be a polemical defense of one form of worship and its attendant structure and leadership, otherwise known as Church government or polity, against other forms. This is not going to directly contrast and compare Anglicanism with Presbyterianism or Congregationalism with Lutheranism and so forth, though there will be general comparisons at various points. I will attempt to be as irenic as possible. The focus of this work is an affirmative statement and defense of why one branch of the Christian Church, Anglicanism, and, of that, one particular representation of that branch, St. Patrick's Anglican Church, worships in the manner in which we do.[2]

This was written for my congregation because it grew out of their questions concerning why we do what we do. It was originally presented in an eight-week Sunday school class. In this book, my intention is to present this position in a positive, affirmative manner. I am not going after anyone. However, because some of my folks come out of a Reformed tradition, I had to address confusion over the terms bishop[3] and elder.[4]

The argument goes that these terms are virtually synonymous and, at the very least, interchangeable. This line of thought is usually presented in an attempt to diffuse the force of the term used[5] that, until very recently, had been translated as "bishop" in the King James Bible but in more recent translations is usually rendered as "overseer." I reject this argument and believe that I can make a case for the two terms being significantly different *enough* to warrant both having particular connotations and denotations. In other words, each term actually means something distinctly different from the other in the context of leadership (particularly where worship is addressed) and church government—enough to support entirely different church offices for each term. I will leave it up to the reader to determine if I have been successful in my argument. But even here, I am not going to stray too far into an overly academic discussion.[6]

---

2   Two of the most accessible works written from an evangelical Anglican perspective are *On the Nature and Constitution of the Present Kingdom of Heaven upon Earth* by John Roland West (London: Kessinger Legacy, 1882) and *Worship in Heaven and on Earth: Responsive, Congregational, Reverent, Musical, and Beautiful* by J. G. Norton (London: Wells Gardner, Darton, & Co., 1884; reprinted by Book Renaissance, www.Ren-Book.com). I heartily recommend these works to all interested in fully pursuing this topic. I am forever indebted to my wife for pointing me to these works in that they confirmed many of my heretofore unsubstantiated ideas.

3   *Episkopos.*

4   *Presbuteros.*

5   ἐπίσκοπον (episkopos).

6   If you're looking for a comparison concerning differing views of church polity, I would rec-

Due to the prominence of this assertion, it is important to address this linguistic matter in a rudimentary manner in an otherwise popular treatment, if for no other reason than to lay the groundwork for a future, more consciously focused academic treatment, which is planned.

With any such work, there are numerous people who not only motivated its production but contributed to the sharpening of some of the concepts and positions held therein. I am unable to thank everyone, but I would be remiss if I did not mention some very formative influences. I must first thank Sam Henrie, president of Wheatmark Publishing, for not only taking a chance on a first-time author but on one who is publishing material quite different from his usual content. You will forever have my gratitude, Sam. Also from Wheatmark, the senior project manager and person directly responsible for seeing this work to fruition is Lori Conser. Without her patience, professionalism, and insights, this work would be significantly inferior. Thank you so much, Lori.

Next, I must recognize Fr. Michael McDonald for his tireless perseverance in listening to me drone on and on about this subject and his perspicuous analysis of some of my arguments. We were classmates at Westminster Seminary, colleagues, and have been friends for over thirty years. Fr. Mike was a minister in the Christian Reformed Church for many years. Without his support, encouragement, and razor-sharp intellect, whatever decent material there is in this book would never have come to the fore. Thanks, Mike. In addition to Fr. Mike, I must express my deepest appreciation for my colleague and fellow co-laborer in God's vineyard, Fr. Ron Murray, our vicar. His patience in allowing me to present this material to our congregation was of immeasurable value in assisting me in organizing and polishing the content of this book. If I mention Fr. Ron, I must also mention Kathleen Murray Banta and Diana Murray, whose sharp insights and unique perspectives helped me figure out how to present this content in a manageable package and eliminate excessive and unnecessary technical jargon. I also must thank Charles Baker, Richard Tilton, and Roger Cooper of St. Patrick's Anglican Church. Their questions, comments, insights, and friendly badgering about this subject practically drove me to write this book.

ommend the book *Who Runs the Church? 4 Views on Church Government*, edited by Paul E. Engle and Steven B. Cowan (Grand Rapids, Michigan: Zondervan Publishing, 2004).

Most recently, I must recognize my long-time Reformed friend, Fr. Neil Edlin, who is the rector of St. Mary Magdalene Anglican Church in Orange, California. Fr. Neil graciously allowed me to present a two-lecture summary of the contents of this book, which was critical in structing the outline of the material contained herein. Additionally, Christian Dove—a young man, budding scholar, friend, and student at my alma mater, Westminster Seminary, who is intending to pursue doctoral studies at the University of St. Louis—has been an invaluable aid in continued clarification of my arguments, sharpening them when needed and driving me to finally get this thing published. I am indebted to him more than I can express. Here it is, brother, with great appreciation and fondness. I also cannot forget Jonelle Prideaux, a brilliant young woman pursuing her PhD at the University of Cincinnati. Her keen eye, attention to detail, and amazing grasp of the English language provided numerous suggestions that made this book much better than my original draft. Greg Myers and Timothy Norheim were also instrumental to improving the manuscript. With much affection, thanks to all.

Of course, special thanks go to my wonderful, supportive, intelligent, beautiful wife, Benita. Without her practical insights on how to communicate certain theological subjects, this work would have been much longer and significantly more pedantic and polemical. Thank you, babe.

I cannot end this preface without mentioning three other people. The influence of the first has been overwhelming, powerful, and pervasive. I have only had passing direct personal contact with him over the years and never actually had the opportunity to sit down and discuss these issues with him (which would have been interesting since, with some of what is said in this book, I believe he would most surely disagree). But through his preaching, teaching, conferences, writings, CDs, DVDs, and overall ministry, I have learned not only what it means to be a truly Reformed thinker but how to be a better Christian. Ligonier Ministries influences hundreds of thousands of people, and I know I'm not alone when I say thank you to the late Dr. R. C. Sproul for all he did for the Kingdom of God and our Savior, the Lord Jesus Christ. Though I (and numerous others) miss him tremendously, he is now with loved ones in Heaven, reuniting and, of course, playing with his beloved dogs.

The second was one of my professors at Westminster Seminary, Dr. John Frame. His example as both a scholar and a man of God is humbling and inspiring. We had a tumultuous relationship when I was a stubborn, hot-headed student. But he behaved in such a Christlike manner that my boorish behavior weighed on me, convicting me of my sin, and resulted in a long-overdue apology. He is an incredibly gracious, humble, intelligent man and an outstanding scholar, and I am happy to be able to call him my friend. His passion for true worship not only resulted in a book, *Worship in Spirit and Truth,* but motivated me to consider this topic more deeply. Although he will probably disagree with some of what is written here, I am sure he will appreciate that someone from an orthodox, Reformed view is taking this topic seriously. Thank you, John; you are deeply admired.

Finally, I must mention a dear friend, scholar, colleague, and brilliant man who took the time to offer his amazing insight to tighten up this work. His humility demanded that I not identify him by name, so I will simply say that you, your beautiful wife, and your two pugs are deeply loved.

Soli Deo Gloria

Introduction:
The Soil of Christianity Is Judaism

ANY AND ALL DISCUSSIONS OF CHRISTIANITY in general and worship in particular must begin with Judaism. This was brought home quite vividly by Edith Schaeffer in her 1975 book entitled *Christianity Is Jewish*. Unfortunately, over the last forty years, this undergirding foundational concept of Christianity has been muted at best and almost lost at worst. It was within the context of Judaism that Christianity arose: all the original Apostles were Jews; the geographical location of its nascent beginnings was in Roman-occupied Palestine; the terms, concepts, and structures were all informed by Judaism; and, of course, its founder, Jesus of Nazareth, the Christ, was a Jew.

This may just appear to be one of those statements where the reader might say, "No kidding." However, it is important to reiterate this at the start for a number of reasons:

1. The further we remove ourselves from our historical roots, the more likely we lose track of our connection to those roots.

2. There appears to be, especially within the Church today, a lack of overt recognition and acknowledgment of the inherent Jewishness of our Christian roots.

3. To understand what is taking place in Christian worship, one must understand from where that worship originated, the Tabernacle, and then the Temple, and then the Jewish synagogue.

In many of the contemporary discussions of worship, there appears to be a distancing of this vital link.

4. The foundational theological concepts of New Testament Christianity, though communicated in Greek, are not in fact Greek philosophic ideas; they are intrinsically Jewish, and to fully and accurately understand these critical theological topics, we must understand from where they derive: Judaism.

5. The entire Epistle to the Hebrews is an elucidation of the relationship between the Old Covenant and New and the superiority of the New, in Jesus Christ, over the Old. This epistle, saturated with Jewish concepts, imagery, and references, was written to Jewish Christians. One would be hard pressed to understand this epistle without recognizing its connection to and dependence upon the Old Covenant.

6. The Apostle Paul makes it perfectly clear, under the inspiration of the Holy Spirit, that only those who are of the seed of Abraham, those who understand and accept that justification is by faith alone, are *true Jews*. The implication, of course, is that all who trust in Christ and are justified by grace alone through faith alone are the *true Israel*.

The apostles themselves continued to function as Jews, though preaching the New Covenant; they worshiped as Jews; they attended temple and synagogue (discussed later in the book); they believed they were Jews, albeit Jews who believed the Messiah had come in the person of Jesus; they had found that Messiah, trusted in Him for their salvation, and preached Jesus as the Jewish Messiah.

Whether one is discussing sacrifice, covenant, atonement, holiness, or worship, though they may have corresponding uses in non-Jewish contexts, the meanings of those terms in Christianity are distinctly informed by Judaism.

One immediately can relate the Old Testament teachings on the idea of shepherds, from, most famously, Psalm 23,[1] to the teaching of

---

1   Psalm 23:1: "A Psalm of David. The LORD is my *shepherd*; I shall not want." John 10:11: "I

Jesus as the Good Shepherd in John 10. The New Testament teaching of the Church as "a royal priesthood" in I Peter 2:9[2] is taken by the apostle Peter from Exodus 19:6 and the Nation of Israel being a "kingdom of Priests." Even the myriad theophanies that appear in the Old Testament are a foreshadowing of the Incarnation in the New Testament.

We are flooded with references to a "bride," "vine," "kingdom," "great meal," "law," and so on, the meanings of which take on a completely different understanding if separated from their Jewish roots. The importance of baptism as a holy rite of inclusion into the New Testament Covenant community, instituted and provided by God to His people—with all its attendant imagery of washing, cleansing, purification from sin, identification, and grafting—if not understood as connected to circumcision in the Old Testament, robs baptism not only of its theological roots but turns it into something other than what Colossians 2:11-12[3] indicates it is.

Jesus Himself took the opportunity on at least two occasions mentioned in scripture, Luke 24:27 and 24:44, to instruct His followers that all the Old Testament pointed to Him. It is also interesting to note that in Luke 24:16, Luke tells us that the disciples on the road to Emmaus had their eyes (variously interpreted as) "holden" (KJV), "kept" (ESV and NIV), "prevented" (NASB), and "restrained" (NKJV) for "seeing" who the Lord Jesus really was. The Greek word[4] that Luke indicates our Lord used here is in the passive tense and means "to be powerless," "to hold back," and so forth. So, by combining these meanings with the passive tense, we have the Lord "holding them back," "preventing" them, or "making them powerless" to grasp the true meaning of who He was. All of this was done so He could open up the Old Testament and take them

---

am the good *shepherd*. The good shepherd lays down his life for the sheep."

2   1 Peter 2:9: "But you are a chosen race, a royal priesthood, a holy nation, a people for his own possession, that you may proclaim the excellencies of him who called you out of darkness into his marvelous light." Exodus 19:6: "...and you shall be to me a kingdom of priests and a holy nation. These are the words that you shall speak to the people of Israel."

3   Colossians 2:11: "In him also you were circumcised with a circumcision made without hands, by putting off the body of the flesh, by the circumcision of Christ, having been buried with him in baptism, in which you were also raised with him through faith in the powerful working of God, who raised him from the dead."

4   ἐκρατοῦντο.

through it to show them how clearly and powerfully He is presented there.

In Acts chapter 2, the apostle Peter, preaching on the Day of Pentecost, asserts that the events that unfolded at that time were a fulfillment of Joel chapter 2. Just prior to Stephen's martyrdom in Acts chapter 7, he preaches a sermon beginning with Abraham moving through the Patriarchs' betrayal of Joseph and Joseph's impact not only on Egypt and Israel but the world at that time. Stephen then addresses Mosaic leadership, the Exodus, Israel's forty years of wilderness wandering, the nation's battles with Moses, and the Mosaic reception of the oracles on Mt. Sinai. From here, he draws this marvelous recollection to a close by tying in the wilderness tabernacle with an allusion to the "true tabernacle," the Lord Jesus. All of this would be, if not virtually pointless, certainly a winding, distracting tale if not connected to Judaism.

In chapter 10,[5] just as he was about to meet with the Gentile Cornelius, the apostle Peter once again, as the focal point of the first half of Acts, struggles with a rooftop vision given to him by God to "take and eat" foods that were, to Jews, ceremonially unclean. Even the idea of ceremonially unclean food would be odd without Jewish roots.

We could continue to provide many more examples; for instance, the entire discussion of the Jerusalem Council in Acts chapter 15 centers around non-Jews coming into the Church and the requirements for them to be considered part of the nascent New Testament Church. Are they to be fully converted Jews and undergo all the necessary rituals in which previous non-Jews had to participate: proselyte baptism, circumcision, and the like? Without a deep conviction of their Jewish identity on the part of the apostles, this would seem out of place in any discussion regarding the criteria of membership in the *new Church*,[6] or, to put

---

5   Acts 10:9–15: "The next day, as they went on their journey and drew near the city, Peter went up on the housetop to pray, about the sixth hour. Then he became very hungry and wanted to eat; but while they made ready, he fell into a trance and saw heaven opened and an object like a great sheet bound at the four corners, descending to him and let down to the earth. In it were all kinds of four-footed animals of the earth, wild beasts, creeping things, and birds of the air. And a voice came to him, 'Rise, Peter; kill and eat.' But Peter said, 'Not so, Lord! For I have never eaten anything common or unclean.' And a voice spoke to him again the second time, 'What God has cleansed you must not call common.'"

6   An excellent discussion of the relationship between the early Christians and Judaism is pre-

it another way, what it takes to be in the Jewish Church of the Messiah who has come. Then there is the overpowering link, which stands at the heart of both Judaism and Christianity, between Passover and Holy Communion, otherwise seen as atonement. There is much more to say about these issues, which are addressed in the upcoming chapters.

When one takes the time to explore this topic more fully and focus first on Heaven, it has the potential to radically revise one's concept of worship. What occurs in the pursuit of this topic, almost immediately, is that how we understand worship from the start begins in our understanding of what transpires in Heaven first. In other words, when most of the material written on worship is presented to readers, it almost always begins in a linear fashion: Old Testament to New Testament, tabernacle/temple/synagogue to church. But when we begin with an understanding of what was going on in Heaven, which was the model, the plan, the paradigm for all of worship on earth, our perspective now moves from the linear to a downward view, the vertical to the horizontal, a transcendent to immanent perspective, if you will; heaven becomes the starting place. This is what the book of Hebrews tells us:[7] that Moses was given the plan for not only a House for God but the way He was to be worshiped, and this plan was predicated upon what was transpiring in Heaven. This plan is what Moses was given on Mt. Sinai: the entire Torah.

When we begin this way, we realize that the reality, that which is true, is the heavenly model upon which the earthly model is based and to which the earthly model will return. To put it slightly differently, we begin with the heavenly blueprint, which is the absolute and true model of the what and how of worship; it then intrudes into the earthly realm via God's divine revelation to Moses. It is this Kingdom on earth that is to be modeled upon the Kingdom in Heaven; this model advances what heavenly worship is to be on earth. This then informs how and what the nascent Church, both Old and New, would do as far as the where and

---

sented by Gerald Bray in his book *The Church: A Theological and Historical Account*. It is thorough without being overly academic.

7   Hebrews 8:5: "They serve a *copy and shadow of the heavenly things*. For when Moses was about to erect the tent, he was instructed by God, saying, 'See that you make everything according to the *pattern* that was shown you on the mountain'" (emphasis added).

what of worship with the obvious caveat being that the content in the New would be Christological theologically, ending up back at the consummation in heaven and its worship, which is where all of this began.

There are, of course, issues of the symbolism[8] and so forth discussed in heavenly worship as presented in the book of Revelation, but that can be handled when we get to the core chapter of this book, "Worship on Earth as It Is in Heaven."[9,10]

Anthony Saldarini, former professor of theology at Boston College, summarizes the Christian understanding of the Jewish connection as follows, quoting:[11]

> Numerous passages attest to this . . . Jewish worship and practice:
>
> 1. Acts 2:46 says that the early Christians were "day by day continuing with one mind in the temple . . ."
>
> 2. Acts 3:1 records that Peter and John were going to the temple because it was the hour of prayer.
>
> 3. Acts 5:21, 42 shows the continued practice of Christians going to the temple on a regular basis.
>
> 4. Paul continued to observe the traditions of Jewish worship: Acts 21:26; 22:17; 24:11-12; 24:18.

---

8   As has been noted by Dr. Sproul, "symbolism always points to a reality greater than itself." Consider, then, all the symbolism of Heaven as it is introduced in the Old Testament Church. The amazing depth of meaning of this symbolism doesn't minimize its significance; it actually emphasizes the true import. Therefore, the reality of a heavenly altar, for example, isn't minimized by the recognition of Christ fulfilling this symbolism in His atonement; it further enhances its power because He is already there, in Heaven, and there is no more sacrifice to be made. Yet we see all of these symbols present in Heaven while Christ is present in Heaven. This is touched on further.

9   Dr. Scott Hahn has written (from a Roman Catholic view) a very informative and helpful book entitled *The Lamb's Supper: The Mass in Heaven on Earth*. If you're up to the challenge of working through the theological differences between Protestant and Roman theology, this book has much to commend itself and a tremendous amount of useful and helpful material. Caveat emptor.

10   It is a shame that, until only relatively recently, the preponderance of material covering this topic has been dominated by the Greek Orthodox and Roman Catholic Churches.

11   Anthony J. Saldarini. Matthew's Christian-Jewish Community. Chicago: University of Chicago Press, 1994: 101.

5. Several passages seem to indicate a continued obser-
    vance of the Sabbath by Paul and others: Acts 13:14,
    42-44; 16:13; 17:2; 18:4.

6. Romans 14:5-6a and Colossians 2:16 may also be re-
    ferring to Christians who continued to follow the Jew-
    ish practice of worship on the Sabbath.

7. Several passages refer to the early Christians gather-
    ing in the synagogues for the purpose of worship and
    teaching others: Acts 9:2; 9:20; 13:5; 13:14ff; 13:42-
    44; 14:1; 17:1ff; 17:10; 17:17; 18:4ff; 18:26; 19:8;
    22:19; 24:11-12; 26:11. James 2:2 uses the same Greek
    word[12] synagogue, but KJV and NASB have "assembly."

8. Acts 2:42 says, "They were continually devoting them-
    selves to the apostles' teaching and to fellowship, to the
    breaking of bread and to prayer" [services taking place
    in synagogues; my insertion here PAFC].

9. The influence of Judaism upon the Christian church
    may even possibly be seen in comparing the functions
    of the Jewish synagogue officers and those of the early
    church. Just as every synagogue had elders[13] and in-
    structors, so also the early church came to have elders/
    bishops [both presbyters and bishops; again, my addi-
    tion PAFC] in every church (Acts 14:23) whose pri-
    mary responsibility was to lead the congregation and
    care for its spiritual needs (Hebrews 13:17). Further-
    more, just as the synagogues typically had men desig-
    nated to gather and distribute alms to those in need, so
    also the early church came to have deacons who had
    similar responsibilities (Acts 6:1-7).

10. Though not a Scriptural point, it is suggested that even
    the architecture of our church buildings today may be

---

12 συναγωγάς.
13 The identification of these elders and what their function was is addressed in chapter 9.

influenced by that of the Jewish synagogues; consider the use of raised platforms and pulpits at the front, as well as rows of benches or pews facing the front of the auditorium.

11.   In the synagogue, the scrolls of the Law were treated with reverence, because through the words written on them, God addressed the people. Before verses from the Law were read, people recited the following versicle: "Blessed art thou, O God, giver of the Torah." The entire Torah (five books of the Law) was read through once every three years [carried over into Anglican practice as the Lectionary; addition mine PAFC]. All synagogues, no matter how geographically scattered they were, were united by these common readings. The leader chose the reading from the Prophets or Writings, which was meant to complement the reading from the Torah. After the readings, the rabbi or another person present was invited to interpret the reading. The readings climaxed with the recitation of the Shema ["Hear O Israel, the Lord thy God is One"; inclusion mine PAFC].

12.   In view of the ancient household pattern, it is likely that the disciples met in houses both when they were members of the Jewish synagogue and after they were expelled and had to form their own assembly (church).[14]

It is important before moving to the next chapter that I alert the reader to a pattern I employ in this book. The pattern is repetition. The position I assume in this book may seem unique to most people; therefore, certain statements or concepts are repeated to reinforce them in the reader's mind due to their newness for some. I am not attempting to insult anyone's intelligence. I am merely trying to ensure that the reader comes away from this work understanding my position, regardless whether they agree with it or not. If repetition irritates you, I apologize;

---

14   ἐκκλησίαν.

just know that I thought it necessary. As Isaiah has written,[9] "Whom will he teach knowledge? And whom will he make to understand the message? Those just weaned from milk? Those just drawn from the breasts?[10] For precept must be upon precept, precept upon precept, Line upon line, line upon line, Here a little, there a little" (Isa. 28:9-10, *NKJ*).

1

The Model of Worship from Heaven

*And see that you make them after the pattern for them, which is
being shown you on the mountain.*

—Exodus 25:40

*Thus it was necessary for the copies of the heavenly things to be pu-
rified with these rites, but the heavenly things themselves with better sacrifices than these. For Christ has entered, not into holy places
made with hands, which are copies of the true things, but into heav-
en itself, now to appear in the presence of God on our behalf.*

—Hebrews 9:23

FOR THOSE OF US WHO ARE a bit older, one of the monumental
changes in the Church is the architecture. Most people today pay no attention to church architecture, and even fewer realize that there is a significant theological statement being made by how a church is designed
and built. Now, I am not going to go into an excursus on church architecture *per se*; however, there is a biblical precedent to the concern with
how a church is constructed.[1]

In 1986, I heard R. C. Sproul ask this question at Mariners Church
in Newport Beach, California. It has stayed with me for all these years for
two reasons: That night was the infamous Bill Buckner error of game six

---

1   An excellent overview of the connection between worship in Heaven and on earth can be
found in R. C. Sproul's book *A Taste of Heaven*. Dr. Sproul is writing from a Presbyterian position, so there will be differences between his treatment and this one; however, it is still a valuable
contribution to the discussion.

between the New York Mets and Boston Red Sox, two teams I despise. He extended this question to those present, and I raised my hand to respond. He then asked me if I was Roman Catholic, and I said, "No, I left the Roman Church years ago," to which he responded, "Ah, you don't count." He was joking with me, of course. But the question he asked was, "For those of you who come from an Evangelical or broadly non-denominational background, have you ever wandered into a Roman, Greek Orthodox, or pre-1970 Anglican church? If so, did you notice the immediate difference in your reaction to being inside? The sudden quiet, reverence, and even sense of awe?" There is a biblical reason for that.

If you take the time to go through scripture with this particular focus in mind, something should immediately jump off the page at you: the place where we are to meet with God, to pray to God, to hear the word of God, and to worship God is known as His house. Not only that, but God designed, presented to Moses, and instructed Moses to model His earthly residence upon His heavenly one. In other words, the model that God gave to Moses—the blueprint, the architecture, the design for His earthly dwelling place—is predicated upon His heavenly dwelling place. The tabernacle and temple in scripture are intended to be earthly replicas of God's heavenly dwelling. Our models, then, of God's dwelling place on earth should replicate, duplicate, and resemble to the best of our ability His heavenly home.

Of course, this replication of the heavenly sanctuary on earth cannot be exact for several reasons.

1. The heavenly sanctuary is perfect. It exists outside temporal space and time; therefore, when we read about it at various junctures in scripture, Ezekiel and Revelation to name two, we must remember that what we are reading is a description of what the sanctuary looks like at the consummation.[2] Since we are still struggling with sin, our ability to understand and perfectly duplicate this will never happen. That does not, however, negate our responsibility to follow God's command and try to

---

2   I am using the term "consummation" here to denote that period when Jesus Christ returns and brings all human history to its completion, and all of existence achieves its fulfillment in Heaven.

the best of our ability, guided by the Holy Spirit, to build God's house on earth as closely resembling His heavenly dwelling as we can.

2. The Book of Revelation presents us with one of the clearest pictures of what the heavenly sanctuary looks like from a New Covenant perspective. Yet it is replete with Jewish apocalyptic symbolism. It then becomes incumbent upon us to make sure that we link the Old Covenant descriptions and commands with the New Covenant descriptions when we attempt to model our earthly buildings for God's house.

3. Even given the symbolic nature of the Book of Revelation, as well as the statements from the Book of Acts that we "worship in a temple made without hands (the Lord Jesus)," we are still required to worship God in some place. The commandment to keep holy the Sabbath has never been eradicated, and we are commanded to meet with our God and not forsake assembling ourselves together (Hebrews 10:24–25). If we fully understand the nature of symbolism[3] in scripture—that the symbol always points to the reality that is greater than the symbol—we must realize that, even if we are unable to fully comprehend the full meaning of the symbol, it is pointing to an even greater depiction of God's house than we can imagine. That symbolism of the temple being nonphysical (Acts 7:48 and 17:24–25), therefore, in and of itself, does not negate any attempt to understand what is being communicated in the Book of Revelation or elsewhere. The concept then, for instance, that we must have an actual physical location to create a dwelling place on earth to worship God in Spirit and truth, as it were, is not mitigated by those passages above (or any others). Shadows, although shadows, are real, and they are projections of the very real object that casts them. Inferior, yes; fleeting, sure; not an exact copy, of course; but imaginary, definitely not.

---

3   In this particular instance, the symbolism in the Book of Revelation that "candles," "incense," "altar," "vestments," and so forth point to is fulfilled in the Lord Jesus Christ.

4. As in many of the connections between the Old Testament and New,[4] the Old Covenant and New, the concept of a specific location to worship God is maintained. In other words, even though we understand that the Lord Jesus is the *true tabernacle*, and that the tabernacle and temple pointed to Him as their fulfillment, worship in a place still occurred. We are commanded to hear the word of God preached. That proclamation, in addition to day-to-day interaction and proclaiming the Gospel, must occur someplace. Ministers, as will be addressed in subsequent chapters, were ordained to minister someplace; the sacraments,[5] baptism, and the Lord's Supper were to be administered someplace, and so on. The command given in Holy Writ is that God is to be worshiped in a specific location, in a specific way, according to specific instructions given by Him. Scripture never, either explicitly or implicitly, abandons this notion. Worshiping Him in whatever way one chooses, wherever one chooses to do it, is not the God-revealed scriptural command. Therefore, we still must build an earthly dwelling for the *true tabernacle*, the Lord Jesus, in order for us to worship Him properly, in spirit and truth. It is imperative that, if we are to build this house of God, we must have some idea as to what it should look like, how it is to be built, given God's explicit revelation in scripture. We do this as Christians taking into account all of the New Covenant theology communicated to us by our Lord and Savior, Jesus Christ. Once again, not the exact spiritual reality but the divinely revealed pattern we are to use on earth, a place to meet with God.

Rather than beginning with some functional or practical concept as to how to build a church, we are to model our churches after the heavenly pattern. The earthly replica should contain the elements that God

---

4   In other words, the connection between circumcision and baptism and Passover and the Lord's Supper.

5   Those from a nonliturgical, traditional background get hives when they read this term. As used throughout this work, *sacrament* means "a visible, physical sign of an invisible, spiritual grace." This is, essentially, the definition given by St. Augustine and has not been improved upon. I am not invoking the Roman Catholic usage.

provided to Moses when He instructed him to build His earthly home. When one reads the Book of Revelation in conjunction with Exodus, Deuteronomy, Ezekiel, and all other descriptions of God's dwelling place on earth, one begins to see that the description of the tabernacle/temple does not begin in the Old Testament but in *heaven*. The fullest depiction of that heavenly place, for Christians, is Revelation; so, even though it is the last book of the New Testament, it should be the *first book* we read (in conjunction with Exodus, Deuteronomy, First and Second Chronicles, Ezekiel, and Isaiah) when we desire to worship God and understand what His house is to look like .

What, then, are some of the elements or characteristics of God's house? I would encourage everyone to go back and reread those passages for themselves,[6] but there are a few that can be mentioned here.

Now that we have outlined much about the correlation between worship in heaven and worship on earth, let us look at the elements of heavenly worship. The first thing that jumps out at us are the materials involved and utilized in this worship. We see lampstands,[7] a throne,[8] incense,[9] a censer,[10] an altar,[11] robed clergy,[12] hidden manna,[13] and a cup (chalice) or offering bowl[14]—everything that one would find in a traditional Anglican worship service, interestingly enough.

Let us now consider the two most common texts dealing with our topic.

Isaiah 6 and Revelation of Jesus to St. John

"I saw the Lord sitting upon a throne, high and lifted up." In the supernatural vision of the heavenly court, Isaiah begins to describe what is happening. "After these things I saw, and behold, a door opened

---

6   E.g., Ex. 25–31, Deut. 12 and 16, and Ezek. 40 and following.

7   Rev 1:20, 2:5.

8   Rev 2:13, 3:21, 4:4, 20:11.

9   Rev 5:8.

10   Rev 8:3.

11   Rev 8:3.

12   Rev 4:4.

13   Rev 2:17.

14   Rev 16.

in heaven! . . . And behold a throne set in heaven and one sat on the throne." For St. John, nothing could be clearer. The veil between heaven and earth, reminiscent of the veil separating the Holy of Holies from the Holy place, was lifted for both Isaiah and St. John. What takes place in heaven, as the model of what is to take place on earth in worship, can only be known by us through divine revelation. So, in the power of the Holy Spirit, Isaiah and St. John tell us what they see and hear.

Imagine the royal train of a monarch, its beauty, glory, splendor identifying the dignitary as someone exalted. Now look at what Isaiah says: God's "train filled the temple." We fail to realize sometimes, when we read this passage, that this temple, this place of God's dwelling, is the heavens themselves. The train of God's royal robes *fills the entire heavens!* St. John adds that the glory of God was like "jasper stone and sardius."[15] How appropriate that both of these were two of the twelve stones affixed to the breastplate of Aaron, the High Priest.

Then Isaiah sees the initial indication of worship, the Seraphim, the highest order of the orders of angels, hovering above the throne antiphonally singing, "Holy, Holy, Holy" across the top of God's throne, back and forth to each other. The entire earth is filled with the glory of God, and as they are singing their praises to God's glory, with their six wings they cover their eyes and feet and use the remaining two to fly. St. John, in his vision, sees four living creatures, all around the throne, *for all eternity, never resting, never ending, never ceasing,* exclaiming, "Holy, Holy, Holy, is the LORD God Almighty, who was and is, and is to come!" Worship, never-ending worship of God! And while all of this is transpiring, the twenty-four Elders fall down to their faces and throw their golden crowns before the foot of the throne, proclaiming, "You are worthy, O Lord, To receive glory and honor and power; For You created all things, And by Your will they exist and were created" (Rev. 4:11, NKJ).

The combination of Isaiah and Revelation presents us with an astounding picture. Four living creatures. The twenty-four Elders, focusing upon, directing their exclusive attention upon, God. They are extolling the unbridled praise, adoration, worthiness, glory of the Eternal God, who created all things by His will. This is *responsive* worship in all

---

15 Sardius is a fiery-red precious stone, most closely resembling a ruby.

its beauty, majesty, and profundity. And this is merely St. John's *intro-duction* to worship in heaven. Does our worship remotely resemble this?

The Spiritual Characteristics of Worship

This Is Holy Worship

We often pay lip service to the fact that God is holy, especially during corporate worship. However, when one thoughtfully considers what passes for worship and a recognition of the holiness of God, one would be hard pressed to find anything closely resembling it in scripture. When one examines the reaction of anyone in scripture, but particularly in Isaiah, one does not see breathy singing, manipulating the emotions and causing people to well up in sentimental tears. What one hears is the booming antiphonal singing of the angels, back and forth, extolling God's Almighty grandeur and glory, and what we see is one of the holiest prophets in the Old Testament prostrating himself,[16] burying his face (along with the angels, I might add) away from the holiness of God because it is impossible for Isaiah to even glance at Him, no less gaze longingly at Him. We see Isaiah uttering the profoundest of acknowledgments: "I am a man of unclean lips, amidst a people of unclean lips." To be truly confronted by the holiness of God is to immediately recognize one's unworthiness, not to stand, cheer, clap, and act as if one is at a party.[17] No other attribute of God, not righteousness, not justice, not omnipotence, not even love, is raised to the superlative level[18] that the Jews would use when they wanted to emphasize a point.

A holy prophet and pure, sinless angels that light the throne of God all covered their eyes and bowed their faces when in the presence of God's holiness. Is this how we worship God?

---

16   Some might assert that the text of Isaiah 6 nowhere states that he "prostrated" himself. However, if Seraphim, who are perfectly sinless, can't look upon God, it is not a stretch to think that the human prophet was so awed by what he encountered that he fell to his face as all Jews would have in worship.

17   Note the human reaction to encountering God: Genesis 18:27, Exodus 20:18, Deuteronomy 5:25, Joshua 5:24, particularly Judges 13:20–22, 2 Chronicles 7:3, Nehemiah 8:6, Job 42:5-6, Isaiah 6:5, Matthew 17:6, and Revelation 1:17.

18   R. C. Sproul, *The Holiness of God*. 25th Anniversary Edition. Sanford, Florida: Reformation Heritage Publishing, Ligonier Ministries, 2001: 30–32.

Loving Worship

Notice the reaction of the Seraphim in their worship of God. Their love was based upon their very nature and because God loved them. Living with Him in His presence in eternity, hovering above His throne, never got old, never stale, never irrelevant.[19] Their gratitude, their love, for God is not the insipid, vacillating, fleeting so-called love of humanity; no, their love of God was deep, powerful, constant, inexhaustible, and eternal, fully consuming them in their worship of Him. Is this what consumes us in our worship of God? St. John adds to this in his comment that the twenty-four Elders tossed their gold crowns at the foot of the throne of God. There is no selfishness here, no "me, me, me, it's all about me" attitude, no thought of oneself at all. All concentration was on our loving God. Can we say our worship is this dedicated?

Willing Worship

From this love of God came the natural willingness to worship Him. There is no division in love and will. How often are we unwilling, for whatever reason, to meet with God to worship Him as He commanded? Is this how we express our love for God—with an unwillingness to meet with Him on Sundays, let us say? Should we not be shouting from the rooftops, as did David in Psalm 122, "I was *glad* when they said, Let us go to the house of the LORD!" Isn't that what we see here: a gladness, a true joyousness, a holy response to even being allowed in the presence of the Holy One? He has saved us; we should be willing to worship Him for that alone. He has given us His grace in His word; we should be willing to worship Him for that alone. He has given us His grace in communion; we most definitely should be willing to worship Him for that alone. Is this the type of willingness we demonstrate in our worship of God?

19　The question then arises: how was it possible for one-third of the angels to sin and rebel? This has to be acknowledged but cannot be addressed here given the context and limited scope of this work.

Perfect Worship

While the worship of the Seraphim is perfect, and ours will never be during our time on earth, should not our worship attempt to emulate theirs? Our God is a perfect God and demands perfection to approach Him. Worship is one of the most significant and prominent ways we approach God. We should be striving to be as perfect in our worship as our fallen human nature is capable of, realizing that it is only in Christ Jesus and His perfect righteousness imputed to us that we can approach God at all. Do we truly desire to get it right? Is this our heartfelt desire in our worship of God?

Joyous Worship

The worship of the Seraphim was joyous, and not only had they never sinned, but they probably did not even know what sin was in some sense. Shouldn't we—being constantly attacked by sin, experiencing sin, being sorrowful for sin, confessing our sin, being forgiven of our sins—worship in the most joyous and joyful manner? Practiced not in some type of artificial happiness but in a response of joy, a true joy, because we know all too well that we do not deserve to be in God's presence in church, save for the grace and finished work of Jesus Christ. It is our lot in life to wage this battle while on earth. What could be more joyous than to know that, on Sundays, we can enter the house of God, experience the grace of God, be forgiven of our sins by God, and truly worship God in spirit and truth? Is this our response in our worship of God?

Impressive Worship

As Isaiah is uniquely blessed and privileged to see the glorious throne room of God, he is overwhelmed by what he sees. How impressive it must have been to his eyes to see God's glory; to his ears to hear the angelic melody of the antiphonal hymn; to his mind to be able to understand the subject he was seeing, in a limited, human way, of course. There was no confusion of what he was hearing. He completely understood the words that were being uttered. And notice that there were no seated spectators; all were involved. Heavenly worship is corporate; it is participatory. How important it is, then, for our worship to be able to be understood; how important it is for our worship to be rational, to follow a divinely written pattern that is presented to us in words or a language in order for us to understand intelligibly not only who our God is but how to worship Him properly. Isaiah was the stranger here, and he understood everything that was transpiring before him. Now reconsider St. Paul's admonition to the Corinthians (in I Corinthians 12–14) in this context.

This experience was so impressive, so penetrating for Isaiah, that it revealed to him his utter unworthiness to be there. He heard God's voice, and that voice moved the door posts. Inanimate matter, lifeless material, moved at the voice of God. The entire throne room, *heaven itself*, was filled with the smoke from incense. Once again, when we truly encounter God's holiness, we truly recognize our unworthiness and sinfulness. Praise Him for Christ, our righteousness. Isaiah had seen the pure, sinless Seraphim praise God with holy lips, unlike his own lips. He beheld God revealing Himself to him—He was revealed, the Infinite, Almighty, Holy One of the universe—and exclaimed, "I am undone!" The word Isaiah uses here means "cause to cease," "to be destroyed." It was the late R. C. Sproul who described it as unraveling,[20] like pulling on the thread of a sleeve and then watching the entire sleeve unravel. Isaiah was so overcome in experiencing God that he fell apart. Are we as impressed by God when we worship Him on Sunday?

The Ritual Characteristics of Worship

It might be jarring to some, but worship in heaven involved ritual and ceremony. The religious nature of the ceremony taking place in heaven contains, by its very nature, ritual. These ritual acts informing this ceremony[21] revolve around the activity focused upon the worship

---

20 *Op. cit.* Sproul, *Holiness of God*, 35.

21 The issue of the nature of and relationship between ritual and ceremony involves centuries of analysis and discussion. For my purposes here, I am using the terms as follows: ritual is the specific acts and elements performed; ceremony is how these acts and elements are incorporated into a larger context. For instance, participating in communion on Sunday involves the ritual of the priests preparing the bread and wine for distribution to the congregation in the broader context of the entire worship ceremony—preaching, singing, reciting scripture recitation, and so forth.

of God: The silent and prostrate adoration of God by the four living creatures and the twenty-four Elders. The twenty-four Elders offering incense (Rev. 5:8) and chanting a doxology. The multitude of the angelic host responding to the twenty-four Elders' doxology by chanting an angelic anthem themselves. Every creature, all living creatures, all the inhabitants of the earth and sea, *every existing thing* responding in a universal, heavenly chorus. In conclusion, the four living creatures singing and ending in "Amen" and the twenty-four Elders falling down and closing worship, as it had started, with prostrate, silent adoration are only some of the elements of heavenly ritual and ceremony.

Observe how elaborately responsive this worship was. The twenty-four Elders offering their doxology were responded to by the angel host; the angelic host was responded to by the entire creation; and the universal chorus of the whole creation was responded to by the four winged,[22] living creatures. Full participation by all of creation was involved in worship.

As I have stated, heaven is the starting place and pattern for all worship on earth. We have seen that worship in heaven is intelligible and responsive. To these we must add congregational.

Congregational Worship

If the point of worshiping God was/is to merely focus attention upon Him due to His glorious, transcendent splendor and nature, one Seraph could have accomplished that without difficulty. However, that is not the exclusive focus of worship. Worship is the recognition not only by a select number of heavenly beings but of all beings: the twenty-four Elders, the four living creatures, all the angels, all created things demonstrating that the glorious, awesome, infinite God of the universe is to be the focus of every second of our worship. The entire created order as well as the heavenly host all had a role in this heavenly liturgy. An infinite number of worshipers all lending their collective voices to worship. All attention is upon Him. Therefore, if all beings are to turn their attention to God in worship, then worship is also to be congregational. As the Seraphs in heaven raised their voices in this great act of worship, as both the prophet Isaiah and St.

---

22   J. G. Norton, Worship in *Heaven and on Earth: Responsive, Congregational, Reverent, Musical, and Beautiful*. London: Wells Gardner, Darton, and Co., 1884: 102.

John demonstrate, they gave witness to the congregational nature of worship. All had a share in this worship. There were no mere onlookers. Every song, every response, every bowed head was joined to theirs. All worship is participatory. Is this heavenly example what our worship models?

Reverent Worship

Many Christians today believe that to worship God in spirit and truth is to concentrate primarily upon praise—singing, guitar bands, solo artists all lending their voices and talents on Sunday morning. I will not comment on the guitars and solo artists, but I will say that praise, adoration, thanksgiving, and joy are all part of proper worship, but they must be expressed properly and in context. While one can find numerous places in scripture where these qualities are present, one would be hard pressed to find them expressed in the same context in heaven as they are on earth. In heaven, God is the intended center of attention. Sorën Kierkegaard once described the worship of his day as follows:

> Many Christians think that in Sunday worship, the minister or singers are the performers; the congregation is the audience and God is the director. The reality is, God is the audience, WE are the players, and the minster is the director.[23]

This was written in the nineteenth century, and it could be equally applicable to contemporary worship settings in most churches. Have you ever heard someone say, "I didn't get anything out of that sermon today" or "I didn't get anything out of church on Sunday"? How sad such an attitude is. Yet is it any wonder that this mindset is so prevalent within Christianity today? Our actions are passive, as if worship is done to and for us; our attention is on the activity taking place on the stage or platform instead of upon God, and the very buildings in which we attend these events are more like auditoriums or convention centers, generating no sense of awe or reverence or the presence of God. Many are even called worship centers. How has utility become the true focus of the house of God? Is it any wonder people have a hit-or-miss attitude

---

23   This is a slight modernization of the quote from the Danish Christian existentialist philosopher Sorën Kierkegaard in his work *Purity of Heart in Edifying Discourses in Various Spirits*.

when it comes to worship in a facility that on Sunday is called "church" and on Monday could be the site of a Comic-Con?

This sentiment misses the entire point of worship. We are there so that God gets something out of our worship, because He is worthy to receive it. He is the one full of worth. We are there for Him. If we acknowledge that and prepare our hearts and minds to worship in that manner, in spirit and truth, most certainly we will get something out of worship. We might even be surprised by what it is: joy, grief over our sin, astonishment with some aspect of God's character, tears over the understanding of the work of Christ on the cross, and so on.

Worship in heaven opens the way it ends: with prostration and adoration. Look at the reverence of the Seraphim in their worship of God. With two wings, they covered their eyes so as not to steal a glance at His infinite glory; with two wings, they covered their feet so as not to presume to approach His majesty in an unworthy manner. The example of the twenty-four Elders showed such reverence in these simple gestures.

These actions of reverence on the part of our heavenly examples stimulate and promote (or at least they should) devotion on our part; they certainly did on the part of the Seraphim. Gestures of these kinds are not superfluous, extraneous acts of the self-centered; on the contrary, they are the actions of one who is moved from the heart to acknowledge where they are, in whose presence they happen to be, and what they should do to express that depth of devotion. These acts do not save; they are the acts of those already saved. Is this the type of reverence we experience in our worship?

Ritualistic Worship (and the Use of Incense)

"The house was filled with smoke." The Elders with their golden censers offering incense, the sweet savor of loving adoration and prayer. This is our reminder on earth of God's presence in His house on Sundays. For us, there is also the added dimension that incense (smoke) presents us with the visible reminder of God's presence in the Glory-Cloud[24] in the

---

24   This concept is a profound understanding of the presence of God. Reflect on the account at Mt. Sinai in Exodus, where the cloud descends upon the mountain. Simply put, this cloud of glory, or Glory-Cloud, is God's divine chariot, where His mobile throne is present. This is

Old Testament. This smoke, which was the presence of God on earth with His people, filled the tabernacle and the temple, indicating He was there in the midst of His people, dwelling with them and leading them. So significant was incense in worship that men died for offering incense not specifically prescribed by God. While the Elders were offering their incense, they were singing. There is also the added benefit of providing a sweet fragrance in the air. If you have ever been in a sanctuary where the air conditioning went out, you will understand. There is one other element of the use of incense in worship, one more reminder. In the world of the early church, incense was used in emperor worship. And when Christianity had victoriously replaced the pagan Roman empire, incense became a vivid reminder that all Christians worshiped the *true* emperor of the universe, Jesus Christ.

In all of these things, the twenty-four Elders in their royal state, seated around the throne of God; the four living creatures around the throne; the seven lamps; the emerald rainbow; the great throne and the King who is seated upon it all demonstrate the continuity between Old and New Covenant worship. Do we see these reminders in our worship?

Musical Worship

As Isaiah first encounters the heavenly scene, he hears chanting: the wonderful, mellifluous, glorious, beautiful chanting of the Seraphim, back and forth to one another. It is an anthem to the holy majesty of our transcendent God. Music is an integral part of all worship; however, it is not the center of our worship. It might seem odd to say that, but if one considers the average Sunday worship service in a Christian service, one would think just the opposite. Bands, instruments, soloists, and more are front and center, directing our attention and gaze straight at them. This appears to be amiss. God is to be the immediate, direct focus of our worship, not bands, soloists, or even the music, yet we see this played out over and over in current worship.

Music as a vital part of our worship gives wings to our deepest, most

---

emblematic of the royal chariots of ancient near-Eastern sovereigns. For a compelling and illuminating explanation of this depiction, reference Dr. Meredith G. Kline's *Images of the Spirit* (self-published, 1980).

intimate emotions. When our words fail us because our minds and hearts have been pierced by the power of the word of God, we need a way to express this in worship. There are times we find ourselves speechless, so overcome with the response to God's word that we are paralyzed. It is music that takes the depth of what we are feeling, draws it out of our souls, carries it on the softness of its dulcimer sounds, and presents it to God via the Holy Spirit's intercession. It is such a magnificent aide in our worship, when given its correct function and place.

Our God understands us to the core of our being and has given us yet another means to properly worship Him: in songs of praise, lamentation, exultation, and adoration. What beautiful means to express the purity of our devotional experience in our worship of Him. Is this the place that music has in our worship, or is it the focus of our worship?

Beautiful Worship

Imagine Isaiah in his normal day-to-day routine. He sees the resplendent beauty of a sunrise, the amazing colors of the heat as it rises from the desert floor in Israel, the glory of the colors of the High Priest's tunic, and the unbelievable refulgent glory of the temple. Woodlands, rivers, seas, flowers, and then, of course, the breathtaking sunset. A living canvas of art. Likewise, St. John, though exiled on the isle of Patmos at this point, would have experienced the visual beauty that Rome added to the region of Palestine. The gold, bronze, silver of the Roman Empire. All of this on earth. Then they are confronted with beauty, splendor, and glory as no currently living man has seen: the indescribable heavenly scene that is set before them. If the amazing glory of the beauty they encountered on earth took their collective breath away at times, can you fathom what they were experiencing at that very moment in their respective visions of heaven and the heavenly throne?

St. John describes streets of transparent gold, city walls of crystal-clear jasper, gates of pearl, and a light so bright that no artificial light is needed to illuminate all of heaven. As he describes the throne, there is a rainbow that looks like an emerald. The emerald is situated upon the High Priest's breastplate, but it is also a call back to the promise—fulfilled in heaven, made to Noah—that God would judge the earth with water no more. Only here there is no more judgment at all. St. John even points out to us that the twenty-four Elders[25] sit in white robes (liturgical vestments) or garments with gold crowns upon their heads. Envision the representative beauty on view: the beauty of the throne of God, the glorious beauty of the emerald rainbow, the seven lamps, the four living creatures, the six-winged Seraphim above the throne, and the twenty-four Elders in their liturgical garments and golden crowns. What an astounding, beautiful sight. Plus the beauty of worship is not exclusively in the accoutrements and physical items but also in the acts of devotion, praise, singing, and adoration as well. It is from here that all the earthly beauty receives its form. Whatever is encountered on earth, one must always acknowledge that it pales in comparison to the source of all beauty: heaven.

Yet all the beauty that they experience in the heavenly court cannot compare with the ethereal sight of the King in all His beauty. Surrounded by the beauty that is to the eye as music is to the ear, beauty that was handed to Moses on Mt. Sinai to be duplicated in the tabernacle and temple because God does not dwell in ugliness.

How often have we heard some say, when they encounter a European cathedral in all its magnificence and splendor—the blinding sparkle of jewels, the bright hue of gold, the shine of silver—"What a waste of money; it's all gonna burn anyway." Then we encounter what is to be the superior replacement of these majestic houses of God: bare, white-washed walls. No color, no splendor, no understanding that the representation of the church is a theological expression of what heaven will look like. Is this the picture of heaven that scripture presents to us? Do the banal, bland, sterile, and plain truly represent God's house? Does this ugliness please Him? Is this what our churches look like?

I understand financial limitations; however, that does not necessitate ugliness. We do the best we can with what we have, all the while realizing that it is for the beauty of God's house that we do it. Does this unattractive concept of worship represent heaven? Our places of wor-

---

25   They represent each of the twelve Old Testament patriarchs and New Testament apostles, though there are those who see them as the angelic court. Given that St. John has already mentioned his vision and description of angels earlier, I hold to the former interpretation; otherwise, why did St. John simply not identify them as angels here? It is not, however, a point over which to divide.

ship, our churches, are to be beautiful, and beauty, it is stated, is in the eye of the beholder, and the eye beholding our churches is also the One who told us what His house is to look like: God.

Heaven Is Glorious in Its Beauty

On top of all of the beauty of the actual worship that was occurring, the very foundation of the holy city itself was beautiful, made of jasper, sapphire, chalcedony, emerald,[26] sardonyx, sardius, chrysolite, beryl, topaz, chrysoprase, jacinth, and amethyst.[27] The obvious point is that heaven, the Holy City of God, our eternal reward, the model of all earthly places of worship, is transcendentally gorgeous. The New Jerusalem was the model for all earthly places where God is supposed to dwell. This, then, is where it all begins. This is where all of what we do on earth should start. Mark D. Vander Hart, professor of the Old Testament at Mid-America Reformed Seminary, a Presbyterian graduate school, once said, "The earth is always required to take its cue from what heaven is doing." In every aspect, in every element, from worship to the throne, beauty and glory are evident. This leads us to earth.

The Tabernacle and Temple Were Created to Be Beautiful

2 Chronicles 3:6 (NKJ): And he decorated the house with precious stones for beauty, and the gold was gold from Parvaim.

If heaven is the model of all earthly representations of how we are to worship, we would expect to see similarities between the two. Consider the following from the Book of Exodus:

1. "From every man whose heart moves him," there are to be contributions of gold; beautiful yarns; the finest woods, oils, spices, and so on (25:1–9).

---

26   Rev. 21:19.
27   Rev. 20:20.

2. The tabernacle is to be filled with beautiful items for worship, including an ark made of acacia wood (25:10–22), a table for the bread of the Presence (25:23–30), a lampstand of pure gold (25:31–39), and an altar (27:1–8).

3. The tabernacle is surrounded by elegant curtains, frames, a veil, and a screen (26:1–37, 27:9–19).

4. The priests are to be clothed in exquisite garments that are to be made "for glory and beauty" (28:40).

5. The tabernacle, the priests, and the people are consecrated by the sacrifice of the most valued animals, including bulls, rams, and lambs (Exodus 29).

6. The place itself is to smell wonderful, perfumed with incense made from "the finest spices" (30:22–38).

7. All of this is to be done "after the pattern for them, which is being shown you on the mountain" (25:40 and 27:8). God's specific guidance will direct the craftsmen.

8. How will this grand project be accomplished? Moses is to "speak to all the skillful, whom I have filled with a spirit of skill, that they make [all that God has instructed]" (28:3, 6, 15, etc.).

One of the first things that strikes the reader is the meticulous detail with which God designed the tabernacle/temple (I am including the temple here for convenience). The measurements of the tabernacle—the curtains, linens, and so forth—are precise and exact.[28] There is nothing slipshod about God's house. The next thing to notice is that it was designed to be beautiful[29] and full of color (which is existentially powerful considering the Jews were a wandering, nomadic desert

---

28   One of the best treatments of this precision of the construction of the tabernacle/temple can be found in Professor Vern Poythress's work *The Shadow of Christ in the Law of Moses*. Additionally, if you read T. D. Alexander's *From Eden to the New Jerusalem*, he indicates that the base of the New Jerusalem, the model for the Holy of Holies, is a perfect cube (which is half the size of the continent of Europe; 20, n. 11). What a gloriously magnificent expression of the unfathomable awesomeness, immensity, and grandeur of our God!

29   Ex. 28:2.

people); there were blue, white, and scarlet with gold, silver, and bronze objects. It was to be a spectacular sight to behold. It was to proclaim, to announce, to shout to God's people and all the world the glory of God.[30]

This is the divine description of His earthly house that Yahweh gave to Moses on Mt. Sinai. It was to be the core of Israel's existence—the worship of God, with all its attendant theological significance, the horror of sin, the need for atonement from sin, the sacrifices provided by God to cover that sin, the reconciliation those sacrifices for sin accomplished, and so forth. In short, it was here that God would meet with His people, His house, to fulfill His commands. Ask yourself this question: does this resemble the majority of churches today?

We and the Church at large lament the constant refrain we hear about the Church being irrelevant. For the sake of discussion, what would happen if we were able to reach a friend or relative (or even a stranger) and invite them to join us for worship on Sunday? If we preached the full counsel of God, if we emphasized that we are actually in God's house, that He is present with us really and sacramentally,[31] and that we are there to give back to Him, to worship Him? And if the church setting, architecture, images, smells, sounds, and so forth all replicated what was presented by God to us via the holy scripture, infallibly, inerrantly, first to Moses and then, by practice and example, to the rest of the Church, Old and New Testaments, a replication of what we have just covered, a picture of heavenly worship on earth? If we confronted everyone, our congregations and guests, with the person and work of the Triune God-

---

30   Ex. 28:40. R.C. Sproul does a wonderful job of presenting this picture in his book *Worthy Worship* and has informed my description.

31   By "sacramental" in this context, I mean that, by the union of the Holy Spirit who indwells us, individually and corporately, the Church, we are united to the "whole person of Jesus Christ" as the Holy Spirit is united to His Head, Christ, the head of the Church. In this union of the believer and the second person of the Triune Godhead, Jesus Christ, by the indwelling of the Holy Spirit, the whole person of Christ is presented to us through the means of the bread and wine. There is no physical or metaphysical change in the bread and wine. They are the vehicles by and through which, given our union with Jesus, we receive Him, the real, entire, whole human and divine person. This connection accomplished by the indwelling Holy Spirit, connecting us to and granting us the grace of the second person of the Godhead, also links us to the transcendent heavenly realm where the Lord Jesus is seated at the right hand of God. Therefore, the Godhead, in Jesus Christ, is present with us through the bread and wine on earth, and we are joined with Him through the same bread and wine as He is seated in the heavenlies. This is the great mystery of communion, the great sacramental presence of God with us in church.

head—Father, Son, and Holy Ghost—in this setting, His magnificent house, do we really think that all present would find this irrelevant?

Also, consider the statement often made in reference to the Lord Jesus's return; how many times have you heard, or have you yourself said, "When Jesus returns, every tongue will confess and knee will bow"? This is a direct statement concerning not only the enemies of Christ but everyone being made to bow, to worship Him. Though it will happen when we get to heaven, somehow, for some reason, we refuse to bow physically to His rule on earth.

There is one additional point to consider. Look at Hebrews 8:1–4.[32] The writer of Hebrews is asserting the Lord Jesus's superiority over the earthly high priest because He is the eternal High Priest. But notice verse 2, where the writer states that He is a "minister" of the true tabernacle. The term used there is the same word from which we derive "liturgy." Jesus is the master liturgist. He is not only the object of our worship but is also the One *leading* it, right now, in heaven. "The earth is always required to take its cue from what heaven is doing," as Professor Vander Hart has ably described. Therefore, every priest celebrating worship on earth is mimicking, following, repeating the very example of the Lord Jesus Christ as He celebrates and leads worship in heaven.

On Earth as It Is in Heaven

Imagine you awake after being glorified and find yourself in heaven. St. Peter greets you at the gates of heaven and begins to lead you to your mansion. As you are walking through the gates, you slowly notice that something is off. There are no streets of gold. You pass it off as merely cosmic rapture lag, the delay in getting your heavenly senses upon being transformed from your earthly body to your heavenly body.

You continue, and the apostle Peter takes you to the Lord Jesus, seated at the right hand of God. As you fall down to worship Him, you are again struck by something that is amiss: there are no candlesticks, no incense, no altar. As a matter of fact, heaven resembles an auditorium,

---

32   Hebrews 8:2: " . . . a Minister of the sanctuary and of the true tabernacle which the Lord erected, and not man" (NKJ).

not a heavenly temple. There is nothing you can see that looks anything like what is described in Isaiah, Ezekiel, and Revelation.

This is my sense when I walk into churches that make no attempt to implement the heavenly pattern, as described in the book of Revelation, upon earth. To see churches that are bare, barren, and devoid of beauty, candles, incense, bells, bowing, kneeling, standing makes me wonder, *What is it that we are supposed to be doing here on earth?* Where is the heavenly pattern?

This is not an attempt to foist an artificial, external, manmade tradition upon anyone. This is an attempt to present a picture of what scripture says, not only what we are supposed to do but what the house of God, in which we do it, is supposed to look like. It is all directly presented in God's infallible, inerrant word.

The Structure

When I read God's word, I notice something quite different than most people with whom I speak. Most people, when they discuss worship and church, begin here on earth , possibly even in Eden, and move linearly through time until we arrive at what we have today: a mishmash of ecclesiastical expressions so different and diverse from one another that it makes one wonder if there is any scriptural prescription for order, architecture, and worship at all.

Rather, when I look at God's word, I understand all of what we do, where we do it, and how we do it as an attempt to mirror as closely and as accurately as possible what is taking place in heaven. Hebrews 9 tells us that what occurred in the tabernacle and temple were shadows of the reality of what was happening in heaven. The great Princeton biblical theologian, Geerhardus Vos, has stated,

> When the Epistle speaks of shadowing, this means shadowing down (from heaven to earth), not shadowing forward (from Old Testament to New Testament). According to this philosophical interpretation, the New Testament is not merely a reproduction of the Heavenly Reality, but its actual substance, the Reality itself come down from heaven, the *aute eikoon* or very

image. The word *eikoon*, besides meaning image, also had the meaning of archetype, and this is the meaning which precisely suits our purpose here. Let us test certain passages with this idea in mind.[33]

Pay close attention to what he is saying. The idea of the shadow that is cast is not primarily from the Old Testament forward, as if when the New Testament arrives the Old Testament shadow suddenly disappears. No, in actuality, it is heaven that is casting the shadow downward, intruding into the earthly realm. He goes on to add,

> But the author of Hebrews, on the contrary, speaks of the Old Testament as the antitype. An antitype, of course, always has a type lying back of it as its model. To find the original type, of which the Old Testament is the antitype, then, we must go back of the Old Testament to heaven. This heavenly type was shown to Moses on Mount Sinai.[34]

In our contemporary understanding of the relationship between the Old and New Testaments, we understand the Old Testament to be the "type" of all things that point to the "antitype." The New Testament, Vos says, corrects that; the real, actual type is heaven itself. One last extended comment from the great biblical theologian:

> In 8:5 we are told that the Jewish priests serve that which is a copy and a shadow (*hupodeigma* and *skia*). The author adds that it is a copy and shadow of the heavenly things. Thus it is not a shadow projected or thrown forward (into the future), but a shadow cast down from heaven to earth. Moreover, the particular use made by the author of the adjective true (*alethinos*) ought to be noted. *Alethinos* is a much stronger word than *alethes*, which is the more common word for true. *Alethinos* means

---

33   G. Vos, *The Teaching of the Epistle to the Hebrews*. Phillipsburg, NJ: Presbyterian and Reformed Publishing Co., 1956: 58.

34   *Ibid.*, 58. For those not familiar with the terms "type" and "antitype," think of partial (type) and complete (antitype) for the sake of simplicity.

not simply the true, but the real, the genuine, the veritable. It occurs elsewhere in the New Testament only in the Fourth Gospel. The true therefore is the real archetypal representation. So in the Fourth Gospel we read of the true bread coming down from heaven, and again of Christ as the Truth coming down from heaven.

This, then, is the one scheme of typology that is peculiar to this Epistle. The Epistle, however, also uses the ordinary conceptions of type and antitype as they are used by Peter and Paul. Thus in 9:8, with reference to the Holy of Holies, the author says that the fact that this was shut off to the people pointed forward to the fact that at a future time it would be opened to them. The Holy Spirit was signifying this, he says; therefore a forecasting was involved in this fact concerning the tabernacle. In 9:9 the author speaks of "a parable for the time then present." The Old Testament things, therefore, were a parable; that is, they were things called a parable in relation to the reality of the things of the New Testament. In 7:18 the author speaks of a provisional commandment contained in the Levitical priesthood. In Christ's own priesthood we have the subsequent and permanent commandment.[35]

This heavenly type, then, informs the Old Testament antitype and rather than weakening the Old Testament pattern, actually strengthens the model derived from heaven. By describing this relationship as a "parable," Vos is reinforcing what is well known in biblical interpretation: all symbols, images, and parables, though taken from real, actual events or material, always point to the greater reality.

When Yahweh descended upon Mt. Sinai in the Glory-Cloud—His heavenly chariot, His heavenly court, His throne—He communicated to Moses an exact, meticulous, precise, detailed description of not only what His heavenly home on earth was to look like but how He was to be worshiped in it.

When we begin to discuss proper, biblical, Godly worship that is

---

35 Ibid., 58–59.

to be conducted in "spirit and truth," we must begin in heaven. It is the heavenly paradigm, the heavenly model, the heavenly structure, the heavenly pattern that is to be prosecuted and emulated here on earth. It is to be precise, exact, not subjectively understood as if we worshiped God any way we felt we wanted to in a place built to our liking. No, we should be looking to heaven and then to the earthly pattern given to Moses by Yahweh in order to worship God rightly in a house built rightly, according to His specifications.

Now look at the tabernacle for a moment once again: it was beautiful with blue, red, purple, and white. It had color; it had beauty. There were candles, and incense, and bells, and veils covered with images, and there was a throne,[36] the ark of the covenant. This is to name only some of the elements of the tabernacle (we could also discuss the perfection of the dimensions, the division of the sections into various spheres of existence, the universe, the earth, heaven, etc., but I refer you to Poythress's book for a fuller explanation).

Where did the elements of this tabernacle derive? Out of Moses's imagination? From the neighboring Hittites? Egyptians? No, they came from heaven, from Yahweh. Look now at the Book of Revelation: in Revelation 1:20 and 2:5, we see lampstands; in Revelation 2:13, 3:21, 4:4, and 20:11, we see a throne; in Revelation 5:8, there is incense; and in Revelation 8:3, we have a censer.

The pattern for what we are to do is from heaven; it is a divine, transcendent, heavenly, divinely revealed, infallibly communicated pattern. This is what was presented to Moses; this is the form of what God's house is to look like. Yes, I understand completely that sometimes there are not the financial means to produce such a structure. However, that does not mean that we cannot do what we are able to do to provide those things that God has instructed be included in worshiping Him. We should make sure that as we develop what we do on earth, in reference to all aspects of worship, architecture, music, clerical attire, the color of our sanctuaries, liturgy, and so forth, we use the heavenly model as our standard, all the while ensuring a Christological interpretation, content, and meaning to all that we do.

---

36   The ark of the Covenant serves as a number of symbols; one is the very throne of the God of the universe.

There are so many more texts to which we could refer regarding heavenly worship,[37] but we must conclude here. As Gentiles, we have been grafted into Israel, into the True Vine, the Lord Jesus Christ, by faith alone, the once-for-all faith delivered to the saints. The theology is no longer Mosaic; it is Christological. However, the pattern remains the same; it is the theology that has changed.

---

37   Also see Job 38:7, the nativity in Luke 2–3, Revelation 11:15–18, Revelation 14:1–3, Revelation 15:2–4, and Revelation 19:1–7.

2

From the Kingdom of Heaven to the Kingdom on Earth

The central motif of Sacred Scripture, I believe, is the concept of the Kingdom of God.

—Dr. R. C. Sproul

WE BEGAN BY ASSERTING THAT THE place to start when we discuss worship on earth is the heavenly paradigm. As we have introduced, the Jewish nature and influence have been pervasive. The terms (covenant, atonement, etc.), the foundation (of substitutionary sacrifice), and the concepts are Jewish and provide a context for our understanding of what we will continue to discuss in an even more influential and profound manner. It is from this necessary heavenly starting point that we begin to unpack all the elements that are part of worship. I contend that if one does not begin here, with heavenly worship and all that that entails (place, polity, etc.), all that follows will be in error.[1]

To illustrate, as ROTC cadets, we were trained in all manner of rudimentary combat arms. During our training, we would cycle through the various units that make up a combat unit; one of those units was artillery. It was here that we were trained to plot grid coordinates on a map. The military takes a map and breaks it up into eight-digit squares

---

1 To be forewarned, while the manner in which the subject matter of this book is presented is generally familiar to many, the presentation itself might appear new or different. For that reason, there will be a significant amount of repetition in order to firmly ensconce the concepts in the reader's mind.

covering a particular local area of the map. These coordinates are based upon the Universal Traverse Mercator longitudinal and latitudinal lines. A grid coordinate, then, is simply one specific square on such a map.

While I was on active duty, eight digits was the most precise coordinate we could plot for any one square. It was so essential that we correctly plotted these points on the map that almost as much time was spent in plotting grid coordinates as actually firing a mortar or 105mm Howitzer artillery round. The reason for the necessary precision, we were told, was due to the fact that being off by just half an inch on the map in plotting the grid for a target could lead to disastrous results.

During our instruction, the cadre said that if you plot your grid and it's off by a mere half an inch on the map from the location where the round was fired, it could be off its target by miles. If we were firing at a target, say, six miles downrange, and we were off by half an inch, we could miss our target by as much as one thousand meters. When engaging a target fifteen miles downrange, one could be off by miles. Imagine the catastrophic results of an artillery round missing by that much. You could have just gone from destroying a munitions depot to destroying a children's hospital or a school.

In the same manner, I believe that if you do not begin the entire discussion of Christian worship with the heavenly model for worship, by the time one gets to the New Testament, they could be off in an enormous and significant way. So we have begun in heaven to get us to our next point, the heavenly Kingdom as the model for the earthly Kingdom as it relates to our worship.

The Heavenly Model

Geerhardus Vos has given us two diagrams to illustrate how we are to understand the connection between heaven and earth and then the Old Testament and New Testament in this context.[2]

---

2   Geerhardus Vos, *The Teaching of the Epistle to the Hebrews.* Phillipsburg, NJ: Presbyterian and Reformed Publishing Company, 1956: 56–57.

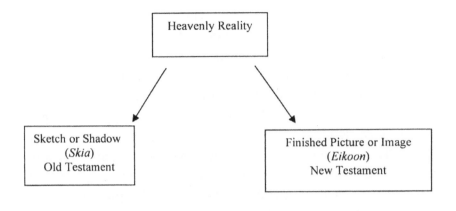

And,

Heavenly Reality

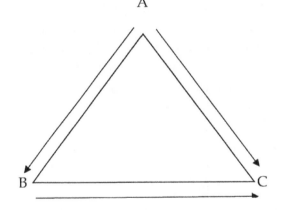

Vos, preferring the second image above, indicates that from A to B is "the shadow of reality coming down," from A to C is "reality itself coming down," and from B to C is "the Old Testament prefigur[ing] the New Testament of reality." For Vos, A represents the heavenly reality; B represents the Old Testament, which is a shadow of the heavenly reality; C represents the New Testament, which is the substance of the heavenly reality; and B prefigures C because B is the shadow of A, and C is the substance of A.[3] In other words, everything the author of Hebrews is stating revolves around the fact that the shadow is coming down from

---

3   *Ibid.*, 57.

heaven, not forward from the Old Testament to the New Testament. The Old Testament is a prefiguring of the New Testament. The shadow cast down from heaven, for Vos, is that copy or shadow of heavenly things.[4] So, as we understand this relationship, that which is in the Old Testament is a shadow of that which descends or intrudes from heaven into the earthly Kingdom and prefigures that heavenly substantial reality that descends or intrudes from heaven into the New Testament Kingdom. Heaven was shown to Moses; it was this manifestation that Moses communicated and that prefigures the substance of the New Testament.

One very important point must be addressed at the outset of this specific chapter. As we introduce the relationship between the two types of Kingdoms, it is critical to keep in mind that we will not see a one-to-one correspondence or identity between them. The reason should be obvious; although the earthly Kingdom is patterned upon the heavenly Kingdom, it is just that: a structure modeled upon a blueprint or pattern. Because heaven is transcendent, spiritual, eternal and the earth is imminent, physical, and temporal (as well as temporary in its present condition), one would not expect an exact replica of heaven in all ways; that would be impossible at this juncture. What we will see is the divine revelation given to man to be implemented exactly as it was revealed. So when we speak thusly of the earthly Kingdom patterned upon the blueprint of the heavenly Kingdom, what we are saying is that this exactness is in the application of the revelation given. God divinely *pre-interpreted* what the earthly representation of the heavenly Kingdom would look like when it was developed. Essentially, He said, "OK, based upon what my heavenly Kingdom looks like, I want you to create this model on earth, exactly as I instruct you to, to represent what my heavenly Kingdom looks like." With that caveat, we proceed.

Inside the Heavenly Kingdom

There is an interesting irony, however, in beginning with heaven as the point of demarcation for all foundational discussions concerning worship—and that is it is not only the place where we begin to engage

---

4   *Ibid.*, 58.

the subject, but it is also the goal, the place where we end in the discussion. Heavenly worship is more than a theological topic; it is a *hope* for all Christians.

There are many, many facets to the nature of heaven and how it impacts our understanding of worship on earth. Therefore, we must necessarily limit our discussion in this chapter significantly and focus on just a few. To be precise, we will focus upon one, the heavenly Kingdom as a kingdom—but a kingdom that has extensive influence on worship. As with all of scripture, when engaging God's word, the depths can never be exhausted. Discussing the heavenly Kingdom can involve politics: what it is to rule, leadership, divinity, monarchy, theocracy, and so on. So what we will discuss is the general structure of the heavenly Kingdom, how that provides a model and paradigm for the earthly Kingdom, and how the heavenly Kingdom's structure provides the bedrock of what transpires on earth, both in the nature of kingdom generalities (actions, elements of worship such as candles, etc.) and how that informs matters of worship.

Our tendency in theological discussions of the Kingdom on earth is to begin with the revelation of God to Moses on Mt. Sinai, and this would essentially be correct. However, while the specifics are communicated by divine revelation there, in Exodus, the concept of kingdom is alluded to as far back as Genesis—in fact, all the way to Genesis 2.

What I want to do in our discussion of the Kingdom of heaven on earth is begin with an overview of how this is introduced in Genesis and moves throughout the rest of scripture, then briefly introduce the place of worship, and conclude the chapter by discussing the general structure of kingdom in scripture as it relates to our topic of worship.

If you have ever been involved in a conversation with anyone about worship, you have probably encountered one of the following statements: "If you're going to begin to understand how to worship, you must start in the Early Church," or "If you're going to begin to understand how to worship, you must start with house churches," or possibly, "If you're going to begin to understand how to worship, you must start with the synagogue," or maybe even, "No, you must begin with the tabernacle or temple," or someone might even go back as far as Eden. Each and every one of these positions has an element of accuracy, of truth, but that is not where you start.

The Kingdom of Heaven Is Transcendent

This is where we must start; we start at the beginning, and the beginning is the Kingdom of heaven. I apologize for belaboring the point and repeating certain elements, but there are two reasons it is crucial to do this and begin in the Kingdom of heaven:

1. Because heaven is atemporal, it is outside of time. Heaven is not constrained or limited by chronological historical movement. It exists independent of the constraints of time. It is transcendent.

2. Because it is in heaven where all that we do on earth is defined. Recall the words of Professor Vander Hart: "The earth is always required to take its cue from what heaven is doing." Therefore, whatever comes to us from heaven, even though it goes through a transition of heavenly meaning to earthly application, does not change; it is eternal.

And we only know what our heavenly cues are when God pulls back the veil and provides us with His infallible, inerrant divine revelation.

The Structure of the Kingdom of Heaven

So, as Christians, we begin our understanding of, well, everything, but specifically for our purposes the Kingdom of heaven on earth (and, subsequently, its worship), in God's realm, God's abode. This must be our starting place. Therefore, and this is one of those concepts that you file away in your mental computer hard drive, we begin with kingdom structure.[5] God intrudes, if you will, the Kingdom of heaven into earth, and it is that kingdom paradigm, that kingdom structure, that informs all of what we will be discussing.

---

5   There are many works that directly and indirectly address this important topic, but I would highly commend to you *Kingdom Prologue: Genesis Foundations for a Covenantal Worldview* by the late Dr. Meredith G. Kline. Agree or disagree with him, he will challenge you.

The Kingdom of heaven involves many theological concepts, but what we're going to be looking at is its structure on earth, elements within that structure as revealed (some of which we've already addressed and will repeat occasionally), and, of course, its worship.

Just as a reminder, the following are the elements of heavenly worship as they are listed in scripture. All these elements of worship are expressed in the Book of Revelation.[6] Remember, I stated that we are starting at the beginning, the Kingdom of heaven, because it is outside of time. Well, the Book of Revelation is one of those books in scripture that spends the majority of the time discussing heaven. Look at what Revelation states about how worship is conducted in heaven:

1. Sunday worship—1:10 (cross reference Acts 20:7 and I Corinthians 16:2 with John 20:19–20).

2. Altar—8:3–4, 11:1, 14:18.

3. Priests (ministers)—4:4, 11:15, 14:3, 19:4.

4. Vestments—1:13, 4:4, 6:11, 7:9, 15:6, 19:13–14.

5. Lampstand (or menorah)—1:12, 2:5.

6. Incense—5:8, 8:3–5.

7. Chalice (bowls, cups)—15:7; 16; 21:9.

8. The *Gloria*—15:3–4.

9. The *Alleluia*—19:1, 3, 4, 6.

10. The *Sursum Corda* ("Lift Up Your Hearts")—11:12.

11. The *Tris-Hagion* ("Holy, Holy, Holy")—4:8.

12. Antiphonal chanting—4:8–11, 5:9–14, 7:10–12, 18:1–8.

13. Scripture reading—2, 3, 5, 8:2–11.

---

6   Though I stridently disagree with his Roman theological position, I must credit Dr. Scott Hahn with this list (with a slight modification on my part in point 1). Keeping in mind that Dr. Hahn is a Roman theologian, if you can parse through his Romanism, you will find much helpful material in his book *The Lamb's Supper: The Mass as Heaven on Earth* (Doubleday, 119–120).

Chalice[7] is the only one of these listed that I want to mention here. When we read scripture, we see "bowls" used in the Book of Revelation, but the term used can also mean "cup," hence, "chalice." Scripture uses the word *bowl* as it discusses the seven bowl judgments. But it can mean chalice, so think about that term, *chalice*, in reference to what we do in church on Sunday morning when we partake of the communion cup. What does that cup signify? Well, it signifies redemption. It signifies the grace of Christ, but it also signifies an element of judgment that must be acknowledged; otherwise, there would have been no need for Jesus Christ's sacrifice, correct? Remember the Lord Jesus's words, "If it is your will, take this *cup* (chalice) from me."

Therefore, every time we participate in communion, every time we receive the cup, we are not only receiving the grace of Christ, but we are also acknowledging and remembering that He has taken upon Himself the very judgment that this cup signifies, which judgment was for us. This is why it was critical that the English Reformation Divines *insisted* that we participate in both the bread and the wine, correcting the prevailing error of distribution in one kind only; this is why it is so essential for each of us to partake of the cup on Sundays. This should look extremely familiar to everyone who practices traditional, liturgical, biblically orthodox worship.

So all these elements are already present in the Kingdom of heaven. They are/were being practiced in worship in the Kingdom of heaven long before earth even existed.[8] This is how worship is conducted in the Kingdom of heaven. The next step, therefore, in our understanding of heavenly worship in the Kingdom of heaven is for this pattern to be duplicated, and it is duplicated on earth. If you have spent any time on biblical studies, what you will find is this, and this is a virtually uncontested truth: the cosmos, the very universe itself, was created to be God's holy temple/sanctuary and a place in which He is to be worshiped.

The universe—the stars, sky, trees, water, mountains; not just build-

---

7   The Greek term for "chalice" is φιάλας.

8   Ponder the depth of this statement by St. John in Revelation 13:8: "All who dwell on the earth will worship him, whose names have not been written in the Book of Life of the Lamb slain from the foundation of the world" (NKJ). The pattern God gave to Moses, which was the pattern upon which the Church was to be built, both in her Old Testament form (Israel) and New Testament form (the Church), has included in it the anticipation of holy communion.

ings—is to be His temple, and the very first place that this is evidenced, the very first place we see God in His creation of the entire universe, where everything contained therein will worship and fellowship with Him, intruding from heaven into earth, is Eden.

The Kingdom Begins at "In the Beginning"

When we discuss Eden, we often fail to realize that it is an elevated location. Eden is a place to where those who desire to minister (initially to Adam and Eve) and worship God must ascend. This is the first area on earth that models the heavenly court in the Kingdom of heaven. Eden, the mountaintop sanctuary/temple in the garden.

Genesis 2:10–14	**Ezekiel 28:13–14, 16**
[10] Now a river went out of *Eden* to water the *garden,* and from there it parted and became four riverheads. [11] The name of the first *is* Pishon; it *is* the one which skirts the whole land of Havilah, where *there is* gold. [12] And the gold of that land *is* good. Bdellium and the onyx stone *are* there. [13] The name of the second river *is* Gihon; it *is* the one which goes around the whole land of Cush. [14] The name of the third river *is* Hiddekel; it *is* the one	[13] You were in *Eden, the garden of God;* Every precious stone *was* your covering: The sardius, topaz, and diamond, beryl, onyx, and jasper, sapphire, turquoise, and emerald with gold. The workmanship of your timbrels and pipes was prepared for you on the day you were created. [14] "You *were* the anointed cherub who covers; I established you; *You were on the holy mountain of* God; You walked back and forth in the midst of fiery stones. (NKJ) [16] "By the abundance of your trading You

Genesis 2:10–14	Ezekiel 28:13–14, 16
which goes toward the east of Assyria. The fourth river *is* the Euphrates. (NKJ)	became filled with violence within, And you sinned; Therefore, I cast you as a profane thing Out of the *mountain of God*; And I destroyed you, O covering cherub, from the midst of the fiery stones." (NKJ)

So God created this earthly realm, this Kingdom on earth, to be a model of the Kingdom of heaven, and the *first* thing He says is, "Eden, my palatial residence on earth, my earthly temple/sanctuary, is an elevated temple/sanctuary." God dwells in His house, His temple/sanctuary: Eden, His Kingdom on earth.

The second element of this creation event, this recreation of the Kingdom of heaven on earth, is the Garden itself. Most people, when they read Genesis and look at this situation, do not make the distinction that there are actually three separate areas being discussed, three different sections to the created order. It is very often overlooked by most people who read this section of Genesis that this triadic or tripartite distinction is built into the very created order; there are three sections presented here.

The first section is the creation itself! In the creation narrative we see two sets of triads – days one thru three, or Yahweh's creation of kingdoms and days four thru six Yahweh's creation of kings.

The next example in the creation narrative is Eden itself, this elevated area where God resides in the temple-Garden, in His temple/sanctuary. The second section is the Garden of Eden, where Adam and Eve spend the majority, though not all, of their time. The third section is the outermost parts of the earth.

Why is this significant? Because this triadic/tripartite concept and explanation of the created order is seen throughout scripture. One can spend an entire chapter on this concept alone. But allow me to give you a few, just a few, pegs upon which you can hang this concept in your cerebral hard drive.

If you are familiar with Old Testament biblical studies, you will immediately recognize that this three-part concept is seen in the tabernacle and temple, which should immediately trip some circuit breakers in your thinking and tell you that the tabernacle and temple were not only specifically designed to be God's house, and for worshiping and fellowshipping with Him, but they were to be a mirror of the entire created order, God's extending the Kingdom of heaven into the earthly realm, the physical realm.

So we have Eden, the Garden of Eden, and the outermost parts of the earth. Everyone remember this interesting biblical account of Noah's Ark? How many decks are there in Noah's Ark? Three. The top deck is where Noah (the representative of God, created in His image) lived with his family. The second deck is where all the animals, without spot and undefiled—in a word, holy—were housed for eventual worship. The third deck is where the rest of all the world's animals were housed. So here we see, in the account of Noah, the tripartite concept presented.

How about Mt. Sinai? The top of Mt. Sinai was the most Holy of Holies. It was here that Yahweh's mobile throne, His mobile heavenly court in the clouds, descends and rests on top of the mount and where He makes His home until the tabernacle is built. The second area is the middle section of the mountain, where Joshua, Aaron, and the elders would wait for Moses, the Holy Place, because they couldn't join Moses at the top in the Holy of Holies. The third area is everything else, where the Nation of Israel and the rest of the world would dwell at the base of the mountain.

So this triadic/tripartite concept exists throughout scripture, beginning in the created order of Eden. Even the standalone synagogues, when they began to become more numerous in late second and third centuries, modeled their architecture after this pattern as they modeled it upon the temple.

Therefore, we see that God is recreating the Kingdom of heaven on earth. We have the Kingdom of heaven overlapping[9] into the earthly realm; we have the Kingdom of heaven being imposed upon the earthly, physical created order, where the Holy of Holies (Eden) is God's resi-

---

9 The late Dr. Meredith G. Kline referred to this in our Old Testament classes as "intrusion" into the earthly sphere.

dence, and the Holy Place (the Garden of Eden) is where God's ministers minister to and serve God. These two areas are to influence, affect,
witness to, and bring the rest of creation into God's divine Kingdom.

Now consider this: in Genesis 3:8, Adam and Eve walked with God,
correct? When God is dwelling with His people in His tabernacle, II
Samuel 7:6–7 states that God says He has "moved about in a tent and
Tabernacle." The Hebrew word for "moved"[10] is the same word used
by Yahweh Himself in Genesis 3:8 to indicate that God "walked" with
Adam and Eve in the context of worship. In the created order itself, in
Genesis 3, the biblical type, the biblical foreshadowing, the anticipation
of God dwelling with man, of man walking with God, of fellowshipping
with God, or worshiping God in Jesus Christ, is built into the very structure of creation. This expectation is in the created order, at the very start,
because the created order is to be a recreation of the Kingdom of heaven.

This is significant for this reason: what happens in Genesis 4? We
have the bang brothers, Cain and Abel. Cain and Abel, bless their hearts,
foreshadow the situation in which we find ourselves today with competing forms of worship: What is the proper way to worship God? What
did Abel do? In the Epistle to the Hebrews, we read, " . . . by faith Abel
presented his offering." Then Cain presented his. Abel's offering was
honored by God and accepted; Cain's was not. But I am getting ahead of
myself. This element of the heavenly Kingdom on earth, the acceptabil-
ity of worship, will be discussed in the next chapter.

Now that we have looked at the movement of the Kingdom of heav-
en to the establishment of its representation as the Kingdom on earth,
the natural questions would be: What would that Kingdom on earth
look like? What are some of the characteristics that are exemplified in
this earthly representation of the Kingdom of heaven?

It is critical to understand that this kingdom concept expressed on
earth had to have some type of physical expression in order for it, at the
very least, to be known or seen. Though there are both spiritual as well
as physical aspects of the Kingdom on earth, unless we realize that a
kingdom does in fact manifest itself in a tangible way, a visible way, all
we are talking about is something ethereal, essentially purely mystical in

---

10   *Mithalek* (מִתְהַלֵּךְ).

a way that is virtually nothing more than a propositional explanation of something. In other words, to reject a physical component to the Kingdom on earth, to consign it to only some sort of propositional knowledge of this earthly Kingdom existing, is to come dangerously close to an attenuated form of Gnosticism.[11] To avoid this, we merely recognize that there is a definitive way to understand the Kingdom of heaven on earth as physical. This is easily seen, then, in the establishment of the Nation of Israel as both the spiritual *and* physical representation of that Kingdom of heaven on earth.

With the establishment of the Kingdom of God on earth in the Nation of Israel, God willed the teaching and saving of man, prior to the Incarnation, by establishing a visible church[12] in the Old Testament.[13] This Kingdom/church, revealed to Moses on Mt. Sinai by God, contained very specific and exact qualities. I must pause for a moment here because it is of the utmost import, it is critical to recognize, what was just stated. God divinely revealed this pattern to Moses. This blueprint for the establishment of a Kingdom was by divine command. Moses received this pattern directly from God and implemented this divinely

---

11 Gnosticism is a multifaceted belief system that competed with Christianity for prominence in the early Church. It is too complicated to expound upon it in any detail here. For our purposes, the two elements of Gnosticism that bear on our discussion are a rejection of anything physical as evil and that truth or salvation is known only by the initiated and is attained by secret knowledge. Please note this is a gross simplification of a very wide-ranging belief system.

12 For those not from a traditional, biblically orthodox theology, the idea of Church being used in connection with Israel would seem strange. The radical separation of Israel and the (New Testament) Church is a nineteenth-century doctrine not easily found in the history of orthodox theology until the advent of an Irish Anglican deacon, John Nelson Darby, in the early 1800s and its popularization in the notes of the Scofield Reference Bible (the original and new editions), where it is referred to as dispensationalism. One of the most prominent advocates of this view today is Dr. John MacArthur.

13 The Greek term for Church, ἐκκλησία (*ecclesia*: called out, assembly), and the Hebrew word for the same concept, לְהָק‎"‘(*kahal:* assembly, congregation), were used interchangeably until late third and early fourth centuries, when it became expedient for the Jews to demonstrably and once and for all separate themselves from their Jewish brethren who identified as followers of the Christ: Christians. See Heinrich Graetz's *History of the Jews* (Philadelphia: Jewish Publication Society of American, 1891), Emil Schürer, History of the Jewish People in the Time of Jesus Christ reprinted by Hendrickson Publishing from the original (T and T Clark Publishing, Edinburgh, UK, 1890). See pages 250–251, where Edersheim points out that *kahal* "indicates their (the assembly of Jews) inner or spiritual connection." *Kahal*" is translated (in the LXX) in seventy places as *ecclesia* and only in thirty-seven as "synagogue." The point is that the very issue that dispensationalists assert separates Israel and the Church and their identification as one distinct spiritual people of God, the linguistic difference between *kahal* and *ecclesia*, is eliminated.

revealed structure on earth in order to create an earthly replication of heaven (with the necessary interpretative accommodations of moving from the heavenly realm to the earthly). One must ask then, "Where and when did God state in scripture that this is to end, this is to cease to exist?"[14] This event is marked by God divinely revealing to Moses these elements:[15]

1. Twelve leaders (the patriarchs).

2. Special covenants

3. Special prophetic (initially both predicative and prescriptive) divine revelation

4. Rite of initiation (circumcision)

5. Instructions of sacrifice

6. A place to meet God

7. Only three orders of ministers to serve God and His people (high priest, priest, and Levite) and lead them in precisely how to participate in worshiping God

8. Rite of continued fellowship (Passover)

9. Specific and precise instructions for the proper implementation of circumcision and Passover (sacraments)

10. A code of moral behavior (law)

11. A physical reminder of His constant presence (pillar of fire)

12. Proper ritual for worship and instructions as to the proper and *only* way God is to be approached in this worship

13. A calendar to remind them that God is the focus of all

14. These elements (sacraments and moral law) are taught and celebrated in a place designated by God, the tabernacle (temple),

---

14   We address the issue of the Lord Jesus's fulfillment of the Old Testament in chapter 8.
15   You will see the elements of this list and corollaries repeated numerous times in this book.

and are then brought to the individual Jewish tribes and passed on.

15. It was this microcosmic replication of the heavenly Kingdom of God, with its heavenly sanctuary containing its heavenly throne, that God's rule would extend through His visible presence, signs, and specific rituals for worship conducted via a paradigm of feasts and festivals presented throughout each and every year as an active involvement of God working in His world and a remembrance of His sovereign reign, rule, and control over all of life.

All of this is contained in an eternal covenant, expressed in various specific covenants, given by divine revelation. All of this must be kept in mind because at the arrival of Jesus Christ, the Lord Jesus makes it quite clear He is bringing with Him *His Kingdom,* and these elements comprising the Old Testament qualities in the kingdom of Israel, the Old Testament Church, are brought into the New Testament Church. Almost immediately after He proclaimed, "The Kingdom of Heaven is at hand," Jesus established:[16]

1. Twelve leaders (the apostles) to preach this Kingdom now at hand

2. A very unique relationship with these men—and them alone (compare Yahweh and Moses). Look at Luke 22:29: "And I bestow upon you a kingdom, just as My Father bestowed one upon Me." The Greek term that Jesus uses here, *bestow/bestowed,* is a legal term for the execution of a will. (This is further discussed in a later chapter.)

3. Special covenant (what we identify as the New Covenant)

4. Special prophetic (initially both predictive and prescriptive) divine revelation

5. Rite of initiation (baptism)

---

16 See the previous footnote, for it is applicable to this list as well.

6. Instructions concerning sacrifice (His, which is never to be repeated but remembered by participation in holy communion)

7. A place to meet God (first the temple and then the synagogue)

8. Only three orders of ministers to serve God and His people, modeled upon the Old Testament structure of high priest, priest, and Levite (carried into the New Testament in the orders of bishop, priest [non-sacrificing], and deacon), and to lead them in precisely how to participate in worshiping God

9. Rite of continued fellowship (holy communion)

10. Specific and precise instructions as to the proper implementation of baptism and communion (sacraments) to covenantally continue circumcision and Passover

11. A code of moral behavior (again, virtually everything He said but specifically the Sermon on the Mount)

12. Proper ritual for worship and instructions as to the proper and *only* way God is to be approached in this worship (as the Lord Jesus came to an already existing Church, the Old Testament Church, and endorsed the pattern and practice of that Church, though not its Mosaic theology, through a Christological prism by His participation in temple worship)

13. These elements (sacraments and moral law) are taught and celebrated in a place designated by God, the temple/synagogue, to become the New Testament Church.

14. With the Lord Jesus's arrival, the Kingdom of heaven arrives in His person. He is true expression of the heavenly Kingdom of God with its heavenly sanctuary. God's rule would extend via His presence,[17] and specific rituals for worship again, brought forward in covenantal continuity with the Old Covenant and understood now Christologically. God working in His world,

---

17   Jesus Himself refers to the temple as the dwelling place of God. Matthew 23:21: "He who swears by the temple, swears by it and by Him who dwells in it" (NKJ).

expressing His sovereign reign, rule, and control over all of life through His Kingdom on earth, the Church.

15. This Kingdom/church is the work of Jesus Christ, not man. He establishes it, not us. The leaders are chosen by Him, not us. Merely because numerous individual Christians gather in one place on a particular day does not automatically mean that it is a church. One does not have the *authority* to create one's own church by amassing large numbers of people to meet some-place.

In the Lord Jesus's ministry, He made it noticeably clear that He was not *eliminating* the Old Testament Church; He was changing its theological understanding while retaining its pattern or structure. The caveat is, where it was obvious that the Old Testament pattern could no longer be maintained even with a Christological interpretation, changes would take place (i.e., the sacrificial system that ended with His death on the cross); in every other respect, the pattern would be kept.

The Church Is Both Visible and Invisible

We now arrive at the last element to be discussed in this chapter: the idea or concept of a visible Kingdom or church. This subject creates much controversy if misunderstood. Geerhardus Vos, again, provides valuable insights into this misunderstood concept. While I'm quite aware that Vos would probably dissent from how I apply his teaching, I believe it affords enough overlap to be useful for the average Christian in understanding not only the idea of the visible Kingdom or church but also a proper understanding of the concept for our purposes. Vos states,

It should be observed that our Lord's teaching relates to two aspects of the same kingdom, not to two separate kingdoms. The ancient theological distinction between a kingdom of grace and a kingdom of glory is infelicitous for this reason. In the parable the growing of the grain and the harvest belong together as connected parts of the same process. There is one continuous

kingdom-forming movement which first lays hold upon the inward spiritual center of life by itself, and then once more seizes
the same in connection with its external visible embodiment.
In the second stage the essence of the first is re-included and
remains of supreme importance. The immanent kingdom as at
first realized continues to partake of imperfections. Hence the
eschatological crisis will not merely supply this soul of the kingdom with its fitting body, but will also bring the ideal perfection
of the inner spirit itself. Our Lord's doctrine of the two-sided
kingdom thus understood is an eloquent witness to the unique
energy with which he subordinated the physical to the spiritual,
as well as to the sobriety with which he upheld the principle,
that the physical is not to be despised, but appreciated in its regenerated form, as the natural and necessary instrument of revelation for the spiritual.[18]

There are a number of critical points Vos makes for us in this lengthy
quote. The first is that the establishment of the Kingdom in the Old Testament, under the aegis of the Nation of Israel and the New Testament
Kingdom brought by Jesus, are not two separate Kingdoms, nor are they
a physical Kingdom *and* a spiritual Kingdom, as such. The Church represents that element of the one Kingdom of heaven that includes, in its
physical, visible manifestation, both "wheat" and "tares." But though
this impurity exists, this Church, this earthly Kingdom, is physically
present, identifiable, and organic.[19] The second is in identifying that the
Kingdoms of the Old and New Testaments form "one continuous kingdom-forming movement which first lays hold upon the inward spiritual
center of life by itself, and then once more seizes the same in connection with its external visible embodiment." This last sentence is crucial.
Lastly, Vos makes one of the most significant statements regarding the
earthly existence of this Kingdom/Church when he asserts, "Our Lord's
doctrine of the two-sided kingdom thus understood is an eloquent wit-

---

18   G. Vos, *The Teaching of Jesus Concerning the Kingdom of God and the Church* (Second Edition, revised, J. H. Kerr, ed.). New York: American Tract Society, 1903: 64–65.
19   The unified diversity of the Church, the Body of Christ, is seen all throughout the New
Testament, particularly in Rom. 12:4–5, I Cor. 12:12, 27, and Eph. 2:16, 3:6, 4:4, 16.

ness to the unique energy with which he subordinated the physical to the spiritual, as well as to the sobriety with which he upheld the principle, that the physical is not to be despised, but appreciated in its regenerated form, as the natural and necessary instrument of revelation for the spiritual."

Again, note the last phrase Vos uses. A physical, visible manifestation of the Kingdom (Church) is "the natural and necessary instrument of revelation for the spiritual." The power and force of this argument cannot be overstated for our discussion. Many simply focus on the first part of Vos's statement concentrating upon the spiritual, but this is an ominous and deadly error. Vos *clearly* highlights the necessary and important interconnectedness between the invisible and visible, the spiritual and physical characteristics of the Kingdom/Church.

He presciently notes that the key is the regenerated quality that is critical for one to be "Kingdom" and the other "Church." In other words, with spiritual regeneration, we have inclusion in the Kingdom; all the while, these regenerated individuals exist, worship, side by side in the physical, visible church with the unregenerate. You simply cannot have an invisible church without a visible church; how would you be able to identify such an object? Especially if, as a matter of course, the Kingdom/Church must contain all the qualities that were described above. There would, of course, be a different theological understanding of these elements from the Old to the New, but the elements must still be there, visibly, if we are to speak intelligently of a Church.

Allow me to present an illustration from an Anglican priest in sharpening our understanding of why, as Vos has pointed out, there must be a necessary connection, a "continuous movement," from the Old Testament Kingdom in all of its spiritual and visible qualities to the New Testament Kingdom and its need for a visible element along with its spiritual character.

If God abruptly altered all His methods of dealing with men and established a "purely" spiritual religion after suddenly discarding a purely formal religion, either in the first instance He was radically mistaken, or immediately after Christ came, human nature underwent a sudden and complete change, was so

amazingly spiritualized that men had to be treated as pure spirits, disembodied souls, or angels, rather than as men who could
be taught through bodily senses, by outward signs and forms,
just exactly as men are taught everywhere today, and as they always must be taught until they get to Paradise.[20]

His hyperbole about "pure spirits" aside, his point is a valid one.
This raises the important and continually misunderstood concept of
fulfillment in interpretation, which we address in another chapter.

From what has been said it appears that every view which would
keep the kingdom and the church separate as two entirely distinct spheres is not in harmony with the trend of our Lord's
teaching. The church is a form which the kingdom assumes in
result of the new stage upon which the Messiahship of Jesus enters with his death and resurrection. So far as extent of membership is concerned, Jesus plainly leads us to identify the invisible
church and the kingdom. It is impossible to be in the one without being in the other.[21]

Once again, the importance of recognizing the interconnectedness
of the Church and the heavenly Kingdom as a visible, current, physical
reality is stressed by Vos. It is *not* exclusively or even essentially a future
acquisition alone. One final pearl of wisdom from Dr. Vos:

But what about the relation of the visible church to the kingdom? Here again we must first of all insist upon it, that our Lord
looked upon the visible church as a veritable embodiment of
his kingdom. Precisely because the invisible church realizes the
kingship of God, the visible church must likewise partake of this
character. We have seen that the power of binding and loosing
given to the church is described under the figure of the keys of

---

20   *The King's Highway*, by Fr. Frank Westcott. While I am not sanguine about Fr. Westcott's
overall theological position, he makes a penetrating point here.
21   *Op. Cit.* Vos, 158–162.

the kingdom of heaven.[22] Our Lord in conferring this power acts in the capacity of King over the visible church. In Matt. 13:41 the kingdom of the Son of man, out of which the angels in the last day will remove all things that cause stumbling and them that do iniquity, is nothing else but the visible church. The visible church is constituted by the enthronement of Christ as the King of glory. Out of the fulness of his royal authority he gave immediately before ascending the great commission to preach the gospel and disciple the nations and instituted the sacrament of baptism. We must say, therefore, that the kingdom-forces which are at work, the kingdom-life which exists in the invisible sphere, find expression in the kingdom-organism of the visible church. That Christ is King in this church and all authority exercised within any church-body derives from him is an important principle of church government, which those who endeavor to distinguish between the kingdom of God and the visible church do not always sufficiently keep in mind.[23]

For Vos, then, Jesus Christ's Kingship is present and current, as well as future (not to mention past), and when we discuss either the Church or the Kingdom of heaven, we are speaking of a ruling Savior right now—a ruling Savior/King, who not only rules from the Right Hand of God's throne in heaven but here, in an actual visible, physical manifestation of that heavenly Kingdom on earth as represented by His Church, the Body of the Whole person of Christ.

The great Reformed nineteenth-century theologian John Williamson Nevin has argued that to truly understand the Christian Church, one must begin with the incarnation[24] of Jesus. Nevin argues that Chris-

---

22 Vos explains the concept of the keys in two ways: first, in the traditional understanding of the imposing and remitting of sins, or, in Jewish communication, forbidding and allowing; second, in the sense of "the keys of the kingdom," "in the sense of having complete and total authority of the one(s) in charge over all of the administrative activities (and by administrative, he means *all activities*) of the house in general" (Cf. Isa. 22:22 and Rev. 3:7). While he prefers the latter interpretation, and allows for both, his driving point is "whichever of these two last mentioned views we may adopt, in either case the kingdom of heaven appears as something *existing, in part at least, on earth*" (emphasis added; *Op Cit.*, 148–149).

23 Ibid., 158–162.

24 That the divine second person of the triune Godhead left His heavenly glory, came to

tianity is not merely or exclusively "a such statue-book of things to be believed and things to be done. It is the law of life in Christ."[25] In the incarnation, the new life that came with Christ now has a unique element, the manifestation of life in the Body of the God-man. Nevin goes to great pains to show how necessarily interconnected the doctrines of the incarnation and Church are. He strives to show that "God does not speak to men's souls immediately and abruptly, as enthusiasts and fanatics fondly dream; that would be magic and give us a Pagan idea of religion, not the Christian."[26] His point is that we must understand, especially when discussing the Church, that there is a need to know what is outside of us before we form mental or spiritual conceptualizations. Once again, "the order of all true supernatural teaching is, the objective first, and the subjective or experimental afterwards, as something brought to pass only by its means."[27]

If we begin with the Old Testament, we can see this outworking clearly. God creates the objective; then He reveals the subjective. He first creates the Edenic temple-sanctuary and then reveals to Adam and Eve their responsibilities. The correlation to the New Testament is in Christ when we address the Church. First, the Lord Jesus assumes a human nature in the incarnation (objective); then He reveals His Church (subjective).[28] Yet, as Nevin forcefully argues, it is from Christ's divine-human nature that the Church flows:[29] "This is the Church. It comes in just here as a necessary postulate of the Christian faith. Standing in the bosom of the Creed, we cannot get around it. It is a mystery, like all the other articles of the symbol, which we are required to believe, because it flows with necessary derivation from the coming of Christ in the flesh."[30]

---

earth, and assumed a human nature.

25   John Williamson Nevin, *Catholic and Reformed: Selected Theological Writings of John Williamson Nevin* (edited by Charles Yrigoyen, Jr. and George H. Bricker). Pittsburgh: Pickwick Press, 1978: 153.

26   Ibid., 376. When Nevin uses the terms "enthusiast" and "fanatic," he is essentially identifying what we would term Pentecostals or Charismatics within Christianity.

27   Ibid., 376.

28   By "subjective" here, I mean that, after the incarnation of the Lord Jesus, He reveals to *us* the existence of His *spiritual* Church (those who are regenerate) and that *subjective* knowledge becomes made manifest to all in the visible, physical Church.

29   Ibid., 376–378. First, the supernatural in Christianity. Then the Church flows from the objective fact of Jesus's incarnation.

30   Ibid., 378.

This understanding of the Church, then, for Nevin (and, of course, Christianity as a whole) determines the paramount significance of all that flows from it: the sacraments, order of ministry, Church polity, liturgical worship, and so on. For Nevin, beginning with the early Church through the Creeds, the nature of the Church is settled. As an extension of the divine-human nature of the incarnate Christ, the Church is the source of all the benefits Christianity offers, particularly to her children. Salvation, grace, sacraments are all found in Christ; therefore, as His body, they are found in the Church, not in the sense that, simply because one is a member of a local church, one is saved. No, in the sense that if one is to truly find and experience all the benefits of Jesus Christ, it must be in the Church. You might have a conversion experience at a Billy Graham rally or by listening to some street preacher, but if you are not a part of a local, physical, visible church, you cannot claim or be *assured* you have any of these benefits of Christianity.

Prior to leaving the venerable Nevin at this point, one more observation is to be made. To buttress his assertion of the "organic" nature of the Church, Nevin cites the analogy used by Apostle Paul of the body with all its constituent parts. The body finds its life in Jesus Christ Himself. For Nevin, it is a dire error to believe that we can in any way, whether discussing the Church or sacraments, separate the Spirit from Christ, particularly when considering the incarnation. We have fellowship with both Spirit and the human-divine, whole glorified Christ, not simply fellowship with Christ only through the Holy Spirit.[31]

The ability, then, to identify the Church must include the recognition that it is *both* visible and invisible in more than a propositional sense but in a real, tangible, physical sense. The import of this cannot be over emphasized, particularly if we understand that the redemptive work of Christ on the cross, in its entirety, also redeems the physical, visible world. What, then, could make more sense than there being a visible, physical Church?

Place this into biblical context. In Matthew 21, we read of the Lord

---

31   John Williamson Nevin, *The Mystical Presence: A Vindication of the Reformed or Calvinistic Doctrine of the Holy Eucharist* (edited by Augustine Thompson, O.P.). Eugene, OR: Wipf and Stock, 1846 (reprint date unknown): 223–241.

Jesus's triumphal entry into Jerusalem. The King is coming to His Kingdom. Can we really assert that this King is coming to only and exclusively a non-visible, totally spiritual Kingdom? How could anyone who wanted to become a part of this Kingdom know they were a part of *the* true Kingdom? And once in some of these myriad visible expressions, how does one know it is *the* correct or true one? How would you know you are truly and really a member of it?

How can the Church, as an expression of the Kingdom of heaven, being an organization (not to mention an organism), as seen in the apostle Paul's explication of the Body of Christ in I Corinthians, organize itself or serve any function of a Kingdom/Church—teach men, convert individuals, support a unified theological position and ministry—without being, in an important and profound manner, necessarily visible? Why did He cleanse this physical temple a second time? After all, He was the true Temple and was going to destroy this one.

How would one find such a thing? Where would it exist? How can one join an invisible Church? Yes, regeneration, conversion, salvation places us in the Body of Christ universally, but how does one ensure they are a part of that universal Church without finding a physical manifestation of it?

If this Kingdom/Church were exclusively invisible with no corresponding visible expression of this true Kingdom/Church, how could anything be adjudicated in spiritual matters where there is no ability to appeal to an actual visible authoritative body? How would the Jews have been able to appeal to the Jerusalem Church during the Jerusalem Council if there was not some form of visible body to which they could appeal? Isn't this one of the major difficulties we experience in Christianity, a misunderstanding of the doctrine of the "priesthood of all believers"?

The Nation of Israel was to be a nation of priests before God (Exodus 19), yet there was an established clerical order for divinely ordained duties in which the nation of priests did not, and could not, administer. The continuity of the covenants would mandate the same principle. There simply are certain functions that are limited to certain people in the Kingdom, whether we are talking about the Old or New Kingdoms.

Are they being taught correct doctrine in it by biblically (not simply denominationally) authorized ministers? Receiving God's grace via His objectively given sacraments in it? Correctly receiving God's Law in it? Correctly being disciplined in it? And if the claim is yes, how does one know if it disagrees with another so-called "church" down the block? Who is correct? Which of the two is right?[32] Does the individual person have the authority, in and of themselves, to determine what is biblically true and what is not? We must not confuse ability with authority.

It is not a question of "Does the church I'm attending resemble the Body of Christ?" or "Does the church resemble the New Testament Church that Jesus Christ ordained and instituted?" The question is "Does the church I attend have the identity and possess the qualities and characteristics of the Body of Christ, the Church of the New Testament that was ordained and instituted by Him?" These are two vastly different questions.

How can we avoid pure subjective relativism in doctrinal matters if there is not a visible church to which one can appeal and an ordained proper authority within that church? (The question of the nature of this authority is addressed in a later chapter.) Isn't this one of the foremost reasons for so much doctrinal discord and division? Everybody has a doctrinal/theological opinion. Everybody claims their doctrinal/theological view is correct. Everybody cites their scriptural support for their doctrinal/theological view. The end result is a doctrinal/theological position claiming equal biblical authority for every group that presents a position with no place to adjudicate who is right or wrong or if they are both/all wrong. When scripture says that God is not the author of confusion, there must be a way He left for us to avoid the doctrinal/theological chaotic anarchy we face.

Please do not deduce from this that I am advocating a return to the Roman Magisterium. I most certainly am not. However, I believe there is a way (which I address in a subsequent chapter) to eliminate much (probably not all) of the theological/doctrinal disunity.

---

32   Another significant point to be seen again as you read on.

Summary

The heavenly Kingdom is our starting place. We see the nascent beginnings of this concept being expressed in Genesis as well traces and allusions to this understanding of Kingdom from that point onward. With the divine intrusion of God's mobile throne room, His divine chariot in the Glory-Cloud that descends upon Mt. Sinai, we are presented with the direct, divinely revealed pattern of everything that this heavenly Kingdom on earth will encompass as it is given to Moses. This precise pattern delivered includes all of the elements we find in the Kingdom of heaven (obviously as they are accommodated for earth); we see all of the practical structures put in place to administer this Kingdom, which ultimately is designed to be a redemptive Kingdom on earth, including, but not limited to, the exact manner in which God instructed He be worshiped, expressly identifying three orders of clergy to celebrate that worship, and that it is to be both a profoundly spiritual Kingdom with an attendant earthly component.

Understanding this, we move to our next and possibly most significant factor of this heavenly Kingdom on earth: the worship due the King.

3

What Do We Mean by Worship?

Since Jesus worshiped in both the temple and then the synagogue, since the apostles worshiped in the temple and then the synagogue, since members of the early Church worshiped in the synagogue until 132/135 AD, and the temple and synagogue have historically recognized patterns of ritual and ceremony derived from God's divine revelation to Moses on Mt. Sinai, where in scripture does it reference or what possible reason does anyone have for abandoning this divinely revealed, mandated worship pattern?[1]

WITH THE STRUCTURE OF THE KINGDOM/CHURCH in place, we turn our attention to probably one of the most divisive subjects, unfortunately, in Christianity today: worship. If it is not challenging enough to unearth the true biblical position of proper worship, we face numerous truly unnecessary challenges from both without and within. It is not bad enough that those of us who believe in an orthodox, traditionally biblical liturgical position have to deal with a position of virtual liturgical anarchy from the vast majority of Christians; we also have to deal with the horrendous and egregious ecclesiastical devastation left to us by the, albeit well-meaning, Reformation Puritans. Additionally, we encounter the heterodox influence of dispensationalism and, if that does not cause your blood pressure to rise, we have an individualistic, subjectivistic, relativistic culture that has so poisoned contemporary expressions of (so-called) Christian worship, and Christianity has so imbibed, that one

---

1   An observation you will read again.

would be hard pressed to attend one of these so-called worship centers and differentiate it from any secular concert in any secular amphitheater.

First, we will explore the various terms used in scripture to define worship and then look at worship historically and biblically.

From the standpoint of personal involvement in Christianity, there can be nothing that exceeds the joy, privilege, and honor of worshiping the Triune God of the universe in His house, on an appointed day, at an appointed time. To understand and experience all that is incorporated in the ability to worship God, to be able to even say we have the humbling privilege and honor to worship God, is inexplicable. We can give snippets, glimpses of what we are experiencing but never exhaust the experience. Joy, dread, elation, praise, love, fear, tears, laughter, happiness, sorrow, and much more can be experienced when we engage in proper worship—properly.

That is one of the many reasons the disunity in the body of Christ, among so many brothers and sisters in Christ, can be so heartbreakingly sad and frustrating, and if we feel that, imagine how our Lord feels that this is the situation in His Body. This is why so many of us are constantly talking about worship; it is that important to get it right.

When we come to examples of worship in scripture, whether it be the Old or New Testament, we encounter many characteristics; however, one that transcends both time and space is the concept of humility and how it is manifested. This concept of humility is communicated via numerous biblical terms that mean prostration, bowing down,[2] venera-

---

2 The term primarily used in the Old Testament is *hishahawah*, which means to bow down, bow down deeply, do obeisance, or to sink down. In the New Testament, numerous terms are employed: *proskuneo* (1) from a basic sense, to bow down to kiss someone's feet, garment hem, or the ground in front of him; (2) in the New Testament, it is used in worship or veneration of a divine or supposedly divine object, expressed concretely with falling face down in front of someone to worship, venerate, or do obeisance to; (a) toward God (Matthew 4:10:),; (b) toward Jesus (Matthew 2:2), (c) toward the devil and demons (Matthew 4:9), (d) toward idols (Acts 7:43), (e) toward human beings given or claiming to have divine power or authority (Revelation 3:9, 13:4b).

tion, adoration,[3] service or serving,[4] and observing religious activities.[5] This last one mentioned is interesting in that we find it used in the New Testament in Colossians denoting formal ritual and ceremony (most probably, given the early date of the epistle, referencing initially the temple and then carried over into the synagogue). The essential point is that worship, as presented in all these terms, is directed outward, away from the individual *to* or *toward* a divine object: God. There's little emphasis placed on the subjective attitude or feelings of the individual in worship. This is not to deny these exist; it is simply to highlight the fact that scripture places the focus and premium on God as the main, exclusive subject of worship and how He is to be approached in worship, not how we feel about worship.

Biblical and Historical Roots of Worship[6]

Summary

The Jews who followed Jesus as the Messiah brought all the elements of their inherited faith to their devotion, to their faith in their newly recognized Messiah. This inheritance of faith was overflowing in Hebrew terms, expressions, and, most importantly, in common worship patterns as practiced in the Temple and subsequently, synagogue worship, as well as longstanding traditions that marked them as a distinct people of God. This pattern or structure is what we term *liturgy* (which will be discussed in detail later).[7]

---

3 *Sebō* is always used for the worship, veneration, or adoration of a deity (Mark 7:7), especially as a religious technical term applied to Gentiles who accepted Judaism's belief in one God and attended the synagogue but did not become Jewish proselytes by undergoing male circumcision; God-fearers, worshipers of God (Acts 17:4).

4 Again, in the Old Testament, the term is *abodah*, slave, servant; in the New Testament, *latroō*, serve by carrying out religious duties (Matthew 4:10, Luke 1:74; Acts 7:7, 42; 26:7; Romans 1:9; 2 Titus 1:3; Hebrew 9:9, 14; Revelation 7:15).

5 *Thraskia*: religion, religious service, or worship (Colossians 2:18), especially as expressed in a system of external observances (Acts 26:5; apparently primarily fear of the gods); in religious worship, especially external forms such as those that exist in ceremonies.

6 The majority of the following material is taken from *Reformed Worship*, by Howard L. Rice and James C. Huffstutler (Louisville, KY: Geneva Press, 2001: 9–18).

7 Ibid., 9.

Principles of Worship

Covenant: The Sinai Event

A. As in the Garden-sanctuary and Eden-temple, and in Genesis 15 and the establishment of a covenant with Abraham and his seed, the initiative to bring a people into a relationship with Him,[8] found in the concept of covenant, lay with God. He took the first step; He called to Himself a people out of bondage and slavery and led them to Sinai, where He divinely revealed His law to them through a mediator, Moses. Then, through this divinely commissioned mediator, He led them to the land of promise.[9] All worship was understood as human response to divine initiative.[10]

B. The covenantal relationship of Israel initiated by God was a binding relationship between the two parties. Israel was bound together as a people with God. This covenantal commitment was understood to transcend time in the sense that it would bind Israel together with all Jews past, present, and future. The entire Nation of Israel, each and every person, was intimately involved in the covenant and responsible for living it out, even though they had not themselves taken part in the Sinai covenant.[11] The truth of the intimacy of this relationship and interconnectedness of this covenantal commitment is seen in the stipulations given on Mt. Sinai that sin, any sin, was seen not

---

8 See the opening of the Book of Common Prayer's call to worship.

9 Ibid, 9–10.

10 *A Geerhardus Vos Anthology*, edited by Danny E. Olinger (Phillipsburg, NJ: Presbyterian and Reformed Publishing, 2005: 362, the entry on worship). Vos is, once again, eminently helpful in our understanding in that he ties together multiple important concepts—the place of worship, the person worshiped, and the why of worship. Vos states, "Even in giving Himself God remains God and requires from Israel the acknowledgement of this. The gift is divine and desires for itself a temple where no other presence shall be tolerated." It is important to note that the concepts of divine gift and place to worship, though discussed in the context of Israel, are still applicable to worship today. After all, isn't worship still a divine gift to be conducted (by that I mean incorporation of all the elements of worship: sacraments, preaching, praying, singing, etc.) in a designated place? (Heb 10:24–25)

11 *Op. Cit.* Rice and Huffstutler, 10.

only as an individual offense against a Holy God but was a communal violation infecting the entire nation. Reference Joshua 7 and the effect Achan's sin had on the people of Israel.

C. The institution of this covenant is replete with numerous symbols. These symbols represented what was part and parcel of the meaning and content of the covenant. The principle signs and symbols were, but were not limited to, circumcision, the Ark of the Covenant, the law, the Land of Promise, the altar of sacrifice, Passover, and the temple itself.[12] These signs were the physical, visible realities pointing to something that could neither be seen nor touched but represented the transcendent elements of the Kingdom of heaven.

D. God's covenant with His people had to be ratified by each new generation. Blood sacrifice, the blood that represented life, was the primary symbol of ratification.[13] This blood ratification was alluded to by the Abrahamic covenant of Genesis 15, where Yahweh placed Abraham in a deep sleep and revealed His covenant to the patriarch. While Abraham was in this deep sleep, animals were sacrificed. They were cut (one of the primary meanings of the Hebrew word for "covenant" is "to cut"), and a smoking pot, representing Yahweh, passed between the slain animals to signify that if He violated the terms of this binding covenant, this cutting should befall Him; likewise, if Abraham or any of his seed, violated the stipulations of this covenant, the same should befall them. What is unique concerning the sacrificial system given to the Jews by Yahweh is that even though blood sacrifice was a common practice in the ancient Near East practiced in all nations, Israel was forbidden to offer human sacrifice.[14] Instead, animals were substituted as the sacrifice on behalf of the sinner for the sin committed by them, reminding them that they, not the animal being sacrificed, were supposed to die for their sins.[15]

---

12 Ibid., 10.
13 Ibid., 10. Also see circumcision in relation to the shedding of blood.
14 Ibid., 10.
15 Ibid., 10. This was further driven home to the Jew for, as he brought his sacrifice to the

E. All the elements of the covenant given to Israel were incredibly important for the spiritual life of the nation; however, all of those rituals and ceremonies were only efficacious if they were from a heart of faith.[16] Both were crucial for the life of Israel; ritual alone could not satisfy the demands of the covenant.[17] One must remember that the prophet's condemnation and God's dissatisfaction with Israel while she was in sinful rebellion were never directed at the system of sacrifice, the system for remitting and atoning for their sins, but at their lack of faith in the One who gave them this system.

Pervasiveness of the Sacred

Sacred Time[18]

All of life for the people of God was to be marked by devotion to Him. Days, weeks, months, years, time itself were to be events to remember God and God's acts in their history. This is seen in that one specific day, the sabbath, was set apart, sanctified to God as a holy day to spend in concentration, focus, and worshiping Him. Major feasts during the year were to be marked in the same way as the sabbath day: set aside, sanctified for holy use to God. There even was a sanctified holy year, the sabbath year. Every fifty years, the Year of Jubilee (Leviticus 25:10) was to be celebrated commemorating the glorious redemption from slavery and Egyptian bondage (symbolizing bondage to sin) wrought by the Grace of God to the Jews, and this gift of liberty was to be passed on by Israel to all in bondage in the Nation of Israel.

But of all these sacred times and days, three stand out as unique in their importance: Passover, the Feast of Tabernacles, and the Day of Atonement. Passover is the solemn yearly reminder that it was on this particular day that Yahweh, as King of heaven and earth, destroyed the kingdom of Satan, the kingdom of darkness, symbolized by the King-

---

priest, the offeror would place his hands on the head of the intended animal sacrifice, identifying himself with the animal—a stark reminder that it was supposed to be him, not the animal, dying.

16   Ibid., 10.
17   Ibid., 10.
18   Ibid., 10–11.

dom of Egypt. He freed Israel from her bondage to sin and redeemed them and brought them into the Kingdom of Heaven, the Kingdom of Light. This is such a profound day of the remembrance of the grace of God in the redemption of Israel that all who participated would reflect upon the past grace of God as they experienced the present grace of God, anticipating the future grace of God in the coming Messiah.

Fifty days later, Israel would celebrate what Christians today call Pentecost. The full force is difficult to accurately calculate. This celebration is mentioned in Leviticus 23, and among all its other characteristics, it is a festival or feast of in-gathering. Israelites would go out and gather the harvest from their fields but would leave the corners so the poor could gather for themselves food to eat. This harvest becomes a type or anticipation of God gathering His people from all nations, tongues, and tribes, as we see in Acts.

We are then inexorably led to the Day of Atonement, that one day of the year when the high priest would enter the Holy of Holies this one time to atone for the sins of the nation. All the sin that would separate the Nation of Israel from Yahweh would be propitiated, atoned for, removed to restore and maintain fellowship with Yahweh, only to be repeated the next year.

Sacred Space

We have seen how time was sanctified by God in the life of the Nation of Israel; space was no less affected and set apart or sanctified. All of earth belongs to God, so it would be natural that He would identify specific places that would be set apart for Him to interact with His people. Two of the most significant are the mountain and the tabernacle/temple.

The mountain, the place of meeting with God and His people, particularly Moses, always held a special, sacred position. One of the names for God, *El Shaddai*, might mean "God of the mountain." Think of the conversation the Lord Jesus had with the Samaritan woman at the well, where she tried to deflect the Savior's words by pointing out the competing mountains of worship between the Jews and Samaritans. Although we encounter the mountain concept all through scripture, we do not often put two and two together.

Consider the following: the idea of mountain is present early in scripture. We see from Eden to Abram, as God moves to redeem mankind through His Kingdom, the focal point of divine revelation progressively reveals how God accomplishes man's salvation through this Kingdom. The concept of mountain, between Eden and Abram as it relates to the progress of salvation, is mentioned three times, twice involving Abram. Also connected with this are the concepts of altar, mentioned six times, and sacrifice, twice, once as offering in Genesis 8:20.

However, after the Abrahamic Covenant is established, things change. From Abraham to Moses, mountain is mentioned thirty-two times (eight times specifically as the "mountain of God"), altar is mentioned nineteen times, and sacrifice seventeen times. Additionally, Abraham was the first person to officially designate a permanent, holy place to offer worship to God.

The significance of this cannot be overstated. God, as He breaks into the earthly realm, as He descends from the Kingdom of heaven to establish His Kingdom on earth, in His earliest interactions with man interacts with him from His lofty, holy mountain, beginning with the Edenic-temple mount. Then Jesus Christ, as the incarnate Son of God, arrives to announce that the Kingdom of God has arrived with Him and *ascends* the Mt. of Olives to teach His listeners, both as mediator and God, as Messiah and King, the law of His Kingdom, drawing the mind of every Jew present to the revelation of the law from Yahweh to Moses on Mt. Sinai. In every word or act, Jesus Christ displayed He was God.

What is the takeaway from the discussion about mountains? Why belabor the point? Well, there is certainly much more that can be discussed here in connection with the mountain concept in scripture. We could also expand the discussion of altar, sacrifice, and even desert. Unfortunately, space dictates we narrow the focus of our discussion.

Our concern is to reinforce the idea that worship[19] of God is built into the very foundational fabric of the created order. Worshiping God was not an afterthought of God. Before the creation of the universe, be-

---

19   Throughout this work, we will be using the term *liturgy*. Liturgy has been commonly understood as the work of the people. It is what we are to do, before God, in worship. There is also a more technical understanding that is specifically related to the responsibility of clergy. That will be discussed in a later chapter.

fore the existence of earth, before the Edenic-temple-sanctuary, even before the creation of Adam and Eve, *worship* was intrinsic to and ingrained in the created order. In Genesis, we read that in Eden, Adam and Eve were to "serve, till,"[20] and "keep, observe, and guard"[21] the Garden of Eden (Genesis 2:15). When we see these two Hebrew verbs found together, they are only found when describing the duties of Levites in the tabernacle/temple (Numbers 3:7–8, 8:26, 18:5–6).

Both of our original parents were to act as ministering priests as they represented mankind in our intended capacity to be a priesthood of believers, ministering before God to the world. They were to minister to God in a precise, exact way, in a precise, exact place, at a precise, exact time (every second of the day). Due to the unfortunate sinful events that transpired, they were punished, expelled, and their roles, their respective individual functions, changed forever. Adam was to assume the primary and sole role as the ordained ecclesiastical representative before God, losing his helpmate in the process in this matter and passing this function down throughout history. Eve was barred from this ecclesiastical function. Able to minister in all other ways before God, Eve was not to function in her pre-fall role as joint-minister with her husband ever again, passing this down throughout history. Such are the consequences of sin. Adam and Eve foreshadowed the very worship and ministry we are now discussing.

Herein is the reason to address what may appear to be a tangential matter: the robust appreciation and understanding of the worship of God. God, in the created order, had already established a particular, precise manner in which He was to be approached, the exactitude and precision to continue, though not unveiled until Mt. Sinai.

With worship existing in the very structure of the created order, to be conducted in a specific place, manner, and time, we can begin to unpack the subsequent revelation of God to His people establishing these foundational principles and build upon them in order to truly understand our argument.

If we consider the mountain or, better, the Holy Mountain of God as of utmost importance when understanding the seriousness with which

---

20   *'ābad.*
21   *Sāmar.*

God approaches the matter of worshiping Him, the revelation of God at Mt. Sinai to Moses would extend that import to the most significant of all places, the tabernacle, and subsequently the temple. The temple carried with it special character when we understand sacred space.

When the ability of man to walk routinely with God in the Garden, as Adam and Eve did, vanished, a burning desire for God's people to return to this relationship arose. Though God did interact with His people from the time of Adam, it was not in the same manner. However, with the God-given instructions to build a home for Him on earth, Moses received a semi-fulfillment of this desire. The entire Nation of Israel, for the first time, as the tabernacle (and then temple) was completed, watched as Yahweh descended from His Holy Mountain and took up residence in His earthly home.

With the symbolism of the entire universe, as with the symbolism of the tabernacle (and temple), Israel was presented with a visual depiction of mankind moving from earth (the outer court), to the heavenly realm (the holy place), and finally into the very presence of the heavenly court, the throne room of God Himself (the Holy of Holies), as they watched the priests come and go daily. Then, on that one day of the year, Yom Kippur, the Day of Atonement, they were given the brief glimpse of the anticipated hope that, one day, they, too, would be able to kneel in the presence of God and see Him face to face, as it were, just as the high priest would enter the Holy of Holies. With a place so sacred and holy, the high priest must have not only been physically perfect, but any unresolved sin would result in his immediate death. The cloud and fire would be continual reminders, day and night, that their sovereign, holy, transcendent God was actually dwelling among them, with them, in their very midst. Their God was identifying with His people by dwelling in a mobile home, a tent, as they dwelt, not living in a permanent home and homeland until they came to the Promised Land.

It was in this physical residence of God on earth that the Jews were made constantly aware of the awful nature of sin and its horrendously hideous consequences. They watched as sacrifices were conducted constantly. And it was not any haphazard, personally chosen, individual, subjective object that was to be offered as a sacrifice; no, it had to be a specific, precise, exactly appropriate sacrifice that was fit to be presented to God. The Jews were well aware from their religious history that, at the very outset, God made it perfectly clear that only a sacrifice of which He approved was acceptable to be offered to Him. You could not approach Him with any old offering simply because you felt it was the right way to worship Him. This is highlighted in an article for *TableTalk Magazine*, written by the late Dr. R. C. Sproul. As he wrote,[22]

The first murder was set in the context of worship—acceptable worship, Abel vs. Cain's offering. Four elements must be noted in this account:

1. Both were engaged in acts of worship.

2. Both presented offerings to God.

3. Both were involved in the activity of worship.

4. But only one's worship was acceptable and pleasing to God— the other's was not. If we see, in the Old Testament, the detailed manner in which God legislates the rules and regulations for how He is to be worshiped by His people, we will begin to understand and sense how seriously God responds to worship. What is also seen in the Old Testament is that plain worship, any 'ole type of worship, is not pleasing to God!' There are times when God is angry with the offerings, the actions, and behavioral patterns of His people. See Amos 5:2.

In quoting the late Roman Catholic Dominican scholar Yves Congar in the same article, Dr. Sproul states that according to Congar, worship is the, "Ascribing of excellency, majesty, honor, and worth to the Creator."

We have a tendency to believe that as long as we are being spiritual, as long as we are within the bounds of scripture, as long as we are not directly violating God's word, we can worship as we wish. After all, we are worshiping in spirit and truth, are we not? However, God's word presents quite a different picture as to how He is to be worshiped. Worship is to be formal, at least in the sense of exactly following the form of ap-

---

22   *Tabletalk Magazine* is published by Ligonier Ministries. "An Honorable Offering" was written by Dr. R. C. Sproul.

proach God directs when in an ecclesiastical context. It is to be precise, not slipshod or random. It is to be well thought out, reasoned, respectful, honoring to Him, not off the cuff as the spirit moves one, when that ultimately means as one feels. Just refer to Cain and Abel. One of them followed the Frank Sinatra liturgy, "I did it my way"; the other, God's way. One's worship was accepted; the other's worship was rejected.

We worship God in Christ our Lord because He removed us from the kingdom of darkness and brought us into the Kingdom of Light. He brought us out of the family of Satan and grafted us into the family of God (Romans 11:16–27, I Corinthians 6:19, Ephesians 1:4), the true Israel, the Church. This church is a spiritual temple erected by God to His glory and for His worship, a holy priesthood. The Church of Christ is summoned into being by God to be a worshiping community (I Peter 2:1ff).

Worship, then, is to attribute worth to an object (Psalm 96:4:8; 99:9). It is the excellent worthiness of God, therefore, that makes our worship possible; this is to be uppermost in our minds: He alone is *worship full*. We ascribe to Him all that is in keeping with His nature and revealed person.

We worship Him because He has revealed His divine character to us. Worship in any other way than in which He prescribes carries with it dire consequences, as we will see. The alternative, any alternative, to how God prescribed that we worship Him is unacceptable. Pay close attention to Jeroboam's actions in this verse; [23] he ordains a feast, offering sacrifices with incense out of his own heart. It was to the Lord but not the way God ordained that He was to be approached in worship.

As we all know, God's divine character is holy. It is this holiness of God that demands we approach Him as He instructs. When in His pres-

---

23   1 Kings 12:33–13:2: "So he made offerings on the altar which he had made at Bethel on the fifteenth day of the eighth month, in the month which he had devised in his own heart. And he ordained a feast for the children of Israel and offered sacrifices on the altar and burned incense. And behold, a man of God went from Judah to Bethel by the word of the LORD, and Jeroboam stood by the altar to burn incense. ² Then he cried out against the altar by the word of the LORD, and said, 'O altar, altar! Thus says the LORD: 'Behold, a child, Josiah by name, shall be born to the house of David; and on you he shall sacrifice the priests of the high places who burn incense on you, and men's bones shall be burned on you'" (NKJ). Also compare Deuteronomy 12:13–14 with Leviticus 17:3–5.

ence, His servants are affected by His awe-inspiring glory and holiness and are conscious of their sinful finitude and human frailty. Abraham (Genesis 18:27), Manoah (Judges 13:17–22), Isaiah (6:1–6), and more all acknowledge they are nothing before their God when directly confronted by Him. In scripture, we see two elements of God's holiness: *tremendum,* the awe-full manifestation of God as wholly other; His apartness, greatness, glory, majesty forcing us to bow down before His presence and humble ourselves.[24] The other is *fascinens,*[25] attracting as well as repelling. We are drawn by all these characteristics, and yet the closer we get, the more we are confronted with God's majesty and our sinfulness, driving us to flee. Our approach, then, should be in the constant awareness of our weakness and sinfulness, drawing near in reverence and fear (Hebrews 12:28–29).[26] One cannot be chummy or flippant with God, who is an all-consuming fire.[27] He is not our buddy, our "bruh," or best friend, and so on. He is the almighty God of the universe, who demands our humility.

Of course, we worship God out of gratitude. Look at what He has done for us for no other reason than He chose to. He frees us from His wrath, judgment, fear, and condemnation and brings us into His family.

Allow me to present another excellent example of this God-ordained requirement (what I refer to as *divinely commanded specification*) as to how He is to be approached, precisely, exactly, circumspectly, in worship. Remember the Exodus? Yahweh enters space, time, and history and physically inserts Himself into the earthly sphere, moving heaven and earth to save His people. He engages the most powerful man on earth, the ruler of the kingdom of darkness as it were, the god of this world, Pharaoh, and his ten deities and, one by one, destroys these false gods, rescuing His people from the kingdom of darkness and bringing them into the Kingdom of Light. He then destroys the god of this world, Pharaoh (as a foreshadow of Jesus Christ's defeat of Satan),[28] and all his armies in the Red Sea. He prepares His people for eventual entrance

---

24 R. P. Martin, *Worship in the Early Church.* Grand Rapids, MI: William B. Eerdmans Publishing, 1964: 14.

25 The Latin literally means "to be enchanted or bewitched."

26 *Op. Cit.* Martin, 14.

27 Ibid., 14.

28 2 Corinthians 4:4: In their case, the god of this world has blinded the minds of the unbe-

into His Kingdom, the Promised Land, by bringing them through the Red Sea, baptizing them, including them in the covenant He made with Abraham, Isaac, and Jacob. He redeems them for Himself.

They cross the Red Sea, not getting their little toe damp, and arrive at the other side. Miriam and Aaron break out into song. The people rejoice. Yahweh descends upon Mt. Sinai in the Glory-Cloud, His heavenly court, complete with throne and all the heavenly host. The people are so excited by all this that they rush to the foot of the mountain.

Remember this event? Because what scripture says next is critical to our understanding of how we are to worship, *approach*, God. The people were so thankful that they rushed to the mountain to worship God. What did Yahweh say? "Oh! How wonderful it is that they are so grateful and devoted to me that they want to proceed up my mountain into my heavenly throne room!" Is that what scripture tells us? Did Yahweh say, "Yes, this is exactly what I had commanded Pharaoh to do, to let you go so that you may worship me in such a manner." I do not recall that. Or how about, "This is my desire: that you express yourselves freely and worship me as you see fit in spirit and truth." Was this God's declaration?

Yahweh said none of these things. As a matter of fact, after God had moved heaven and earth, destroyed the Egyptian nation, brought His people through the Red Sea, and set them upon the foot of the mountain, the people were so excited for their redemption that they rushed the mountain in a spirit of joy and thanksgiving, and Yahweh said the following (Ex. 19:3–14, ESV):

…while Moses went up to God. The LORD called to him out of the mountain, saying, "Thus you shall say to the house of Jacob, and tell the people of Israel:

> 4 You yourselves have seen what I did to the Egyptians, and how I bore you on eagles' wings and brought you to myself.
>
> 5 Now therefore, if you will indeed obey my voice and keep my covenant, you shall be my treasured possession among all peoples, for all the earth is mine;

---

lievers to keep them from seeing the light of the gospel of the glory of Christ, who is the image of God (ESV).

6 and you shall be to me a kingdom of priests and a holy nation. These are the words that you shall speak to the people of Israel."

7 So Moses came and called the elders of the people and set before them all these words that the LORD had commanded him.

8 All the people answered together and said, "All that the LORD has spoken we will do." And Moses reported the words of the people to the LORD.

9 And the LORD said to Moses, "Behold, I am coming to you in a thick cloud, that the people may hear when I speak with you, and may also believe you forever." When Moses told the words of the people to the LORD,

10 the LORD said to Moses, "Go to the people and consecrate them today and tomorrow, and let them wash their garments

11 and be ready for the third day. For on the third day the LORD will come down on Mount Sinai in the sight of all the people.

12 And you shall set limits for the people all around, saying, 'Take care not to go up into the mountain or touch the edge of it. Whoever touches the mountain shall be put to death. 13 No hand shall touch him, but he shall be stoned or shot; whether beast or man, he shall not live.' When the trumpet sounds a long blast, they shall come up to the mountain."

14 So Moses went down from the mountain to the people and consecrated the people; and they washed their garments.

Notice:

1. The people were excited, emotionally moved, and wanted to worship God.

2. God mandated a specific way in which He was to be approached.

3. His presence made the mountain holy to the point where the

mountain is identified with God (look at the personal pronoun in verse 13).

4. No one, no matter how devout, was allowed to approach Yahweh in any manner other than the way He commands He be approached.

Right here, this is the moment where the foundational principle of heavenly worship, which we previously discussed concerning Genesis 4 with Cain and Abel, is reestablished in Exodus 19. Exodus 19 is essentially a reiteration of what took place in Genesis 4. And it is this foundational principle, this *divinely commanded specification*, that informs all biblically correct worship moving forward. Genesis 4 is the disobedience of Cain and the acceptance of Abel; Exodus 19 is the disobedience of those Jews who followed Aaron and the acceptance of those who followed Moses.

Let us now look at what we are referring to concerning divinely commanded specification. This will be familiar to many, but it is important to include this concept at this juncture to establish the running principle as the biblical thread informing the practice of worship.

A wandering sheep strays to the top of Mt. Sinai, and Moses chases after it. He gets to the top of Mt. Sinai, and he is confronted with something no one has ever seen before: a bush on fire that is not burned up. Yahweh has descended, in the Glory-Cloud, to the top of Mt. Sinai. Suddenly, Moses hears this voice, "Remove your shoes; you're on holy ground."

Moses is now in the mobile throne room of God. He is in the midst of God's mobile, heavenly court; he is now in the Holy of Holies. The dirt was not sanctified. The ground was only holy because God's presence made it so.

Suddenly, Moses is confronted with the experience of seeing the practice of divine worship in the very heavenly court itself. Everything we see after, everything described in scripture, no matter how meticulously precisely it attempts to describe what Moses saw, cannot come close to describing the reality that Moses saw at that moment.

Notice, in Genesis, in Exodus, in Leviticus, in Deuteronomy, in

Numbers, that Moses never completely explains what he saw because he was incapable of describing it in all its fullness. All he was able to do was duplicate the Kingdom of heaven on earth according to the exact pattern that God, the Master builder, gave him on the top of Mt. Sinai.

Now, it is here that the intrusion of the heavenly Kingdom, to which we have previously referred, which we have seen in type and shadow, comes to physical manifestation. This heavenly Kingdom is now put on, if you will, a Power Point display for us throughout history, as God gives detailed instructions to Moses as to what worship is to look like.

God does this through the establishment of the Nation of Israel. The Nation of Israel, the Old Testament Church, is going to take God's heavenly Kingdom on earth and win back the world that was treasonously turned over by Adam and Eve to Satan. There will, of course, be a special, unique order of priests that He will choose from a particular family that will have special, peculiar duties and responsibilities in order that correct worship is followed.

That is what the entire Christian Church is doing, day by day, moment by moment; we are, by our witnessing of Christ, winning back the Kingdom—at least I hope and pray we are.

It is here where Moses enters the Holy of Holies, the top of Mt. Sinai, and is given the instructions for establishing the heavenly Kingdom on earth in order to recreate a copy of that Kingdom of heaven on earth, with its attendant instructions for worship. And the blueprint of that Kingdom, a microcosm of the universe and God's Kingdom palace, is specifically manifested in the tabernacle (and later the temple), His dwelling place, His home on earth.

Think about that; God gave to Moses specific instructions on what to build, His house, and His house represents everything that He has created. This house is the microcosm of the heavenly Kingdom, and God dwells there with His people. He is physically there. They "see" Him, day and night. Is it becoming clearer now why we take the physical, visible elements of a place, a visible church, not merely an invisible one, so seriously? It is not only a replica of the heavenly Kingdom but also the place where God dwells with us and, in precise detailed fashion, tells us how He is to be approached in His house.

The tabernacle and temple are consecrated areas. God set these areas specifically apart so He could dwell with His people, so that these areas would be purified, holy, and so that they would be worthy of His presence.

The visible church on earth is consecrated and set apart for the very same purpose. Have you ever wondered why people bow, why they genuflect, why they make the sign of the cross when they enter a church sanctuary? Because our understanding of who God is and how we worship Him does not exist solely between our ears. It is not purely a mental or propositional form of worship. We are not Roman Catholics in that we think the tabernacle on the altar contains God. Not at all. We do, however, recognize that churches, set apart, sanctified by the proper ecclesiastical authorities, are in some way beyond our human comprehension, God's dwelling place on earth. We believe in mystery. And these places bombard us with the awesome, holy, majestic, divine presence of our transcendent God.

We recognize the reality of the presence of God in every aspect of our existence, and it should affect every second of our day. That is why the visible church should be taken so seriously. When we walk through the doors of a church, out of the narthex (lobby) and into the sanctuary, we are not simply walking into a building. We are walking into the actual house of God and into His presence. He is there. Let me repeat that: *God is actually present there!* No, I cannot rationally explain how any more than I can rationally explain how one person can be both 100% human and 100% divine or how one God can be three persons yet one unified God. I simply know it to be true because that is what God's divine word, scripture, tells me. But, once again, I am getting a bit ahead of myself. This will be addressed in another chapter.

So God demands He be approached in worship in a very specific, exacting way. He demands no deviation, nor allows any—hence, His dissatisfaction with His people, the Jews. It was not the ritual and ceremony that was the problem; it was their lack of faithful obedience. They were never going to fully or perfectly keep the Old Testament law; that was not the purpose. Its purpose was to be a teacher, a schoolmaster, to drive them to their Messiah, Jesus Christ.

The Lord Jesus then arrives, and with Him He brings His Kingdom. How, then, did He worship? Is there any instruction by Him; or the apostles; or the disciples of the apostles, the church fathers, where we find a detailed pattern of worship in the New Testament? If you are looking for a passage in scripture where the Lord or the apostles say, "Here, do . . . ," you're not going to find it. However, there most certainly is a biblically established form of worship in which the Lord, the apostles, and even the Early Church fathers would have participated.

We should begin now to see how what we have mentioned previously begins to connect. The Kingdom/Church interconnectedness presents us with an already established structure, from the inception of the Old Testament Church, Israel, throughout Old Testament redemptive history, arriving in the New Testament with Jesus and the Kingdom. The elements of the Old Testament Kingdom/Church were present in the New Testament Kingdom/Church inaugurated by the Lord. Covenant continuity links the two theologically and historically. We see in this connection another important, foundational connection that is often bypassed, the indisputable Jewishness of covenant continuity. Of course, in all of this, there is the overwhelming principle of divinely commanded specificity: God is to be approached, worshiped, and obeyed exactly as He has commanded, in exactly the way He commanded it.

Jesus Christ then spends His entire life, from early childhood right up until His crucifixion, worshiping in, participating in, and acknowledging this church established in Eden and formally defined on Mt. Sinai. He participates in temple sacrifice. He attends Jewish High Holy ceremonies (all the required Jewish feasts). He even apparently participated in some Jewish traditions that were not even mandated in Leviticus.[29] In every way, He not only accommodates but continues and advances the Jewishness of His life and ministry.

With the presence of His Kingdom/Church, and having commissioned His most intimate disciples, the apostles (all of whom are Jews), the Lord begins teaching them and brings them gradually into the Christological understanding of all these Jewish practices, transitioning them from a Mosaic understanding. They, with their Messiah, worship in the temple alongside Him. They participate in all the Jewish ceremonies and

---

29   John 10:22–23: "At that time the Feast of Dedication took place at Jerusalem. It was winter, [23] and Jesus was walking in the temple, in the colonnade of Solomon" (ESV). This is the Festival of Lights; non-Jews are more familiar with the name Hanukkah.

festivals in which He participates, all the while, coming more and more to the realization that *all* these Old Testament ceremonies and practices are being fulfilled in the Lord Jesus Christ, right before their eyes.[30]

The Jewishness, with the Christological understanding of all their Jewish traditions and history, is passed on from the apostles to their disciples, the Early Church fathers. After the destruction of the Temple in AD 70, these people now needed a new place to properly worship the Triune Godhead. The synagogue was the natural location. Existing side by side with the temple for the better part of five hundred years at this point, the synagogue was not the place of ecclesiastical, liturgical worship but prayer, Bible study, fellowship, teaching, and so forth. However, once the Temple was destroyed, the synagogue became its replacement.[31] The conversion of numerous Jewish priests, as stated in Acts 6, would provide a normal, natural, almost seamless transition from temple worship, with its attendant theology of sacrifice, to worship of Jesus in the synagogue. This would be the location from which the apostles would launch their evangelistic endeavors to fulfill the Great Commission given to them by the Messiah. The existing Jewish synagogues would be the landing spot for Apostle Paul in virtually all his missionary journeys (until, of course, he finally turned to the Gentiles exclusively). As some synagogues became followers of the Messiah, others did not, which required the apostles to develop another location for the proper biblical worship of God. It would accommodate Gentile converts to the "new" faith in Jesus the Messiah, yet the Jewish liturgical structure and pattern would naturally be brought by the apostles to the new synagogues for uniformity of worship between Jew and Gentile Christians.

This, then, is how worship developed in the New Testament. The Lord Jesus worshiped in the temple and taught and prayed in the synagogue. The apostles worshiped in the temple and taught and prayed in the synagogue. The disciples of the apostles, the Early Church fathers, worshiped in the Temple (until its destruction in 70 AD) and taught

---

30   I deal separately with the concept of Jesus's fulfillment of the Old Testament and how it is misunderstood in a later chapter.

31   The temple, synagogue, and so-called house churches and their function and place in worship will be discussed a later chapter. Even though this was the case, there were still patterns and structures implemented and followed, in other words, liturgy.

and prayed in the synagogue until this was no longer possible in the early second century.

For over one hundred years of New Testament history, this was the unarguable manner in which Christians worshiped. One must then ask, in relation to worship today, why do we not worship as the Lord Jesus, the apostles, and the early Church worshiped? Why does contemporary worship so radically distance itself from this clearly taught form of worship in the New Testament?

Consider the following New Testament passages; all are actually written prayers or hymns carried over from temple/synagogue worship, practiced in the early Church, and inscripturated in our New Testament.: Revelation 15:3–4, *The Song of Moses from Exodus 15*; Luke 1:46–55, referred to as *The Magnificat*; Luke 2:14, *The Nunc Dimittis*; Revelation 4:8, *The Trishagion or Sanctus from Isa 6*; Ephesians 5:14, taken directly from Isa 26:19, 60; Philippians 2:6–11, or *The Hymn to Christ*, which was prayed or sung by the early Church; Colossians 1:15–20, another *Hymn to Christ* prayed or sung by the early Church; I Timothy 3:16, which is understood to be an early Christian hymn or confessional statement uttered by the Church; Hebrews 1 (virtually the entire chapter comes from the Psalms and was used in worship in the Church); and, finally, both *amen* and *abba*, brought directly into the New Testament from Aramaic as precomposed liturgical forms.[32] The point is this: God gave us a pattern in the Old Testament, and the Lord and the apostles brought this pattern not only into their worship in the New Testament, but by inspiration of the Holy Spirit, they wrote it down for us to use in the New Testament. It was brought, in this written form, into New Testament worship exactly as the pattern appeared in Old Testament worship.

To reinforce the previous assertion, examine this group of passages from the New Testament that uses the definite article, "the": in Acts 2:42, the Greek tells us that the Church continued in *the prayers* of the

---

32   This is a partial list taken from Martin, *op. cit.,* 39–52. A more detailed presentation can be found there. *Amen* is found here, at the end of the glorious doxologies of the New Testament authors in praise of Christ: Romans 1:25; 9:5; 11:36; 16:27; Galatians 1:5; Ephesians 3:21; Philippians 4:20; I Timothy 1:17; 6:16; II Timothy 4:18; Hebrews 13:21; I Peter 4:11; 5:11; and Jude 25. The first four of the abovementioned texts are directly recited in Anglican worship and biblically practiced liturgical patterns.

apostles, the formal, synagogue prayers used by the disciples of the Lord Jesus; Philippians 2:16—*the* word of life; Romans 6:17—*the* form of doctrine; I Timothy 4:6—*the* good doctrine; II Timothy 1:13—*the* pattern of sound words; II Timothy 4:3 and Titus 1:9—*the* sound doctrine; Philippians 1:27—*the* gospel; Ephesians 4:5—*one* Lord, faith, baptism; Colossians 2:6–7—in *the* faith; I Timothy 6:20–21—*the* faith; Colossians 1:5—*the* word of *the* truth; Colossians 2:6—*the* faith; II Thessalonians 2:13—*the* truth; II Timothy 2:18, 25; 4:4—*the* faith (twice); and I Corinthians 11:2; 15ff—*the* traditions. Those elements were written down and passed on to be used in worship following the Old Testament pattern established by God.

This was not some manmade tradition but the tradition of practicing God's word, first Old Testament and now New Testament, because it was eventually written down and handed on to generation after generation to ensure that God is properly worshiped.

This is what Galatians 1:9, "what you have received," and I Thessalonians 4:1, "just as you received," mean (also II Thessalonians 2:15, "the traditions"). This was not worship that was made up as they felt led by the spirit. This was a worship that incorporated written prayers from their Jewish heritage (Ephesians 3:3–14 is a corporate prayer of the apostle Paul in three stanzas);[33] a faith that was once delivered to the Church, written down, and then practiced; creeds and doctrinal confessions to be learned, recited, repeated, and believed in order to be a member of this New Testament Church (see Acts 8:28–35 and I Corinthians 15:3–5, which are understood to be Early Church baptismal creeds). Then once the New Testament Church separated itself from her Jewish brethren, this pattern of written liturgical practice was continued. In summation of the preceding scripture points, Martin states, "The N.T. church is a believing, preaching, worshipping, confessing church indicating the existence and influence of a body of authoritative doctrine (I Corinthians 15:31). This helps explain the churches identity and eventual separation from the Jews."[34]

---

33   Ibid., 33.
34   Ibid., 54–56. To state it another way, it is the divinely commanded specification God mandated, the pattern, structure, and practice of divine liturgy.

Some final observations must be made in this regard concerning I Thessalonians 5:16–22 and I Corinthians 14.

1. Look closely at I Thessalonians 5:16–22. Most of the Greek verbs that Apostle Paul uses begin with P, giving the sense as though each verse were the heading of a section of the service.[35]

2. Consider next I Corinthians 14. The apostle Paul is counseling his Corinthian readers on the proper biblical exercise of corporate, public worship. Compare verses 14–27 with I Thessalonians 5:16–22 (particularly I Corinthians 14:14–15 with I Thessalonians 5:19, I Corinthians 14:27 with I Thessalonians 5:16–22, and I Corinthians 14:40 with I Thessalonians 5:21). Notice the pattern Paul presents and then the admonition, in both I Corinthians 14:40 and I Thessalonians 5:21. Corporate, public worship is to be structured after the temple/synagogue pattern and to be done decently and in a specific order. Is it any wonder why the apostle Paul prohibited speaking in languages (so-called tongues) in a public, corporate setting?[36]

3. In Colossians 3:16–18, once again the apostle Paul uses the same verb that he does in I Corinthians 14:34b (it is also seen in the parallel passage, Ephesians 5:19ff).[37]

4. Part of the necessity for this dignified biblically structured corporate worship in public is because the Early Church virtually always celebrated the Eucharist, holy communion, and the Lord's Supper when they gathered together to hear the word of God.[38] It was a solemn, holy, powerful spiritual moment in the life of the Church to celebrate, participate in, and receive the grace of God in the Body and Blood of Christ, by means of the bread and wine. The Didache, almost recognized by the early Church as part of the New Testament canon and dated in the first century, identifies the main emphasis of Church worship

---

35 *Op. Cit.* Martin, 135–136.
36 Ibid., 136.
37 Ibid., 136.
38 Ibid., 137–140.

at this time in being upon communion, while the service was administered utilizing set prayers during its celebration.[39]

If Jesus Christ, in bringing the Kingdom of heaven, replaced this liturgical pattern of worship with something new to occur someplace new, where is it? More directly, where are His instructions that all that the Jews knew of worship and liturgy ceased? It cannot be stated enough. He worshiped in the temple and synagogue. The apostles worshiped in the Temple (until its destruction) and synagogue. The disciples of the apostles worshiped in the synagogue. They were Jews. They thought of themselves as the true Israel, true Jews; they would never have substituted something different for the temple or synagogue. They would never have replaced it, especially since that is where the Lord Jesus sanctioned worship, unless there were explicit instructions to do so.

If the Lord were going to disavow all that had gone before and claim that His fulfillment of all of the law and prophets completely set aside and eradicated what had come before in the Old Testament Church, we would have expected Him to make a strenuous, pronounced, clear renunciation of the Old Testament Church to His orthodox, monotheistic, temple-attending Jewish followers. Did He not do this constantly in relationship with the Pharisees? He told the people, "You have heard it said, but I say to you." Look at the reaction to His statements about destroying the Temple in three days. Why did He not just say, "Destroy this Temple in three days, and something new and more glorious from My Father in heaven will replace it"? No. Rather, He made the direct connection between it and the true Temple, His Body. So Jesus Christ did, in fact, build a Church. It had a particular, definitive, historically established liturgical structure and order. But it was His Church in the first place. It was an extension of and modeled after the existing Church He built in the Old Covenant but informed by this new Church content.

It always seems odd to me that God was so meticulous, so detailed, so insistent upon how He was to be worshiped in the Old Covenant, but now virtually anything goes. He made sure people worshiped Him exactly as He commanded in His law given to Moses,[40] which was so

---

39   Ibid., 139.
40   It is critical to keep in mind the distinction between theology and practice. One can see

important that people were killed if they did not worship God exactly as He commanded. He made sure His house was built according to precise specifications that He gave to Moses. This pattern was carried out from the tabernacle, to the temple, to the synagogue, and then we are supposed to accept that suddenly, after the Lord Jesus's ascension, all of that vanished, disappeared? Now, in contrast to thousands of years of biblical and church history, we get to do whatever we want, however we want to do it, in buildings we want to create devoid of biblical input, only to return to the original pattern given to Moses on Mt. Sinai when we arrive in heaven.

What happened between the Lord's ascension and our glorification that changed God's mind and His desire to worshiped as He instructed in the first place? Worship begins in heaven. The infallible, inerrant word of God records numerous instances of the drama of heavenly adoration taking place before the very throne of God. It may be that for the person familiar with scripture, some of these are so apparent that they are overlooked. The concept of heavenly worship begins in the created order and is expounded with God's revelation to the children of Israel about the building of the tabernacle and the manner of worship to take place within it. It continues throughout Old Testament redemptive history and brings us directly to the Messiah, Jesus Christ. His ministry was a ministry of acknowledgment and participation in this worship, a liturgical pattern He bequeathed to His apostles and they to their disciples. This revelation formed the basis for the Old Testament worship of the Jews; it was the foundation for the New Testament worship practiced by Jesus Christ, the apostles, the early Church fathers, and the Church because this worship on earth was to reflect worship in heaven, a pattern of worship to which and in which we all hope to participate at the consummation. It makes one reflect on Antonio's comment from *The Tempest*: "Past is prologue." Maybe we should say, "Heaven is prologue, epilogue, and all in between."

---

total theological fulfillment of the Mosaic economy by Jesus while still maintaining the liturgical practice, albeit with the necessary Christological understanding. We do not need to carry each and every liturgical element from the Old Testament pattern in order to retain the liturgical pattern informed by Christology.

4

The Tie That Binds—Covenant: Part 1

*"And I will make My covenant between Me and you, and will mul-
tiply you exceedingly." Then Abram fell on his face, and God talked
with him, saying: "As for Me, behold, My covenant is with you, and
you shall be a father of many nations. No longer shall your name be
called Abram, but your name shall be Abraham; for I have made
you a father of many nations"*

—Genesis 17:2–5 (NKJ)

WHENEVER THE CONCEPT OF WORSHIP IS discussed, there is always, underlying the discussion, a foundational matter that is often
glossed over. The question of church polity or how a church should be
structured, and who was to lead it, has been a point of contention since
the close of the Reformation era. What is the true or correct biblical paradigm of church organization? Which of the three prominent (though,
unfortunately, not exclusive) forms of government is correct: congregational rule, elder rule, or Episcopal rule?

Writing as an Anglican, I, or course, subscribe to Episcopal rule as
the correct biblical form of church polity. In a later chapter, I specifically
address this question. But here I bring it to one's attention in preparation
for a more detailed discussion.

Two other critical and interesting factors in this connected discussion between worship and polity, which are often only superficially
addressed, are the heavenly pattern and the covenant. We have already
addressed the issue of the heavenly pattern, so in this chapter, I focus on

the second point: the covenant. The inclusion of the covenant in this discussion may shock and surprise some; however, if I were to reword it as that which provides the link between Old and New Testaments (Covenants), it might seem a bit clearer.

Before launching into that discussion, let us recap what we have addressed thus far. We have seen that, to accurately address the various issues of worship, polity, location, and so forth, we must begin in heaven with the heavenly Kingdom. Here is the paradigmatic structure that defines and informs everything that happens on earth. We have seen that in all things, earth takes its cues from heaven. While the theological concepts of kingdom and what it looks like and worship and what is included in that were built into the creation order; the detailed descriptions of both kingdom and worship were specifically and precisely given to us in God's revelation to Moses. There on Mt. Sinai, God presented all that the Kingdom of heaven was to Moses to be duplicated on earth and defined by God Himself. In other words, what Moses received from God, the blueprint of the Kingdom of heaven to be presented on earth, was explicitly explained or interpreted for him. God told him what heaven looked like, what was practiced there, and how it was to be understood and duplicated on earth.

This description of the heavenly Kingdom, what was practiced there, and how it was to be translated into an earthly Kingdom comes to us by infallible divine revelation. This revelation presents very precise, detailed instructions on what the earthly Kingdom is to look like and how God is to be worshiped in it. This precise revelation is what I have called *divinely commanded specificity*,[1] which includes, but is not limited to, a dwelling place/house exactingly and precisely built to God's specifications and a system of government/kingdom with officers, administrators, laws, sacraments for inclusion and continuation, rules for worship, a sacrificial system, and three orders of clergy. All these things provide the foundational setting for what is to follow in redemptive his-

---

1   What I mean by divinely commanded specificity is, in Church polity and worship, that the how, why, where, what, and who are already revealed and commanded by God to be duplicated exactly as instructed. All that we do in these areas of Church government and worship is very specific.

tory. What connects the Old to the New Testament in redemptive history is covenant.

When we begin to discuss the idea of a covenant, it is important to make some preliminary comments. The concept of covenant has many nuanced applications and meanings. It could mean covenant theology, the principle by which we understand the integral and unified development of God's working in redemptive history. We could also be referring to specific covenants in which God has engaged man, such as the Adamic covenant, Noahic covenant, Abrahamic covenant, Mosaic covenant, and more.

Given the complexity of the term *covenant*, the understanding I would like the reader to grasp is the basic meaning of the term. A covenant as I am employing the word is a contractual relationship between two parties, binding each party to the other and incorporating rewards for faithful adherence and penalties for violation. In our case, this contractual relationship is between the Lord God of the universe and a specific people into which He has unilaterally chosen to unite Himself. This covenantal arrangement was intended to be perpetual and was ratified by a sacrifice or the shedding of blood. We see this in Genesis 15 in the interaction with Yahweh and Abram. This perpetual covenantal relationship enacted by God can only be rescinded or broken by God Himself or one who is greater than God.[2]

Mention could be also made of the three important overarching theological expressions of God's covenant relations, first within the Triune Godhead in eternity, the Covenant of Redemption, made with the Son (and, by extension, involving the Holy Spirit). As Derek Thomas explains:

> The Covenant of Redemption (sometimes called the covenant of peace) is an arrangement between the Father and the Son in which the Son promises to act in the place of sinners, becoming a security for His people, obeying and suffering in their behalf, and by His obedience to the law and its penalties, gaining for-

---

2   Now, with this understanding, think about the New Covenant or Testament instituted by the Lord Jesus at His last supper. Only God had the authority and power to establish a new covenant to supersede and fulfill the previous covenant.

giveness and redemption for His people. Biblical warrant for such a covenant is derived from such passages as Pss. 2:7, 9; 89:3; 2 Sam. 7:11, 16; and Zech. 6:13. Additionally, Scripture views the work of Christ as a fulfillment of the will of His Father in heaven: Jesus came to obey His Father and receive the blessings promised for such obedience (cf. John 5:30; 6:38).[3]

From there, we would entertain the two main covenants dealing with mankind, the Covenant of Works and the Covenant of Grace. Again, Dr. Thomas offers his insights:

The Covenant of Works is sometimes called the covenant of life or the covenant of creation/nature. According to this covenant, Adam is the federal (representative) head of humanity, meaning that his obedience or disobedience is reckoned as humanity's. So when Adam fell, his guilt was imputed to his posterity, including those who have never sinned (e.g., infants). Though the term covenant does not occur in the Genesis account of Adam, all the essential features of a covenant are present, including such things as divine condescension to be in relationship with particular people; promises of blessings for obedience and curses for disobedience; and covenantal signs (the tree of life and the tree of the knowledge of good and evil). Furthermore, some have seen a reference to the covenantal nature of the Adamic administration in Hos. 6:7: "But like Adam they transgressed the covenant."

The Covenant of Grace represents God's undeserved favor toward the believer, archetypically viewed in God's covenant with Abraham and his seed (Gen. 15:18; 17:2, 4, 7, 9, 13, 19, 21), though operative throughout redemptive history from the fall onward. The other covenants of the OT (Noahic, Mosaic, Davidic) are subsumed under this covenant, wherein God graciously condescends to dwell among His chosen people and to do good to them. The covenant of grace has sometimes been

---

3   Derek Thomas, "Covenant Theology" in *The Reformation Study Bible*, Orlando: Reformation Trust, 2016: 2451. Use by permission of Ligonier Ministries, Inc.

confused with the covenant of redemption (as in, e.g., Westminster Larger Catechism 31). In these instances, the covenant of grace is viewed from an eternal perspective in which the requirement (condition) of faith on the part of the believer is seen as God's (gracious) gift rather than a condition/requirement on the part of the believer.[4]

There are many other elements of the concept of covenant that we could discuss, but for our purposes here, I focus on the broad concept of covenant in general and, as such, limit our interaction to the idea that at the core of the covenantal concept is the promise summarized in the statement, "I will be your God and you will be my people" (Gen. 17:6, 8; Ex. 6:7; 20:2; 29:45; Lev. 11:45; Jer. 32:38; Ezek. 11:20; 34:30; 36:28; 2 Cor. 6:17, 18; Rev. 21:3).[5] As Dr. Thomas states,

> This promise includes fellowship and the supply of everything that we will ever need, both here and hereafter. In particular, God's covenant is deeply personal, exemplified by the use of personal pronouns: "I will establish my covenant between me and you and your offspring after you throughout their generations for an everlasting covenant, to be God to you and to your offspring after you ... and I will be their God" (Gen. 17:7, 8).[6]

Of all the challenges the Church has had to face over the years, one of the most overlooked is that of understanding the biblical relationship and ties between the Old and New Covenants. One might say, "But Father Paul, I have heard numerous theologians, pastors, and teachers talk about the relationship between the Old Testament and New Testament." I am sure that is the case, but my point is that while there might be an overwhelming amount of discussion on this topic, I think the presentation of the connection breaks down at points. Many either overstate the

---

4   Ibid., 2451–2452.
5   Ibid., 2452.
6   Ibid., 2451.

connection[7] or exclude it almost completely.[8] Yet I am firmly convinced that this relationship is vital to virtually every doctrinal position presented in the New Testament. Imagine speaking about the atonement of Christ without a proper understanding of the Old Testament sacrificial system. Or try to speak of Jesus as Messiah without knowing about the Old Testament teachings and prophecies related to the Messiah. Try as you might, you cannot explain the ministry of John the Baptist unless you truly understand his connection to Elijah's ministry. Then there is the profound difficulty in comprehending the concept of worshiping Jesus on Sunday unless one comes to grips with the idea of Sabbath and what Sabbath rest actually entails (hint: it doesn't mean rushing home after church and watching your favorite sporting event, TV show, or movie). All of this leads us to how understanding the connection between Old and New Testaments prepares and informs us to understand one of the most important, vital, and misunderstood doctrines of Christianity: worship. Thus, covenant is seen (citing Dr. Thomas again) as:[9]

> ... a relationship between two parties involving stipulations and a clear promise or threat depending upon compliance. A covenant relation is a commitment that binds the parties to each other, and whether it is negotiated (as in marriage or business contracts) or unilaterally imposed (as in all of God's covenants), mutual obligations are accepted and pledged by both parties.

As mentioned earlier, when they begin this discussion, most people usually start anywhere other than heaven. They begin in the wrong place. This not only leads to a distorted view of what worship is but how to conduct worship and why it is to be conducted in that way. It is because of the covenantal continuity that exists between the Old and New.

When we read the doctrines in scripture, they involve God's inter-

---

7 Those who too closely link the Old Testament to the New, such as extreme forms of Christian Reconstruction or Theonomy.

8 Those who radically separate intrinsic connections between the Old and New Testaments, such as the continuous link of the one people of God manifested as the Nation of Israel in the Old Testament and the Christian Church in the New. There is only one people of God. This radical separation is evidenced in dispensationalism.

9 *Op. Cit.,* Thomas, 2451.

action with His people, directly or indirectly, and with a sinful world. These two groups form the drama that plays out in human history. Within this drama, God has expressed how He will deal with His people and, by extension, those who are *not* His people (at this juncture in redemptive history, we will concentrate upon saving one group). God deals with His people via a covenant relationship. He has determined that He will proactively and unilaterally initiate and engage in a binding relationship with a select group of humankind. This began in the widest possible manner with His relationship with Adam and Eve, our first parents and our federal representatives, the representatives of all humanity. However, from the moment of the fall, that relationship took on a different context. From Genesis 4 onward, God selected, chose, and elected a very specific group of individuals. His people would come first through Abel; then Abel's brother Seth, and all others, would be identified through Cain. Mind you, this does not mean that God suddenly ceased to deal with all people. What it means is that He has determined to identify a special category of people that He would call His own. This would historically unfold through successive generations, where the various covenants previously mentioned would come into play, until we arrive at Abraham.[10]

With Abraham and the establishment of the Abrahamic covenant,[11] the special nature of God's relationship took on another significantly profound aspect, that of covenantal promise. God directly reveals to Abram (subsequently changing his name to Abraham) that He would establish an everlasting relationship with him and make him the father of many nations. This promise was enacted, as first encountered in Genesis 15, by certain signs that would ratify or seal and implement this covenantal promise. First there was a sacrifice to be performed, by

---

10   Salvation is to God's remnant and comes through the Jews. Matthew 10:5:[5] "These twelve Jesus sent out and commanded them, saying: 'Do not go into the way of the Gentiles, and do not enter a city of the Samaritans.[6] But go rather to the lost sheep of the house of Israel.'" Matthew 15:24: "But He answered and said, 'I was not sent except to the lost sheep of the house of Israel'"(NKJ).

11   Some of the material here will be familiar repetition, with slight tweaks, of material mentioned earlier. While it might be a bit wearisome to reread similar material, given the import of the topic and the historical misunderstanding of the application of some of this material, I found it critical to drive home the points repeatedly to avoid any further future confusion and make sure my position is clear.

which God was indicating that this covenantal promise would remain inviolate, and if either party violated this covenant, the cutting of the animals seen in Genesis 15 would be the punishment leveled against either perpetrator. To break this covenant was a sin, and the wage of sin was death. At its core, then, one of the most important elements of covenant is a solemn religious sanction.[12] God, in this encounter, was represented by the smoking pot passing through the bifurcated animals as the sign that He, too, was holding Himself to the requirements of this agreement. The next sign God would give to Abraham to reconfirm that this was a relationship between Himself and Abraham's seed was the sign of inclusion into the covenant, the sign that whoever desired to be a part of this relationship between God and man, whoever wanted to be a part of Abraham's family (as it were), whoever wanted to have this special relationship with God and be called one of His own would receive the sign of this covenant of promise, the sign that they are God's, the sign of salvation: circumcision.

The importance of these events cannot be overstated for, through them, we have the unbreakable tie connecting God's people in both Testaments and under both covenants. In this we have the unfolding of what is necessary to be a part of God's covenant community. The promise was given to Abraham that he would be a father to many nations. This promise states that all who are his seed, the seed of righteousness by faith alone, and who, by this righteous faith, receive the gift that God gave to Abraham (circumcision), will be a member of the covenant. They will be included in the family of God, and by receiving this sign, by faith, they will be saved. Note that for one to be saved, one must come to Abraham; in other words, for one to be saved, one must be part of the seed of Abraham. There was no other way to salvation. This procedure would eventually blossom into converts coming to the Nation of Israel. But make no mistake: salvation came as a gift of God to be experienced only if one were to become a Jew.

This gift was to come through only one of Abraham's two sons, Isaac. This gift of salvation, this blessing to be called one of God's own, this Covenant of Grace, would be experienced only as one receives this

---

12   Geerhardus Vos, *The Teaching of the Epistle to the Hebrews*. Phillipsburg, NJ: Presbyterian and Reformed Publishing Company, 1956: 31.

grace through Abraham and then his younger son, Isaac. Isaac and his wife, Rebekah, would then have two sons, Esau and Jacob, and it was through Jacob, "the supplanter," the "deceiver," the "one who grasps at the heel," that the promise would be perpetuated. God uses a sinful man, not the macho hunter, to demonstrate, among other things, that He is sovereign over all, even over the conditions under which He chooses to save mankind. God would eventually change Jacob's name to "Israel, one who wrestles with God," a name pregnant with irony and foreshadowing the tumultuous nature of man's relationship with God. Man, the sinner, perpetually strives with God, yet God is always the one who initiates all aspects of the reconciliation and redemption of this relationship.

The Nation of Israel, then, would be the means of salvation for the whole world. No matter one's race, to be saved, it would be through this small group of nomadic people chosen to be the vehicle of redemption for a fallen world.

I hope, at this juncture, you are beginning to see the importance of truly understanding the connection between the Old and New Testaments. The manner in which one defines one's relationship with God will ultimately revolve around how one understands the covenantal connection and covenantal continuity between the Testaments. God uses one method to bring His people to Himself, and that is through His covenantal people. That is the norm. Those who come to God by faith alone are of the seed of Abraham.[13] Those who are of the seed of Abraham will inherit the covenantal promise. Those who inherit the covenantal promise are a part of the covenant community. Those who are part of the covenant community are saved. Do not be misled; by covenant community, I mean they who are in the Covenant of Grace.

---

13   Romans 9:1–8 (particularly verses 6–8): "I tell the truth in Christ, I am not lying, my conscience also bearing me witness in the Holy Spirit, [2] that I have great sorrow and continual grief in my heart.[3] For I could wish that I myself were accursed from Christ for my brethren, my countrymen according to the flesh, [4] who are Israelites, to whom *pertain* the adoption, the glory, the covenants, the giving of the law, the service *of God*, and the promises; [5] of whom *are* the fathers and from whom, according to the flesh, Christ *came*, who is over all, *the* eternally blessed God. Amen."

   [6] "But it is not that the word of God has taken no effect. For they *are* not all Israel who *are* of Israel, [7] nor *are they* all children because they are the seed of Abraham; but, 'In Isaac your seed shall be called.'[8] That is, those who *are* the children of the flesh, these *are* not the children of God; but the children of the promise are counted as the seed" (NKJ).

It is this Covenant of Grace, this covenantal promise, that forms the foundational principle by which we understand God's working with His people, which transcends or crosses over, if you will, from one Testament to the other. It is within this covenantal connection that the promise of the Messiah comes and with Him, the gathering of His people into one body or covenantal community. Therefore, when we see God interacting with His people in the Old Covenant, it is imperative that we make sure we rightly apply His work with them to us. We are one people of God. God works with one people in this covenant relationship. All that took place in the Old Covenant was preparatory for what was to come, with the Messiah, in the New Covenant. Although, with His coming, the Messiah, Jesus Christ, fulfills[14] all the imagery and typology of the Old Covenant, His fulfillment in no way abrogates, eradicates, or destroys it.

Now that we have established the covenantal continuity between Old and New, let us take another look at what we stated in an earlier chapter. Those participating in tabernacle and temple worship, along with the synagogue, worshiped according to a particular, distinct pattern. There was a distinct set of instructions, rules and regulations, officers, and sacraments (Hebrews 9:1). The temple is where the Lord Jesus liturgically worshiped. The synagogue is where He and the Jews participated in prayer, scripture reading, "bible" study, and fellowship, as well as preaching when not worshiping in the temple. This earthly worship was a representation of heavenly worship, complete with images or icons, candles, incense, a throne, and so on.

The exact dimensions[15] of the tabernacle and temple were given by God Himself to Moses on Mt. Sinai. Moses was to ensure that not only was the tabernacle to be built precisely as God instructed it to be built, according to the blueprint that God gave him, but that worship was to be conducted exactly as God commanded, in a manner acceptable to God.

With the arrival of the Lord Jesus Christ, fulfilling the covenant

---

14   Once again, I briefly deal with the biblical meaning of πληρόω (play-row-oh), "fulfill," the misinterpreting of which has caused numerous mistakes in this discussion of continuity.

15   Again, it cannot be overemphasized: notice the exacting precision in these dimensions revealed to Moses. God does nothing in a free-for-all manner.

promise, ensuring covenantal continuity, bringing with Him His Kingdom, He begins His ministry not by creating something totally new and
nonexistent, not by rejecting temple worship, not by asserting that with
His arrival, all of this ends. No, He immediately goes to His house, the
temple, and as the one true Temple, He begins to institute His Kingdom
on earth. He has His disciples worship with Him there in the temple. He
preaches in the temple. He prays in the temple. He evangelizes in the
Temple. He has his disciples participate with Him there in the temple.
Even after He is brutally murdered on the cross, this is where His covenant people continue to worship. The apostles continued to worship in
the temple while using the synagogue for prayer, Bible study, teaching,
and fellowship. Remember, it was only in the temple where the sacrifices
for the forgiveness of sins were authorized to be conducted. Therefore,
worship, in the narrow sense of atonement for sins, would be practiced
in the temple. The apostles would take this and immediately reinterpret
this practice to having been fulfilled on the cross, never to have another
sacrifice again.

Why, then, after the destruction of the Temple in AD 70, would the
Church, the covenant community, realizing their covenant continuity
with the Old Covenant saints, reject what they knew as the proper pattern of worship and exchange it for a free-form pattern of worship? They
were fully aware of what happened in the Old Testament when individuals did not follow God's pattern as to how He was to be approached
(see Exodus 19), where, post-redemption, the children of Israel were
denied the ability to approach Mt. Sinai (Yahweh's dwelling) until they
were purified, even though their approach by all accounts was out of joy
and gratitude. Nadab and Abihu,[16] who did their own thing and offered
strange fire to the Lord, are another example of the consequences of not
exactly following God's divinely specified commands as to how He is to
be approached. Pay close attention to this incident. All the speculation
about what the "strange fire" they offered was is irrelevant. The point is
it was not what God had specifically commanded them to do in order to

---

16   Leviticus 10:1: "Then Nadab and Abihu, the sons of Aaron, each took his censer and put
fire in it, put incense on it, and offered profane fire before the LORD, *which He had not commanded them.* ² So fire went out from the LORD and devoured them, and they died before the
LORD" (NKJ).

properly and obediently approach Him. And they were Aaronic priests being executed for incorrectly approaching God on their day of ordination. Even the example of Uzzah[17] demonstrates that the approach to God is on His terms, and there are others. Uzzah was a Kohathite. The Kohathites were the Levitical tribe responsible for the care of the Holy elements of the tabernacle, so they were fully aware of what they were allowed to do and not to do. They were most certainly not allowed to touch the Ark of the Covenant. Yet Uzzah, having been fully trained in the handling and care of the ark, reacting instinctively, without thinking, touched the ark with his sinfully defiled hands. For not following God's divinely specified command, Uzzah was executed.

In addition, after rejecting the pattern God had established for thousands of years in the Old Testament, why return to that very pattern of worship in heaven after the second coming of the Lord Jesus Christ? This concept of heavenly Kingdom intrusion undergirds or overarches the entire discussion of the Kingdom on earth, or the Kingdom of heaven/God on earth with its attendant covenantal content.

Eden and the extending Garden are seen as God's extension of His heavenly Kingdom on earth, His earthly dwelling, as it were. Eden was His sanctuary on earth, and the Garden was the extension of his temple on earth. Adam and Eve were His vicegerents, His representatives of earthly rule. God was establishing an order of priestly kings to rule His Kingdom on earth.

With Abraham comes the Covenant of Promise of a great nation (i.e., Kingdom). Inclusion in this Kingdom came with an initiation rite: circumcision.

The arrival of the mediator of this Covenant of Promise, Moses, brings with it and him the detailed blueprint of a nation of priests functioning in the context of the replica of the heavenly Kingdom on earth. This covenant Kingdom of God on earth, known in various ways as the Church, Israel, God's people, the Bride, and so on, is both a spiritual and physical kingdom, with the attendant temple/sanctuary in its midst,

---

17   2 Sam. 6:6–7: "⁶And when they came to Nachon's threshing floor, Uzzah put out *his hand* to the ark of God and took hold of it, for the oxen stumbled. ⁷ Then the anger of the LORD was aroused against Uzzah, and God struck him there for *his* error; and he died there by the ark of God" (NKJ).

and manifests itself, as we have seen, with the following characteristics (essential to be reiterated here):

> » It has an act or rite of initiation: circumcision.

> » It has ordinances of sacrificial worship (burnt offerings, grain offerings, peace offerings, sin offerings, etc.).

> » It has an act of continuation: Passover.

> » It has specific instructions as to the implementations of these sacraments of worship.

> » These specific instructions of worship are performed and led only by three properly designated offices, ministers, or orders.

> » It contains a specific moral code or law.

> » These elements, sacraments, and laws are taught and celebrated in a specifically designated place, tabernacle (temple).

> » These specific instructions of worship mandated a specific manner of how God is to be approached.

> » This Tabernacle/Temple was the place where God dwelt on His throne, manifested His presence, met with His people through His designated ministers.

> » It was at this microcosmic replication of the heavenly Kingdom of God, with its heavenly sanctuary containing its heavenly throne, that God's rule would extend via His visible presence, signs, specific rituals for worship and conducted via a paradigm of feasts and festivals presented throughout each and every year as an active involvement of God working in His world and a remembrance of His sovereign reign, rule, and control over all of life.

In establishing His Kingdom/Church on earth, God brings man back (from the Adamic treason) to Himself via His Kingdom by saving and teaching them in this established visible church in the Old Testament (which anticipates the Incarnation). This visible church would include but not be limited to:

1. Special covenants

2. Special revelations

3. Two unique sacraments

4. Rituals and ceremonies

5. A tabernacle/temple or physical location

6. Only three designated ministerial orders or offices

7. Laws, precepts, ordinances, and so forth

And it would be called the Nation of Israel. When the Incarnate Son of God, who came for His people, preached the arrival of God's Kingdom in Him, the realization of the anticipation of God's covenant Kingdom on earth, the fulfillment of the reality of the type of God's Kingdom in the Old Testament, had actually, physically, visibly intruded into the earthly realm. Now this fulfillment of God's Kingdom on earth, this fulfillment of the true Israel, is called the Church, the Body of Christ.

As a fulfillment of the Old Testament Kingdom of God, the true Israel, it is historically, biblically, theologically, *covenantally* connected to the Old Testament Kingdom. Therefore, with it, Jesus the Messiah brings:

1. An organized Kingdom

2. An active, living Kingdom

3. A visible Kingdom, a place where people go for salvation (again, refer to Matthew 23:21)[18]

---

18   *Op. Cit.* The great biblical theologian Geerhardus Vos, in his book *The Teaching of the Epistle to the Hebrews*, states, " . . . the nature of the relationship of the people to God is that of a *lateria* (worship). According to 9:14, 15 this is the essence of service to God" (41). "This is intended in the sense of *drawing near to God and worshipping Him*" (*emphasis is mine;* 43). He goes on to say, "All through the ninth chapter the worshipper is represented as one who serves. This service is organized on the same *principle* as the Old Testament service. It is a service in a *sanctuary*, with *priest, altar* and *service*" (emphasis is mine; 43).

God's covenant of promise, though realized through a man, was made with His Church in mind. To experience that covenant, to be blessed by all the grace that that covenant offers, to share in that covenant, one had to be a member of that covenant. Remember, God never dealt with the individual Jew alone in saving him, *per se,* but always as a member of His Body, His Church, the Nation of Israel in the Old Testament and the Church in the New Testament.

Do not forget that Jesus Christ Himself was a member of this Church. He fulfilled all the requirements of the law and moral code of this Church. He was circumcised on the eighth day. He attended the yearly Passover in Jerusalem, was presented at the temple when He was twelve (presumably for His bar Mitzvah or, for Christians, confirmation), and was taught the law. He attended worship and prayer at His local synagogue. He kept all of the Old Testament festivals and Jewish traditions that didn't violate the law,[19] by His own conscious, deliberate choice, as an example of His wonderful, submissive obedience to God's Law to men and maintained that obedience on our behalf (as a substitution for us). All of this took place within the Church, the covenantal body.

Not only this, but Jesus emphatically and vigorously upheld the authority[20] of the Church to everyone, especially His apostles and disciples: "The scribes and the Pharisees sit on Moses' seat, so do and observe whatever they tell you, but not the works they do. For they preach, but do not practice" (Matt. 23:2, ESV).

"And Jesus stretched out his hand and touched him, saying, 'I will; be clean.' And immediately his leprosy was cleansed. And Jesus said to him, 'See that you say nothing to anyone, but go, show yourself to the priest and offer the gift that Moses commanded, for a proof to them'" (Matt. 8:3, ESV). Jesus did this to ensure adherence to the Levitical purification code so that the healing was to be certified by the priest as well

---

19   Jn. 10:22–23: [22]"And it was at Jerusalem the feast of the dedication, and it was winter.[23] And Jesus walked in the temple in Solomon's porch" (KJV). Jesus not only, presumably, participated in bar Mitzvah (Luke once again) but also participated, here, in Hanukkah; neither tradition is a mandatory Jewish feast or festival per Old Testament Law. Tradition, for Jesus, was not the problem; it was false tradition, hence, His constant refrain, "You've heard it said, *but I say to you.*"
20   We will be subsequently looking more closely at the issue of ecclesiastical authority as it plays an important and, once again, often misunderstood role in worship.

as to indicate fulfillment of the prophecy of the arrival of the Messianic Kingdom.

Why was Jesus baptized? In addition to all the other theological reasons, it was to "fulfill all righteousness." Jesus stated, "I have not come to destroy the Law and the prophets, but to fulfill them" (Matt 5:17). And fulfillment, or "to make full," does not mean to eradicate but to complete. Apply the same concept of removal or eradication to the fulfillment of Old Testament prophecies.[21]

The fact of the matter is the Church was *already in existence,* albeit in its form as the Old Testament Church, the Nation of Israel. The structure, the organization, was never to be changed, only the theology, theological practice, and theological meaning of such practices (i.e., sacrifice). Remember, Jeremiah (31:33) said that God would put His law in our hearts, a New Covenant, which is what Jesus was teaching in the Sermon on the Mount. All of this takes place within a visible, physical context: the Church.

If the Church suddenly, with the arrival of Christ, undertook to revolutionize God's previous methods of saving men, then surely it cannot be God's work, or else God's previous work must have been a failure. Refer to Paul's teaching in Romans 3–4. What benefit is it, then, to be a Jew?

Paul makes it clear in Galatians that the law was a schoolmaster intended to bring, drive, force men to Christ. This was preparatory for the New Testament Church. But how can you have a schoolmaster if you do not have a school? There was nothing wrong with the structure of God's Church in the Old Testament; it was the sin of man that created the problems and abuses, and it was this Old Testament teaching that was fulfilled in the New Covenant in Christ Jesus.

But once again, we hear the tired, worn, hackneyed refrain that Christ did not prescribe in the New Testament any explicit directions for making any one Church. On its surface, this claim appears to be true. The problem with this claim is it is incorrect in its substance. For all of us who recognize the covenantal continuity between the Old and New Covenants, there would be no need for any specific instructions for the

---

21   To be discussed at length in a subsequent chapter.

creation of a New Church because of that very continuity. A Church, as previously mentioned, already existed. In the same manner that there is no overt argument necessary for infant baptism due to the continuity between covenants—and baptizing infants would be a natural extension of circumcising infants—especially if, as God revealed, the New Covenant would be superior to the previous one, there was no need to give specific instructions for a New Church because of the covenant continuity that existed between Old and New.

On the contrary, given Jesus's involvement, support, teaching, attendance, and complete participation in both the temple and synagogue practices; given that we see for decades the apostles and their disciples (the Church fathers) teaching, attending, worshiping in the Temple (until its destruction) and the synagogue following Jesus's example (until finally forced out in ca. AD 135), we would have expected exactly the opposite. If fulfillment meant eradication, where is the disavowal by Jesus? If all that had gone before were now no longer an element of Jesus' ministry or New Covenant worship, where are His instructions to that affect? If the Old Testament Church and all its' elements, no longer had any import for these orthodox, monotheistic, temple-attending Jewish followers of Jesus, where is His compelling, perspicuous, definitive statement to that point? Are we to believe that those who devotedly, dare I say, militantly, protected their Jewish heritage and identity, would relinquish that without so much as an attempt by Jesus to persuade them of such? I repeat what I stated earlier, just consider the reaction His audience had when He said He would destroy the temple! Rather than making a bold new claim altering the historical theological position of Jewish identity with the temple and citing some better structure would be with what the Jews would identify, He made the connection between it and the true Temple, His Body. That His Body was the true temple, doesn't change the force of this argument.

Then there are all the other things that are done that aren't explicitly stated or taught by Jesus: dedicate their kids on the first day of the week, observe the first day of the week for worship, baptize women, give communion to women, and so forth. If one responds, "Well, a reasonable inference can be drawn from scripture," game over. Everything for which I have argued so far carries more than a reasonable scriptural inference; it carries scriptural reference and connection.

Besides, Jesus came to assume His throne, in His house, in His holy city. The reason there was no Ark of the Covenant in the second Temple was because the Temple was waiting for the true Ark of the Covenant, Jesus, to return to it.

So do you think Jesus established a visible Church? One more time, remember:[22]

1. Jesus came preaching the Kingdom of God is at hand (in Him, among us). In His parables, Jesus likens the Kingdom to a net, to wheat and tares, to sheep and goats, where there are good and bad.

2. This Kingdom, as we have seen, is organized with all attendant elements and personnel.

3. It has laws for governing its function, purpose, and perpetuation. It has officers to execute these laws.

4. It has a means by which to include or naturalize foreigners; we call it salvation.

5. It has physical space, location, and boundaries.

6. Citizenship has duties, responsibilities, and privileges.

7. It is its own type of civilization.

It is not a subjective belief, moral philosophy, speculation about a book, a group of rival republics competing for the title of true Kingdom, or a ghostly collection of invisible souls that no one can locate or identify.

Simply because the Kingdom of God is within (or, better, *among*) us, per our union with Christ, that does not exclude its existence outside of us. Ask any loyal British subject if the Kingdom of Great Britain

---

22 I understand completely that I've repeated this a number of times, but due to the historically inaccurate interpretation of this entire subject, I choose to hammer this home, as it were, due to its significance. I apologize if the repetition of this concept has become tedious.

exists only within their heart. The triumphal entry of the Lord Jesus is a perfect example of a King coming to His Kingdom and throne. That is what we celebrate on Palm Sunday.

How do people enter the covenant? Via baptism. If one can enter the Kingdom of God via the rite of baptism, then certainly it would be an easy matter to tell who members were and who were not; therefore, it must be a visible Kingdom.

The first thing Jesus did after making His proclamation that the Kingdom of God (i.e., the Church) was at hand, He established its structure:

1. He ordained twelve to preach to this Kingdom and gave them a technical name: Apostles (Mk 3:14, Matt 10:7).

2. He established a unique relationship of authority with them and them alone (Luke 22:29: " . . . and I assign[23] to you, as my Father assigned to me, a kingdom," ESV).

3. This Kingdom, Church, is the work of Jesus (Matt. 16:18–19).

4. He chose those who would lead and build His Church (John 15:16). In other words, Christians do not get together just because they are Christians and create their own Church.

So, as previously mentioned, the Lord Jesus did in one sense, in fact, build a Church with a particular structure and order. It was a modification of the Church, the Old Testament Church, that was already in existence. But, as has been argued, even if there were an early Church, it was hopelessly corrupt immediately after the death of the apostles; didn't the gates of hell prevail against it contrary to Jesus's explicit teaching? And if the argument for rejecting this early Church is impurity, and the Reformation was an attempt to return to a pure Church, didn't it fail miserably as well? As long as humans are involved in the Church, there will always be impurity, sin, rebellion, and failure, but we do not jettison God's divinely revealed blueprint, His divinely commanded structure and pattern for worship due to sin, rebellion, and failure. God did not re-

---

23 *Diatithamai* (διατίθεμαι). This word literally means "to designate someone to officially and formally, to act in the role of ruling. To be the executor to dispose of a will."

ject what He revealed to the Nation of Israel; He rejected them for their abuse of the glorious gift He gave them. We know then that the gates of hell could never prevail against His Church, so another understanding must prevail.

In summary, our Lord took the following steps to establish His Church:

1. He chose twelve men and called them apostles.

2. He instructed them about His Church.

3. He instituted the sacrament of holy communion and commissioned them to celebrate it until He returns.

4. He commissioned them to teach, baptize, forgive sins, administer discipline, all in His name and by His authority. He did this via ordination, transmission of the Holy Spirit.

5. He promised the perpetuity of apostolic authority until His return to the uttermost part of the world.

6. He promised to ratify in heaven their earthly ministerial acts.

7. He promised the blessing of His perpetual presence.

In the persons of these twelve apostles, we have the ministerial nucleus of the covenantal Church chosen by Christ, commissioned by Christ, with the promise of Christ's continual presence, to do Christ's work, in Christ's name, until Christ shall return, in Christ's Church, because Christ builds His Church, not men.

In the next chapter, we look at two key components of this covenantal continuity, baptism and holy communion, but before we leave this discussion, let us conclude with reference to Dr. Thomas's excellent article, one final time, as he describes for us the vital importance of covenant:[24]

Failing to hold to a covenantal understanding of God's redemptive work leads to distortions of key biblical concepts:

---

24   *Op. Cit.* Thomas, 2452–2453.

1. Without it we have a distorted view of God. The covenant of redemption signals that God's covenant with us
   images in some way His own communion within Himself. The intra-Trinitarian fellowship of Father, Son,
   and Holy Spirit (Gk. *perichōrēsis*; Latin *circumincessio*)
   evidences communion and the presence of the persons
   with and in one another in ways not unlike those seen
   in covenant relationships. It stands to reason, therefore, that man, created in God's image (Gen. 1:26, 27),
   would share a similar form of communion.

2. Without it the gospel is distorted. The danger is that we
   might then view different ways of salvation in different
   administrations (as various forms of traditional dis-
   pensational hermeneutics do) or balk at Mosaic law as
   somehow inconsistent with the gracious nature of redemption and therefore suggest a return to a covenant
   of works (as various forms of "Mosaic recapitulation of
   the covenant of works" views do).

3. Without it we cannot make sense of the Bible as a
   whole. We then cannot understand the flow of history—from Genesis to Revelation—or understand why
   Jesus would Himself take discouraged disciples on a
   walking tour through Moses and the Prophets to un-
   derline their consistent message as culminating in Him
   (Luke 24:27). This point of view is summarily stated
   this way: "Man, by his fall, having made himself incapable of life by that covenant [the covenant of works], the
   Lord was pleased to make a second, commonly called
   the covenant of grace; wherein he freely offers unto
   sinners life and salvation by Jesus Christ; requiring of
   them faith in him, that they may be saved, and prom-
   ising to give unto all those that are ordained unto eternal life his Holy Spirit, to make them willing, and able
   to believe" (Westminster Confession of Faith [WCF]
   7.3). Crucial is the understanding that both old and

new covenants are administrations of the one covenant of grace: "There are not therefore two covenants of grace, differing in substance, but one and the same, under various dispensations" (WCF 7.6).

4. Without it, we have a distorted view of baptism. A consistent covenantal theology notes the following: (1) salvation is essentially restorative, healing the family disruption and blame-shifting culture brought about by the fall (Gen. 3; 4); (2) all God's covenantal dealings have involved children, as exemplified by Ps. 68:6: "God settles the solitary in a home"; (3) Peter's words on the day of Pentecost are therefore precisely what covenant children expect to hear: "For the promise is for you and for your children" (Acts 2:39). An underlying principle of administration continues in the era of the new covenant, a perspective that makes perfect sense given the overarching principle of covenant theology. Credobaptists operating with a covenantal hermeneutic, who ordinarily see a great deal of continuity in how God has dealt with His people across all eras of redemptive history, must at the point of baptism see discontinuity at the level of the administration of the sign and seal of the covenant to infants in the transition from old to new covenant. Similarly, attention is drawn to the Lord's Supper as a covenantal sign and seal (Matt. 26:28; Mark 14:24; Luke 22:20; 1 Cor. 11:25).

5. Without it, we have a distorted view of duty and obligation. The obedience that faith requires stems from the gracious relationship: "I bore you on eagles' wings and brought you to myself. Now therefore, if you will indeed obey my voice and keep my covenant, you shall be my treasured possession among all peoples, for all the earth is mine; and you shall be to me a kingdom of priests and a holy nation" (Ex. 19:4, 5). Covenant faithfulness is the condition and means of receiving the

covenant benefits. Justification leads to sanctification and perseverance, and this need not be viewed as a return to legalism. Unfaithfulness on our part disrupts fellowship and prevents blessing. Far from lessening the requirement for obedience, the new covenant era warns of more severe curses (Heb. 10:28, 29).

5

The Tie That Binds—Covenant: Part 2

*In Him you were also circumcised with the circumcision made with-
out hands, by putting off the body of the sins of the flesh, by the
circumcision of Christ, buried with Him in baptism, in which you
also were raised with Him through faith in the working of God, who
raised Him from the dead.*

—Colossians 2:11–12 (NKJ)

*And as they were eating, Jesus took bread, blessed and broke it,
and gave it to the disciples and said, "Take, eat; this is My body."
Then He took the cup, and gave thanks, and gave it to them, saying,
"Drink from it, all of you. For this is My blood of the new covenant,
which is shed for many for the remission of sins."*

—Matthew 26:26–28 (NKJ)

Inclusion in the Covenant: Circumcision/Baptism

We are regularly, falsely told that holding to baptism is something
we do, something we contribute to our atonement;[1] it is a subjective
response acknowledging God's saving work in our lives. It is an act
of obedience (essentially a good work) by the Christian after their
profession of faith to testify publicly of their conversion to and belief
in Jesus Christ. So, fine. Let us pretend such folks are right and swap
baptism with it being something we do, such as the phrase "our good

---

1 It usually is not stated using that particular term, but theologically that is what it amounts to.

work." Replace baptism with "our good work," and we have the Bible saying:

Acts 2:38: repent and *do our good work* for the forgiveness of sins.

Acts 22:16: get up and *do your good work* to have sins washed away and call on the name of the Lord

Romans 6:1–4: you were buried with Christ *in your good work* and raised with Him to newness of life.

Galatians 3:26: those *doing a good work* into Christ are clothed with Him.

1 Peter 3:21: *our good work* that saves us now.

Mark 16:16: those who believe and *do a good work* will be saved.

There is no orthodox Christian who can, in any way, subscribe to this theological position. This turns God's sovereign, redemptive saving work, in Christ, into nothing more than a type of works righteousness, works salvation. Now, we can discuss how and what baptism *actually does* accomplish, but there is no way we can claim that baptism is something we subjectively do that achieves or accomplishes anything connected with our salvation; baptism is the objective gift of God given to His covenant people to graft them into His covenant community. We do not "get saved" and then decide to get baptized into God's covenant community. We are baptized into God's covenant community and then, through catechism, biblical training, fellowship, preaching, prayer, Godly counsel by our ministers, and congregation, come to the point of confirming this covenant relationship that our parents have willingly performed in obedience to God and acknowledge that it is ours. Obviously, this applies to infants and doesn't apply to adult converts.

Baptism provides a clear understanding of the covenant and its working in general and the sacraments in particular. One of the best texts to use to understand these topics is John 15.

Baptism, as understood theologically, is the sacrament of inclusion into the covenant. The apostle John, however, provides a vivid explanation of what actually is going on in this covenant inclusion. The apostle John goes to great lengths to describe Jesus as the "Vine" into which we are grafted as Christians. For a people that participates in agrarian endeavors, every Jew would have understood exactly what John meant by his metaphor. This chapter, however, has been misunderstood by Christians at times when relating it to baptism.

Additionally, though the metaphor is familiar, it is also dissimilar to the process used historically at this time. Traditionally, when a vine-dresser wanted or needed to rescue a dying vine, he would cut off a healthy branch from a viable vine and graft it into the dying vine. The life-giving properties from the healthy branch would be infused into the dying vine and, in the course of time, resuscitate or revive it. This procedure would have been known by every Jew of the period.

However, when one reads John 15 closely, one sees him explaining the metaphor quite differently; in fact, he explains it in exactly the opposite manner. The apostle tells us that rather than a healthy branch being grafted into a dying vine, it is the dying or dead branch that is grafted into the healthy vine. This dying or dead branch would receive all the nutrients and nourishment from the healthy, thriving, living vine and not vice versa.

This becomes one of the best and clearest explanations of how baptism functions, in relation to the covenant as a whole in scripture. The Lord Jesus is the healthy, life-giving vine. We are the dead branches. By the act of the Holy Spirit, we are grafted into the living vine, the Body of Christ, His entire person, the Church. The Church then, through the indwelling and living Holy Spirit, provides those grafted into her with nourishment, the means of grace (God's word preached and read, prayer, the sacraments, fellowship, etc.). The grafted-in child, growing up in the Church (Christ's Body), will hear the word preached, see the sacraments administered, hear the prayer of the faithful both individually and corporately in the liturgy, experience the grace of the fellowship of believers, and in all of this, move more and more toward life, salvation. This is what we call conversion today, but during the Reformation, it would be called regeneration.

Notice how this clearly explains being a part of the covenant community, yet simply because one is in the covenant community, one is not automatically saved. No, that comes somewhere in the conversion or regeneration process.

Here, Matthew 13 becomes instructive. In this parable, the Lord Jesus gives us four types of seeds and explains each. The first dies immediately, the second sprouts for a short time and dies, and the third is the "good seed." Notice a couple of elements that relate to the covenant in general and baptism in particular. First, there is no timeframe given or referenced. This is particularly important for the first two seeds. We do not know when they might happen. Second, we all know of children that were baptized and never enter the door of the church again (the same can be said with equal force and validity of adults who are baptized). While our sovereign God can do anything, and will lose none of His elect, these can be likened to the seed that dies immediately. Second, we have all been in churches where we have sat next to or fellowshipped, debated theology, or discussed the sermon with a parishioner. Sometimes this goes on for quite a while, maybe even years. Then suddenly they are gone; they apparently fall away and never attend church again. Once again, our sovereign God can do anything and will lose none of His elect, and apart from relocation to another church, we can liken these to the second type of seed. Or we see the evidence of fruit initially, but it disappears and, while the individual does not leave the church, they just remain a dead and dying branch.

For us Anglicans, here is where we see the value of what we call the minor sacrament of confirmation. The child, baptized, grafted into the covenant community, participates in everything within the Body of Christ; the Church provides the full means of grace. They, hopefully, through faithful parents (and in some cases, godparents), are trained, discipled, and mentored in all the things of Jesus Christ until that day, and we have no idea when that day *actually* occurs, when the child comes forward to be confirmed in their baptism, making their covenantal faith their own. They may have been regenerated well before their confirmation, but it is in their confirmation that they get to stand before the world and profess their identification with Christ.

This ingrafting addresses the concern of apparent apostasy. If we understand the above scenario, baptism is not stating that the child is saved;[2] it is stating that the child is a part of the covenant community and will now begin the journey of experiencing their conversion or regeneration until such time as they come to the full knowledge of Christ personally. If they do not, well, they are pruned, a dead branch that possibly has lived among the thriving vital branches but in the end must be cut off.

Validation of the Covenant: Passover/Eucharist

If, as Colossians 2:11–12[3] states and the Church has taught throughout her history, baptism is the New Testament extension of circumcision, the Eucharist or Holy Communion or the Lord's Supper, whichever you prefer, is the New Testament extension (with some necessary modifications) of Passover.[4]

It is important to understand Passover, at least in its broad strokes, to truly understand the significance of the Eucharist. Passover was a sacred observance of the Jews, commemorating the tenth and final plague in the Book of Exodus, when Yahweh judges Pharaoh and all of Egypt by killing all the firstborn animals and humans but "passes over"[5] the firstborn of Israel (Exodus 12:12–13), resulting in the Israelites' deliverance from slavery in Egypt, symbolizing their redemption

---

2   However, if God *did* want to save a child at baptism, He is perfectly capable and within His right to do so.

3   "In whom also ye are circumcised with the circumcision made without hands, in putting off the body of the sins of the flesh by the circumcision of Christ: [12] Buried with him in baptism, wherein also ye are risen with *him* through the faith of the operation of God, who hath raised" (Col. 2:11–12 KJV).

4   There has been much scholarship debating whether what Jesus celebrated in the Upper Room was in fact a Passover celebration or some variation of the Haggadah or Seder meal with elements of the Kiddush. The number of cups Jesus used is mentioned as a demonstration that this wasn't a Passover celebration. However, for our purposes, we will confidently retain what Jesus Himself stated as the purpose of this meal and what the Church has taught for two thousand years, that Jesus was celebrating His last Passover with His closest friends, and leave the speculation for another discussion.

5   *Pasach* (פָּסַח, -psh).

from "the kingdom of darkness" (Exodus 12:14–17). Immediately, we see three critical elements of Passover, life, and death. On the one hand, Passover symbolized the judgment of God against Egypt (the "kingdom of darkness"), resulting in death. On the other hand, Passover represents the blessing, protection, deliverance, and redemption provided by God for His people. The third aspect of Passover that often is either downplayed or overlooked altogether is that it was for God's people alone. Notice that the Jew, by faith, had to apply the blood to the doorposts and lintels (making a symbolic cross), thereby receiving God's protection and salvation. It was not given to Egypt or any other people. One could receive God's passing over, as it were, only by accepting by faith Yahweh's, the Hebrew God's, gift, either by entering a Jewish household and receiving their protection or becoming a member of the Nation of Israel by, by the same faith, applying the blood to their own doorposts, thus expressing their dependence upon Yahweh. However, make no mistake: the redemption given by God was to and for His people. A consequence of this gift of redemption from God was that the firstborn of all Israelites were to be sanctified, set apart, given to the Lord in service; we will come to know them as the priestly tribe of Israel, Levites. Out of a nation of people called to be a "Kingdom of priests" (Exodus 19:6), a special group, the firstborn, were called out to function in a special ministry before God to lead them in the worship of God, both as God's ministers to them and as a part of them, to represent them before God.[6]

With the establishment of the camp at the base of Mt. Sinai and the reception of the law from God to Moses on behalf of the Nation of Israel, the sacramental gift was a reminder to every Jew of the consequences of sin and what the blessings of faith were. This was to be celebrated yearly on the fourteenth of the first month of the Jewish year (Nisan or Abib).[7]

The celebration of and participation in Passover came with, as one

---

6 It is critical to note this separation and function. All believers were to be, in some sense, priests or ministers of God's word (the gospel) to a fallen world, but not all were called to that special, unique ministry of leading in liturgical worship. These were called "priests" in a very different sense.

7 Which, according to the sacred Jewish calendar, is March or April, depending on the planetary cycle.

should by now expect, very specific regulations and requirements primarily found in chapters 12 and 13 of Exodus but also in numerous places in the Pentateuch. The instructions immediately relevant for Israel's survival of the tenth plague included:[8]

1. Selecting a lamb,[9] an unblemished male, for sacrifice, typically one per family, on the tenth of the month (Exodus 12:3–5).

2. Sacrificing the lamb at twilight on the fourteenth of the month (Exodus 12:6).

3. Putting the blood of the lamb on the doorposts and lintel of the house (Exodus 12:7).

4. Roasting the lamb with fire, not eating it raw or boiling it (Exodus 12:8–9).

5. Eating the roasted lamb with unleavened bread[10] on bitter herbs[11] (Exodus 12:8).

6. Eating all of the lamb that night and burning any leftovers (Exodus 12:10).

7. Eating the meal in haste, ready to leave home at a moment's notice (Exodus 12:11).

The point of including a discussion of Passover is not merely for review or reflection but to highlight those elements that are critical in understanding:

1. How it relates to forgiveness, redemption, and atonement.

2. How it forms the foundational covenantal principle of the actual participation in a meal, a covenantal meal with God.

3. How this meal communicates not only a fellowship with God,

---

8   The following is taken from the entry on Passover in the *Lexham Bible Dictionary*, by Douglas Mangum (Logos 8 Bible Software).

9   *Seh* (שֶׂה,).

10   *Matstsoth* (מַצּוֹת).

11   *Merorim* (מְרֹרִים).

but the actual reception of what God intends to offer us in this meal.

4. The dynamic and powerful imagery of the grace included in this participatory Passover meal as it foreshadows Christ's giving of Himself for and to us.

Once again, these images provide us with a robust amount of interpretative information in understanding the New Testament Eucharist or Holy Communion. We see the imagery of the cross in the application of the blood on the doorposts and the lintels, but do we see the profundity of that imagery as applicable only to God's people? Do we truly understand that to attain the blessings of all that Christ Jesus has done, is doing, and will do for us, one must be in, be a part of, be participating in the covenant community? It presumes or presupposes an already existing covenant relationship. This sacrifice, whether in the Old economy or New, is efficacious not directly to each and every individual in the world but only to the world as it is understood to be each and every individual who becomes grafted into the covenant community.

This is the only manner, the only way, the Angel of Death passes over anyone. If one is not in the covenant community, receiving the grace that is provided by God, first in this Passover event and then in Jesus Christ's sovereign, omnipotent, effectual work on the cross and our participation in that work in the Eucharist, one must fully understand and be prepared for that time when the Angel of Death will visit them.

Exodus 12 ends with a few more explicit stipulations related to the Passover observance:[12]

1. Outsiders—including foreigners, temporary residents, or non-Israelite hired workers—are not allowed to eat the Passover meal (Exodus 12:43, 45).

2. Slaves or foreigners living among the Israelites had to be cir-

---

12   *Ibid.* "Passover" in the *Lexham Bible Dictionary,* by Douglas Mangum (Logos 8 Bible Software).

cumcised before they could participate in Passover (Exodus 12:44, 48).

3. The Passover meal had to be eaten in one house and could not be taken out of that house (Exodus 12:46).

4. No bones of the Passover lamb were to be broken (Exodus 12:46).

Of such profound import was Passover to God and the Jews that God made it one of the three Jewish festivals that were mandatory for each Jew to participate in.[13] The Jewish historian Josephus gives us accounts of Passover's importance; it drew such great crowds of Jews in Jerusalem that it made the Roman authorities nervous.[14] In the synoptic gospels, the Lord Jesus is presented as traveling to Jerusalem to participate in the Passover celebration (see Matthew 26:2, 17–30; Mark 14:1–2, 12–26; Luke 22:1–2, 7–23) and in the apostle John's gospel on two occasions (John 2:13, 23; 12:1, 12; 13:1).[15]

Note the astounding intimacy as you read these accounts of the Lord Jesus sharing Passover, particularly His final one on earth with His disciples. They "reclined at table" (Matthew 26:20), drank wine (Matthew 26:29), dipped bread (Mark 14:20),[16] and "leaned on His breast at the Last Supper" (John 21:20). What a magnificent description of the type of closeness, bonding, love, and grace to be able to draw near, this near, to the second person of the Triune Godhead. The imagery is so rich, so glorious, it always makes me wonder why Christians, even some of my Anglican brethren, do not want to participate, experience, receive this heavenly blessing every time they enter Church.[17]

---

13   As a reminder, the other two were the Feast of Weeks (Pentecost) and the Feast of Booths or Tabernacles.

14   *Op. Cit.* "Passover" in the *Lexham Bible Dictionary* (Logos 8 Bible Software), specifically referencing Jewish war (6.420–27) and antiquities (20.105–107); compare Mark 15:6–15. Also see Luke 2:41 and John 11:55.

15   *Ibid.*, "Passover" in the *Lexham Bible Dictionary* (Logos 8 Bible Software).

16   *Ibid.*

17   In his *Institutes of the Christian Religion,* John Calvin argued for Communion *at least* (emphasis mine) once a week (Book IV, chapter XVII, section 43) and, in fact, anytime the word

Here is one of the most intimate expressions of God's love for His people as our Lord Jesus engages in His final meal on earth with His closest friends, His disciples. The apostle John paints the divine mosaic that, here in this final Passover meal, preparing for the Feast of Passover, the true, divine, final eschatological Passover Lamb is giving Himself for His people. As He sits at the table, looking over at Saints Peter, James, John, and so on, what He is telling each and every one of them by His actions is, "As you eat this meal with Me and drink this wine with Me, *know* that the Lamb being slain by the Jews is pointing to Me, and I am doing this. I am giving Myself as your Passover Lamb, Peter! You, James! You, John!" This Passover sacrifice will end the need for any further Passover sacrifice. Pay close attention to what the Epistle to the Hebrews tells us:

> For if the blood of bulls and goats and the ashes of a heifer, sprinkling the unclean, sanctifies for the purifying of the flesh, [14] how much more shall the blood of Christ, who through the eternal Spirit offered Himself without spot to God, cleanse your conscience from dead works to serve the living God? (Heb. 9:13–14, NKJ)

The sacrifice of animals made them clean. It sanctified them. It covered their sin, if only for a year, but it was effectual. This was and is what a sacrifice accomplishes in its enactment in a covenant transaction. It made the testament effective. Geerhardus Vos states, "The idea uppermost in the mind of the writer in Hebrews 9, however, is not that the death makes the thing unchangeable, but that it makes it *effectual.*"[18] Christs work on the cross was effective and successful; it accomplished exactly what the Triune Godhead had covenantally agreed it would accomplish when He entered into this agreement: it would actually save His people. Not hypothetically, not possibly, not incompletely, not inefficiently as if something more needed to be added. No. On that cross, Jesus Christ was taking the place of Saints Pe-

---

was preached (section 44). Edited by John T. McNeill, translated by Ford Lewis Battles. (Westminster Press, 1960: 1420–1421).

18   *Op. Cit.* Hebrews Vos, 39. Emphasis is his.

ter, James, John, and the rest, including those of us today who are His people. This is the power of the covenant into which God entered with mankind, and this is the extent to which the Godhead went to ensure this covenant would accomplish what they intended. It was the Lord Jesus, our Passover Lamb,[19] who would pay the ultimate penalty for our rebellion and violation of God's covenant, in our place, in order to guarantee that God's promised word would not fail. If baptism is our inclusion into the covenant community, participation in the Eucharist, Holy Communion, is our validation that we belong and remain in that community.

If we understand Genesis correctly, one of the prime reasons for God setting Adam and Eve in the Garden was to establish His Kingdom on earth and fellowship with mankind. The pattern of the creation narrative is informative: God creates elements of nature each successive day. In each day/realm, God then creates various creatures to rule. Then at the end of the cycle, God creates man to rule (as His representative) over all that has been created. The sequence in nature culminates with the animals; the animals culminate with man; man, of course, culminates with God. But the fall broke this interconnected fellowship, and since then, redemptive history has been the plan of God to return to this setting. If God is the culmination of man in fellowship and identity (created in His image), and fellowship has been broken, there must be an interceding step to bridge the divide: the incarnation of Jesus Christ. In the incarnation, the Lord Jesus not only took upon Himself a human nature for our redemption, but, in that redemption, He restores the fellowship between God and man by being the God-man. As God-man, He not only reestablishes the broken pre-fall relationship, but He ensures this connection by giving us His very person in communion. The incarnation not only guarantees the Christian is communing with God once again, that fellowship has been restored again, but that one of the ways this restoration is accomplished is by our partaking of the whole Christ, the person. Not just

---

19 I Corinthians 5:7; I Peter 1:19; and Revelation 5:6 and following. Interesting fact: the term for lamb, ἀρνίον, appears twenty-eight times in Revelation alone; of those, only Revelation 13:11 does not directly refer or allude to Christ.

the divine Christ, not just the human Christ, but the entire person of Jesus Christ, the God-Man.

Our Lord, seated at the right hand of the Father, gives the entirety of Himself, human and divine, to His people through the instruments of the bread and wine. As the believer approaches the communion rail to receive communion, he/she through faith receives Christ right there at the rail. Not because Christ is brought down from heaven and taken off His throne but because, as the head of His Church, indwelt by the Holy Spirit, they, the Holy Spirit and the Lord Jesus, are never separated from one another. The head is always connected to the body. Jesus Christ is always connected to the Holy Spirit. The Holy Spirit always indwells the Church and each Christian. Therefore, Christ Jesus is always connected to the Church, and as the believer is a living, spiritually vital member of the covenant Church, grafted into her at baptism, when the believer receives the elements of bread and wine, it is through these creaturely elements, by the power of the indwelling Holy Spirit, that he or she receives the whole person of Christ and His grace.

It is here, in the context of the covenant community, where the Christian is brought into the covenant via baptism. It is here where they are grafted into the person of the body of Christ (the Church) through the incarnate Christ Jesus, human *and* divine. It is where the believer is sustained, nourished, and his/her membership in this covenant community is validated and continued, by the grace of Jesus Christ in the eucharist, by the grace of the God-man. As our Lord, Christ is the culmination of man by His restoration of the sequential Genesis pattern in His incarnation: nature/man, Christ/God. We are blessed with the most amazing gift often overlooked by Christians: God's gift of allowing us, in and through Jesus Christ, to partake of the divine nature (II Peter 1:4),[20] to be partakers of the Holy Spirit (Hebrews 6:4).[21]

---

20   2 Peter 1:4: "…by which he has granted to us his precious and very great promises, so that through them you may become partakers of the divine nature, having escaped from the corruption that is in the world because of sinful desire" (ESV).

21   Hebrews 6:4: "For *it is* impossible for those who were once enlightened, and have tasted the heavenly gift, and have become partakers of the Holy Spirit" (NKJ).

From the nascent moments of the New Testament Church, Christians have understood the eucharist ultimately from the paradigm of mystery regardless of it being discussed in terms of a spiritual feeding of the Christian, or the instrumental efficacy of the bread and wine, or in terms of a remembrance of the once-for-all sacrifice on the cross by Jesus "made actual in the eucharist and presented to God the Father in and with the continual intercession of the risen and glorified Christ."[22]

We have seen the astounding glory of God's blessing to us realized through His covenant with man. We have seen how it is this covenant that is the foundation of the sacramental connection between Old and New. Circumcision becomes baptism, and Passover becomes communion. The disciples of the Lord Christ, the early Christians, were not only of Israel, but they considered themselves the true Israel because the Messiah had arrived, and the Messiah was prophesied to come to God's remnant, the true Israel, by faith. As such, they would have naturally continued all the Jewish patterns and practices learned from their teachers as passed down from the patriarchs, prophets, and priests. Not only would they have *not* needed to be instructed on new patterns or forms of worship to replace Old Testament patterns, but it would have been strange to read in the New Testament where the Lord Jesus would have sat down and reiterated these patterns of authority and worship with which they were raised. Why reinvent the liturgical wheel? On the contrary, all that was required and supplied was not a change in pattern and external authority but a change in theological content to match the previously established patterns—Christological theological content to fulfill the Mosaic theological content passed on to them from their youth.

---

22   H. R. McAddo and Kenneth Stevenson, *The Mystery of the Eucharist in the Anglican Tradition*. Norwich, UK: Canterbury Press, 1995: 3.

6

Here's Where We Pray: Houses of Worship / Synagogue Churches

"For the Son of Man is Lord even of the Sabbath." Now when He had departed from there, He went into their synagogue.
—Matthew 12:8–9 (NKJ)

HAVING ADDRESSED THE TABERNACLE/TEMPLE IN REFERENCE to its function as the dwelling place of God for worship, it's important to discuss another location that has been typically, but erroneously, identified with worship: the synagogue. Allow me to reiterate once again: when we speak of worship in the context of the discussion of this book, we are speaking of that participation of worship that involves concepts brought forth throughout redemptive history such as sacrifice, atonement, and liturgical structure in the presence of God in His house of worship. This form of worship is to be led and conducted by clergy called by God, who are recognized to have the necessary gifts and qualifications to perform such service on behalf of the people of God. All believers are required to worship God in all aspects of their lives, every minute of every day of their lives. It is our obligation, in love, to give to God what He requires, not to mention what He commands. But there is a special, particular form of worship that only takes place before God in a special, particular place.

The disciples, like Jesus Himself, were observant Jews, and though at first after the crucifixion they cowered behind locked doors, their subsequent encounters with the risen Lord transformed their lives (John

20:19–20). In the very last verse of Luke (24:43), after the Ascension, the apostles went up "and were continually in the Temple blessing God." The Temple of Jerusalem, replacing the tabernacle, had been the center of Jewish worship since the time of Solomon.

In Acts (2:46), the three thousand who were baptized following the apostle Peter's sermon on Pentecost, day by day spent much time together in the Temple. After this, these baptized Jews would've returned to their customary Jewish pattern of worship much in the way, after Pentecost, "Peter and John were going up to the Temple at the hour of prayer, being the ninth hour."

Except for sacrifice, the social and religious functions of the temple were taken over by the synagogue.[1] Still, the power of temple images must not be underestimated, especially when the images usually emerged as a particular interpretation of the earthly reflection of a heavenly sanctuary. Even when the contrast to, as opposed to the connection with, the temple is emphasized, the images remain powerful, not to say controlling.[2]

The relationship the Jew had with the synagogue was quite different. Outside of Jerusalem, the apostles, other disciples, and other followers of Jesus, "as His custom was" (Luke 4:16), would worship (read scripture, pray, fellowship, hear a visiting Rabbi, etc. but not present a sacrifice for their sins) in the synagogue. St. Paul would initially visit the synagogue upon his arrival in whatever new city he was visiting. When the apostle Paul and Barnabas journeyed to Cyprus, "arriving at Salamis, they preached the word of God in the synagogues" (Acts 13:5); then, in Pisidia of Antioch, attending another synagogue, they participated in a service consisting of readings from the law and the prophets. When the leader of the synagogue was finished, he asked if the apostle Paul

---

1   Margaret Barker has done incredible work in showing not only the influence of Temple theology upon the synagogue but by interaction, connection, and outward development, its influence upon the Church as well. See her works *Temple Theology, The Gate of Heaven, The Great High Priest,* and particularly *Temple Themes in Christian Worship.* Full disclosure: she is neo-orthodox; however, it is actually quite easy to sift that out from her outstanding contribution overall. *Caveat emptor.*

2   Alan Doig, *Liturgy and Architecture: From the Early Church to the Middle Ages.* **UK:** Ashgate Publishing, 2008: 1. The majority of material here is from this work unless otherwise noted.

or Barnabas had a word of encouragement, whereby the apostle Paul preached (Acts 13:14–15).

At first, Christians were one of several minority Jewish sects. Just as Jesus been opposed by the Jews in the synagogues, so, too, Jewish Christians would soon meet serious opposition in the synagogue, ultimately placing them in a situation where they would either leave of their own accord (which would eventually occur in the mid to late second century), or be forced out and banded together.[3] Yet even with this uncomfortable divorce, we see from second-century material the difficulties inherent in separating Christianity from its religious and cultural place of origin. The later lines of demarcation were not drawn sharply in the first century.[4]

It is important for our purposes, however, not to recapitulate the history of the hostility between early Jewish Christians and traditional synagogue Jews but to determine what, actually, the synagogue was in respect to the Church and what it looked like. These two elements are intricately related. What is often not discussed concerning the nature of synagogues in reference to their relationship with the Church is the actual difference in the early existing first-century synagogue in comparison with the much later developed synagogue of the fourth century.

The synagogue of the first century functioned on many levels. It was a place of social interaction, welcoming important personages, familial interactions, and, of course, religious service. Since we are most interested in this last element, let us examine what a synagogue service would look like before we discuss where we would find a synagogue, which isn't as obvious as we might suspect.

First, let us identify what would actually be included in a synagogue service before we look at how it would be arranged. There would be variations depending on the wealth of the leader of the synagogue or its patron (see the Gentile God-fearer Cornelius as an example of a wealthy patron), but generally the established pattern would resemble something of this nature:

---

3   Ibid., 2.
4   Anthony J. Saldarini, *Matthew's Christian-Jewish Community.* Chicago: University of Chicago Press, 1994: 8–9.

1. The service would begin with an opening prayer called the *She-ma* or *Keriath Shema* and consisting of two introductory benedictions ("good words").

2. Somewhere in this service would be a psalm chanted or sung.[5]

3. It would be followed by the reading of the Ten Commandments and several sections of the Pentateuch, namely, Deuteronomy 6:4–9; 11:13-21 and Numbers 15:37–41.

4. The reading of the "Law and Prophets" would be followed by the eighteen prayers and benedictions (*Berachoth*).

5. Prayers were then offered by a reader, and the congregation responded, "Amen."[6]

6. The teaching and preaching part of the service was based on the Hebrew scriptures. A lesson from the Law (called *parasha*), and one from the Prophets (*haphthara*) were read in Hebrew (rather than Latin or Greek) and followed by a paraphrase or commentary and homily (*midrash:* Jewish Biblical exegesis) in the vernacular Aramaic or Greek.

7. A benediction and the "amen" of the people closed the service.

This pattern, first evidenced in the temple and carried over from temple worship, is the bare-bones format for all subsequent Christian liturgy. If one has been to virtually any form of Christian worship, these essential elements, though not using the above terminology, are most likely present: opening prayer, then a hymn (song), scripture reading, another hymn or song depending on your jurisdiction, more scripture, general petitions to God (prayers), sermon, offering, hymn (song), and

---

5   *Op. Cit.* Doig, 3: "Scriptural 'hymns to God' doubtless included the psalms, a rich and wonderfully resilient element of Temple worship. The strength of the form is such that the musical chant has shown remarkable consistency for 3,000 years from Temple to Gregorian to Anglican Chant."

6   Compare with 1 Corinthians 14:16: "Otherwise, if you bless with the spirit, how will he who occupies the place of the uninformed say 'Amen' at your giving of thanks, since he does not understand what you say?" (1 Cor. 14:16 NKJ).

then a benediction (closing dismissal). It is upon this platform that our worship is structured.

If this is what a synagogue service looked like, what did the synagogue itself look like? At first, this appears to be an irrelevant question. Who cares what a synagogue looked like? What does it matter? The answer to that question actually addresses a common refrain in many evangelical circles: the assertion that we must return to the early Church meeting in houses. The answer to this refrain comes in the form of describing where the first-century synagogue actually met.

When we come to the discussion of the synagogue during the ministry of Jesus and then later into the first and second centuries, we bring to it our understanding of what a synagogue is based on our modern interpretations. This, however, is as incorrect here as it would be in any interpretation of an ancient concept. We often see the synagogue in contrast to what we understand a church building to be: a free-standing or standalone structure for worship. However, this would not be correct in the first century. This type of synagogue did not appear until well into the fourth century during the diaspora. Archaeological evidence shows that dedicated synagogue buildings only became common in the third and fourth centuries in Palestine.[7] According to archaeological research, first-century synagogues were, in reality, homes.

Although over a hundred sites have been identified as ancient synagogues in Palestine, only six can be securely dated before Constantine (who became emperor of Rome in AD 306), and those are in the diaspora.[8] In other words, we can only identify six ancient Palestinian synagogues present prior to the fourth century, and these are not free-standing buildings. They are homes.

This becomes significant because what has been claimed to be the proper place of worship in the early Church, house churches, were in actuality synagogues. To put it another way, during the ministry of Jesus and following, both Jews and Jewish-Christians held services in synagogues that were in houses. After the destruction of the Temple in AD 70, these "house synagogues" became the new place of worship for ev-

---

7   Anthony J. Saldarini, *Matthew's Christian-Jewish Community.* Chicago: University of Chicago Press, 1994: 13.

8   *Op. Cit.* Doig, 2.

eryone. This fostered a sense of community, intimacy among members, a family where all were known by name. Consider this when you read in scripture about households being baptized.

These synagogues would have varied depending on the financial resources of the homeowner.[9] Richard Krautheimer offers this description:

> Regular gatherings would of necessity be held in private, in the house of one or the other of the brethren, 'breaking the bread from house to house.' Since the core of the service was a meal, the given place of the meeting would be the dining-room. And as the congregations were recruited by and large from the lower and middle classes, their houses would have been typical cheap houses. Such houses are known to us, if not from the first and second centuries, at least from the fourth and fifth. In the Eastern provinces, they were apparently one-family buildings up to four stories' high. The dining room on top was the only large room, and often opened on a terrace. This is the upper floor, the *anageion* or *hyperoon* frequently mentioned in Acts, the room 'high up, open to the light,' of which Tertullian still speaks after AD 200.[10]

This was the setting up until the 300s. Professor of theology Dr. Anthony J. Saldarini of Boston College concurs: "Synagogues became more thoroughly institutionalized and erected dedicated buildings regularly only in the third and fourth centuries in Israel."[11] Also,

> Early Jewish and gentile believers-in-Jesus met for worship and instruction in house-based groups. In Asia Minor and Greece, the evidence from Paul's letters for household gatherings is ample. Other N.T. literature testifies to the importance of house-

---

9   Again, reference Acts 10:22 and Cornelius.
10   Richard Kratheimeir, *Early Christian and Byzantine Architecture.* Baltimore, MD: Penguin Books, 1965: 2. Recall Apostle Paul preaching for so long that the young man fell out of the window on the upper floor (Acts 20:7–9).
11   *Op. Cit.* Saldarini, 100–101.

holds as well. The household codes in Col 3:18-4:1; Eph 5:22-6:9; and I Pet 3:1-7 are notable, as is the language concerning house and home in I Pet.[12]

The "house meetings" to which Doig is referring are simply the Christian application of the house-synagogue principle they would have learned by being discipled in a synagogue by a Jewish-Christian apostle. The Last Supper itself had been celebrated in such an upper room of a house borrowed for the occasion (Matthew 26:18; Mark 14:14; Luke 22:11); see also the healing of the paralytic man (Mark 2:1–6). After Pentecost, new Christians broke bread together in their homes (Acts 2:46), and in Jerusalem, as later in Corinth (Acts 18), there would appear to have been a number of loosely associated house-churches.[13]

"Eventually, a part, or even the whole, of a house would be given over permanently to worship . . . The synagogue was adapted within a private house still in domestic use, towards the end of the second century."[14] So even moving into the second century, so-called "house churches" were synagogues. Therefore, "in view of the ancient household pattern, it is likely that the *disciples* met in houses both when they were members of the Jewish synagogue and after they were expelled and had to form their own assembly."[15]

As the Church grew, and more and more converts were won, there would have been the inevitable change of liturgical practice and architectural design. Along with this, the move out of the house-synagogue would be unavoidable.[16] Christianity, as a minority sect of Judaism but still a sect of Judaism, would have enjoyed the normal religious protection provided by the Roman Empire. Once the separation became publicly obvious and essentially permanent, Roman protection would have evaporated, and Christianity would have begun to experience what history has shown it experienced in her early stages: persecution. With the move out of the house-synagogues, another location for worship was

---

12   Ibid., 101.
13   Op. Cit. Doig, 3.
14   Ibid., 3.
15   101. *Ekklesia* is the Greek word for "assembly" and eventually came to be translated as "Church."
16   *Op. Cit.* Doig, 4.

required. The combination of these factors would ultimately lead Christians into hiding and the catacombs.[17] Here, given the limited space, need for secrecy, and fear of arrest, modifications to worship began to take shape. While keeping the basic principles of worship and architectural design as foundational principles, we see the form of our more modern church design taking root: a narthex for catechumens (those seeking baptism), to where they would be escorted out, not able to receive communion just yet; the pillared nave with the font for baptism at the back of the Church as you enter the sanctuary; the raised chancel with altar, and so forth.[18] Yet even with all of this—the separation from Judaism, persecution from the state, and development of a new identity solely as Christians, not Jewish-Christians or Gentile-Christians but simply Christians—coming to the place where there was no connection at all with Judaism was a long process and varied from location to location. Some Christians attempted to hold on to their link to Judaism well into the late third century.

With this link, we have an important biblical connection that is not acknowledged or, in some cases, even known. The general rule was if one had ten adult males willing to gather for prayer, scripture reading, instruction, and preaching, this counted as a synagogue.[19] Those of diminished financial means would use whatever the largest room in the house was; the wealthier members would meet in anything from an upper room to accommodate numbers greater than ten (see Mark 2:1–4 and recall Jesus with the disciples according to John 13–17) to larger anterooms adjacent yet connected to the home (see Luke 7:1–10, especially verse 5 onward, and Acts 18:7–8; note in this passage that one may own the house-synagogue yet not be the ruler of the synagogue).

Notice how many times Jesus enters a house to teach or heal or perform some other religious function. The constant use, by Jesus, of the phrase "house of God" and its synonyms is a powerful foundational idea connecting house with worship in a unique sense (Matthew 21:13;

---

17   The underground catacombs of Rome and France are replete with hundreds of burial chambers and wall paintings depicting the life of early Christians underground during the Roman persecutions.

18   For a more detailed commentary on this development as these churches synthesized elements of Roman households with Jewish structures, see, *op. cit.,* Doig, 4.

19   Jews referred to this as a *minyan.*

Luke 6:4; Luke 19:46; John 2:14–17). Pay close attention to the phrase "breaking bread," a not too veiled reference to the sacramental meal of Communion taking place in the house (Acts 2:42 and 46). We also see how prominent teaching was in these houses (Acts 5:42; 20:20).

Now merge this with the apostle Paul's ministry. He would go to the synagogue ("teaching house to house") of each town he visited; he would fellowship, teach, preach, "break bread," and so forth in these (houses) synagogues; there would be Gentile converts; Christ would be proclaimed as fulfilling Mosaic theology; the pattern was established, and the theology updated. After the apostle was rejected by the Jews and turned to the Gentiles, he would've gone to houses to establish new synagogues, or what we call churches (I Corinthians 16:19; Col 4:15; and Philemon 1:2). The development of Jewish-Christian house-synagogues to Jewish/Gentile-Christian synagogues to Gentile house-churches would have been a natural development given Paul's ministry and gradual move away from Mosaic theological requirements (circumcision, proselyte baptisms, etc.) to Christian Christological doctrine. This is merely the tip of the proverbial iceberg when dealing with this specific matter. There is so much more that can be said and so many more scriptural references to be cited, but it would make this work much longer and not advance the discussion significantly.

One final point before moving to our next chapter. In chapter 2 (p. 47, footnotes 12 and 13), I briefly addressed the identification of Israel and the Church as two expressions of one concept, the one people of God. Before concluding this chapter, due to its importance in understanding God's dealing with His people throughout redemptive history but particularly via covenant, I would like to further sharpen the point made earlier in this work.

Dr. Saldarini presents one of the clearest and strongest cases for the term "ecclesia" or "church" not being a technical term. Allow me to quote the good doctor:

> The Greek term is primarily a political term and refers to any assembly of citizens duly summoned by the herald. It is also used, along with a number of other Greek terms, such as *sunagoge*,

sullogos, sunodos,[20] for the meetings of various Greek voluntary associations. These groups often met in private houses, as did Jewish assemblies (synagogues) and early Christian assemblies (*ekklesia*[21]).

However, *ekklesia* was not a technical term for a cultic group. It was an available term which could include a variety of communities and groups, including those involved in cultic activities.[22]

Notice in the third sentence, he specifically identifies the synagogue (*sunagoge*) as a synonym for ecclesia or church. He adds,

In Acts, the late first-century author uses *ekklesia* to denote several types of assembly believers-in-Jesus, including the still very Jewish assembly of believers-in-Jesus in Jerusalem (5:11; 8:1), the Jewish-gentile group in Antioch (13:1), and Paul's gentile communities in the diaspora (14:23; 16:5).[23]

In other words, in Acts, Luke uses the term *ekklesia* to identify a still "Jewish assembly of believers in Jesus in Jerusalem," a mix of "Jewish-Gentile believers in Antioch," and the apostle "Paul's gentile communities in the diaspora." The first two could easily have been called synagogues.

Allow me to conclude Dr. Saldarini's instruction with one final quote:

The following conclusions can be drawn from this broad and varied usage of the Greek word *ekklesia*:

1. One cannot assume that a full-blown corporate understanding of the Christian Church is necessarily implied by the term in the first century. It is not a univocal, technical term.

---

20   *Sunagoge, sullogos, sunodos:* assembly, gathering, company respectively.
21   *Ekklesia:* called out, gathered together, assembly.
22   *Op. Cit.* Saldarini, 116–117.
23   *Ibid.,* 117.

2. *Ekklesia* is used most frequently of assemblies outside
    of Israel and Syria. Only Luke (in Acts) uses the term
    of mid first-century believers-in-Jesus in Jerusalem and
    Antioch.

3. *Ekklesia* is a Jewish, Biblical term and cannot be simply
    contrasted with *sunagoge* as though one were Christian
    and the other Jewish. *Ekklesia* and *sunagoge* are both
    Greek words for an assembly. Both are frequently used
    in Greek literature, including Jewish and Christian lit-
    erature, for a variety of gatherings. Neither Christian
    nor Jewish meaning nor any fixed content can be as-
    signed to the word *ekklesia* without detailed argumen-
    tation from context.[24]

Thus, linguistically, according to the usage of the Greek word, one
cannot make a linguistic nor theological separation of Israel and the
Church, as much of evangelical theology does, unless one has substantial textual and contextual proof.

So why have I torturously belabored this chapter and these points at
the risk of boring people and driving them off? Two reasons: My hope
(and prayer) is that as I go along and present these points, the reader
is following along and connecting the dots. Some of those, which have
been the gist of this chapter, are as follow: Heaven is the place from
which all our content about worship, kingdom, and church is derived;
this content was divinely revealed to Moses on Mt. Sinai, and through
the inspiration and illumination of the Holy Spirit, Moses interpreted
what he was given by God to form what we see clearly presented in
scripture, a very detailed place where God is to dwell and be worshiped,
a very detailed delineation of what this earthly representation of the
Kingdom of heaven is to look like, complete with administrators, clergy,
rites of sacrifice, sacraments for entrance into and continuation in this
kingdom. We have an incredibly exacting set of instructions as to how
God would be worshiped. Secondly, many argue for Christians to return
to the way the early Church worshiped: in houses. If what was taking

---

place was, in actuality, synagogue worship (because synagogues met in houses), then Christian worship should and must draw its practices from these house-synagogues and their subsequent new form, house churches, with all of the attendant structure, theology, and influence of the temple.

All of this was given within the framework of a covenant between God and His people, the people of His covenant. Therefore, if there is no separation of the people of God into two types of believers, Israel and the Church, then all that went before, conceptually, applies to both groups as one people, not two different peoples of God. It is critical to recognize this fact not merely for the purposes of understanding this chapter nor for the purposes of moving forward to the culminating argument of the book (and it is, mostly definitely, important for that purpose), but it is critical to recognize this in order to have a proper theological understanding of redemption.

7

Who Is in Charge Here? The Structure

"When you come to the inevitable conclusion that the only true authority is that which is derivative from and instituted by the Lord, you realize that church polity cannot be a matter of adiaphora. Then biblical theology makes clear through which structure that authority is communicated."[1]

AS MENTIONED IN CHAPTER 5, WHENEVER the concept of worship is discussed, the question of church polity or how a church should be structured, and who is to lead it, is often glossed over. Questions about the true or correct biblical paradigm of Church organization create tension in some circles. Which form of government is correct: congregational rule, elder rule, or Episcopal rule? Additionally, once one determines which of these forms of polity one will advance, the crucially interconnected issue of authority or how authority is determined must be addressed.

As indicated in several places, I am an Anglican and subscribe to Episcopal rule as the correct biblical form of church polity. Therefore, what I would like to do is lay out my argument as to why I believe the statement "There is no specified form of Church polity indicated in scripture" is incorrect and why the idea that how a Church is organized is a matter of conscience and that we should not get exercised about it is unbiblical. If my argument is accurate, then the type of Church polity is

---

1   This was asserted by a friend who, at the time of this writing, was a student at Westminster Theological Seminary/California. His name is Christian Dove, and you will be hearing much from him in the future.

not only important enough about which to get exercised, but it actually becomes a matter of scriptural correctness or, to say it another way, a matter of obedience to the divine command of God.

Though the topic of elders plays an integral part of this discussion, I look at the terms used, elder and bishop,[2] separately in chapter 10. I will do all that I can to not get too far into the linguistic weeds, so to speak.

When one broaches the subject of authority, in general and within the confines of Christian dialogue specifically, there is significant disagreement and often harsh pushback. The question of authority in many arenas is one that, as humans, we chafe at (this is an area where our inherent Pelagian alter ego makes its most vociferous presence known), but, as Christians, we face an even more blatant, almost insidious enemy: duplicity. Or, to be more polite, inconsistency and contradiction. On the one hand, we laud, praise, trumpet, and shout from the rooftops that "Jesus is Lord" (evidently not grasping the full impact of what it means for Him to be Lord). We proclaim with a loud voice, "God is the sovereign ruler over all the universe." However, on the other hand, when we apply those sentiments to each of us, in our own individual circumstances, we suddenly become demigods: "I am my own authority; no one tells me what to do" and so on.

Again, tying this back to chapter 5, and connecting the discussion between covenant and worship and polity, are the twin concepts previously addressed as critical foundational principles in our discussion: the heavenly pattern and the Covenant of Grace.

Allow me another illustration of the difficulty being discussed, specifically the question of the legitimacy of an organization. I am a former marine. Imagine that I form an organization resembling the US Marine Corps; we memorize the Marine Corps creed; we adopt the principles of the Marine Corps: God, duty, honor, country; we even adopt their insignia: the eagle, globe, and anchor. Would this organization I have created be a part of the great fraternity that is the USMC? Could I, or any of my members, claim to truly be marines? In any way could I say what I have created is a branch, an extension, of the Marine Corps? Absolutely not. I do not have the authority to do such a thing, to create such an en-

---

2 The term "elder" is *zaqen* in the Old Testament and *presbuteros* in the New Testament, and the term "bishop" is *episkopos* in the New Testament.

tity. This is the same difficulty we have when we see individual after individual, because they claim some sort of biblical support, start a Church. I am not speaking of a church plant or a mission church; I am speaking of a group of people creating their own organization, a denomination.

The issue of the relationship of ecclesiastical offices between the Church (both Old Testament and New Testament Church) and synagogue; among (Old Testament) high priest, priest, and Levite and (New Testament) bishop, priest, deacon, and (synagogue) president,[3] minister, deacon; was the natural outworking of bringing those who functioned in the Temple (high priest, priest, Levite) to the synagogue, especially after the Temple's destruction. This would then provide the foundation for the bringing in of Jesus's "other sheep," the Gentiles. There would be a natural development of the pattern of worship for the New Testament Church, based upon the Jewish patterns established in the tabernacle, temple, and synagogue, as the representation of the true worship that takes place in heaven. The reason no specific form of church government is taught or mentioned in the New Testament is because, as I have indicated, as a covenantal continuation of the Old Testament, there would not need to be. Not to be repetitive, but Jews who had placed their faith in Jesus as Messiah, who had grown up practicing temple and then synagogue worship, would have assumed even as Jewish-Christians that the question of how they were to worship would have remained structurally the same.[4]

If the assertion is that unless something is expressly stated in scripture (read New Testament), it cannot be practiced, all manner of difficulties arises. Based on that logic, one can argue that because any number of things are not explicitly mentioned or taught directly, they are not biblical. The term "trinity" is not in the Bible; therefore, we should stop using that term based on this line of reasoning. The same can be said for baptizing women or offering the eucharist to women, especially since, in the ancient world of the New Testament, women had no legal status

---

3   Another common term among the Jews for the leader of a synagogue was *archisynagoges*, simply "the head of a synagogue." Think of "archrival" or "archenemy." The *archisynagoges* is the highest administrative person in the synagogue.

4   This concept cannot be reiterated enough due to the pernicious influence of dispensationalism in ecclesiology.

among the Jews, and the Church was Jewish in its nascent beginnings. Granted, the Lord Jesus hung out with women, but He never directly stated or taught to baptize them; nor did He invite them in the Upper Room, where He instituted the eucharist.

Why, in the Gospel of John, did our Lord participate in Hanukkah (John 10:22–23)?[5] That was an intertestamentally created Jewish tradition; it is not taught anywhere in scripture, certainly not in the law where all the Jewish feasts and festivals, including the three major festivals, are presented.

Obviously, there is a sufficient, reasonable case that can be made for each of the omitted items from scripture. But that is never the force of the above assertion. It is almost always cited as an absolute.

Thus, much as it is assumed that, as children of believers were circumcised in the Old Testament, children of believers would be baptized in the New Testament, and also that women would be baptized and given communion (there is no express command for either of those acts in the New Testament either), the same argument is applicable to how the Church is structured, ecclesiastically with three orders, ensuring proper leadership in worship, governance, theological continuity, and fidelity. If this covenant continuity is maintained, preservation of the three clerical order structure would be required. We see that in the New Testament orders of bishop, priest, and deacon. Vos and others have made it very clear that the concept of kingdom is a "continuous kingdom-forming movement" from old to new.

With that being the case, the elements of the Kingdom, revealed to Moses on Mt. Sinai, have never been abrogated or eliminated. In their fulfillment in Christ, they have traversed from a Mosaic theological understanding to a Christological understanding. The exact, precise pattern then, given to Moses on Mt. Sinai, a pattern of only three orders—high priest, priest, and Levite, changed to bishop, priest, and deacon.

This directly answers two questions then: What form of polity is the correct form? Why there is not an express statement of what that polity is?

The correct form of polity, first, is three orders. The reason the Lord

---

5 Jn. 10:22–23: "²²Now it was the Feast of Dedication in Jerusalem, and it was winter. ²³ And Jesus walked in the temple, in Solomon's porch" (NKJ).

Jesus or the apostles (or the Church fathers, for that matter) did not initially offer up a detailed defense of polity, once again, was that they did not need to. Much as there was no need to defend baptism because covenant continuity identifies baptism as the New Testament successor to circumcision, there was no need for the Lord or the apostles to reinvent the polity wheel[6] because Jews already knew what type of polity they had. The Lord Jesus, worshiping in the Temple, offered sacrifices in the Temple, as did the apostles as Jews of faith. To reiterate polity at this point would have been redundant because as orthodox Jews, they would be completely familiar with who was the ecclesiastical authority, how it was structured, and how they were to worship.

As I pointed out earlier, the synagogue was the place of prayer, fellowship, scripture reading, teaching, and so on(not that these didn't occur in the Temple as well), but it was not a place of liturgical worship in the technical sense because the core of Judaism and Christianity is incarnational atonement, offered through sacrifice, and this couldn't be done in the synagogue. Once the cross occurred, what changed, again, was not the structure of worship but the meaning. After the destruction of the Temple, and under persecution, there needed to be a transition, a place to worship. The synagogue, with all of the Jewish priests who converted to Christianity, per Acts 6, would be the natural place.

We also know, from archaeology, that the synagogues, early on, contained elements of the temple in their architectural structure. As they developed and were built by wealthier patrons, they took on more and more of the temple imagery.

Unless one comes with a preconceived bias stemming from the Reformation, there is no other form of polity than that which was carried over from the three offices in the Old Testament. Peter Toon's argument still stands and has never been refuted: episcopal polity was firmly established no later than AD 200, and from then until the sixteenth century, no other polity was known to the whole of the Christian Church.[7] Episcopacy it is. Period. Development and restructur-

---

6   Much as they did not need to reinvent the liturgical wheel.

7   Peter Toon, "An Episcopalian's Response" to L. Roy Taylor in *Who Runs the Church? 4 Views on Church Government* (edited by Steven Cowan and Paul Engle). Grand Rapids, MI: Zondervan Press, 2004.

ing along Christological lines would be natural as the fledgling Church found her identity first as Jewish Christians and then gradually as Christians. Jewish Christians believed they were the true Judaism. This was how the apostles worshiped; this was how the Church fathers worshiped until they were literally driven from the synagogues in the bar Khocba revolt in the early second century—and even with that, some *still* hung on into the late second and third centuries.

Even if episcopacy was false, where's the pushback, the assertion of false teaching, error, heresy in scripture or in early Church history? There was none; it is nonexistent. Heresies arose early and often and were almost immediately addressed. If episcopacy was so egregiously erroneous, where is the rebuttal?

The late patristic scholar and Roman Catholic theologian Johannes Quasten (AD 1900–1987) has definitively proved that at least Ignatius and most likely Polycarp, following the Old Testament model, believed in a monarchial bishopric.[8] Acts 1:20 points out that the office[9] to be fulfilled was to be differentiated from that of priests.[10]

Additionally, to argue that Ignatius and Polycarp, disciples of John, would teach a form of Church polity they didn't learn from their beloved "father" and go off in some other direction would require very profound and serious documentary support, especially given the reverential status the apostle John had even with Romans. The apostle John was still alive, old, but living when these men wrote. Is one honestly going to argue that they would have challenged their apostolic father's teaching, while he was living, with some false view of polity?

Referring back to the previous chapter, if with the arrival of Christ the Church suddenly changed the method by which God chose to save, how can anyone be assured that this new method is of God? There is the added dilemma of attempting to determine which is correct since there is now no covenantal continuity. If there isn't a consistent covenantal link between the old and new covenants, how can we say that God hasn't failed and hell indeed has prevailed? Once again, the apostle Paul's rhe-

---

8 Johannes Quasten, *Patrology* (four volumes). Westminster, MD: Christian Classics Inc., 1990: 66.

9 The Greek word used here is *episkopoi*.

10 Again, the Greek is *presbyters*.

torical question in Romans 3–4, is poignant; What benefit is it, then, to be a Jew?

As already stated, the purpose of the law, according to the apostle Paul in Galatians, was to be a schoolmaster purposed to inexorably funnel men to Christ. The law then, was intended to set the groundwork for the New Testament Church. For one to have a schoolmaster, whose purpose was to educate and inform, one needs a school. The structure of God's Old Testament Church was perfect because He created it. It was man's sin that defiled the Old Testament Church. Man's willful disobedience, idolatry, and abuse of God's gift, that was what was in error. However, Jesus, in bringing the New Covenant, fulfilled the Old Testament teaching of the structure.

Yet, even though we present these arguments, we are confronted with the assertion that Jesus did not explicitly command, present, or prescribe detailed instructions for one particular form of Church polity. While superficially accurate, it is incorrect at its core. It either ignores or is ignorant of the impact and force of the continuity between the old and new covenants. The moment one consistently applies the principle of covenantal continuity, no need for a detailed blueprint for a new Church or new form of Church polity is required because the very nature of continuity assumes extension. To put it another way, because the old and new covenants form a connecting link, the elements in the old covenant need not be repeated in the new because they are known. Therefore, since this continuity is intrinsic to both Churches—old and new—not only would one not see a repetition by Jesus as to how to construct the New Testament Church, one wouldn't need any new instructions because of the continuity that existed between Old and New.

On the contrary, given the Lord Jesus's involvement, support, teaching, attendance, and complete participation in both the Temple and synagogue practices; given that we see for decades the apostles and their disciples (the Church fathers) teaching, attending, worshiping in the Temple (until its destruction) and the synagogue following Jesus's example (until finally forced out in ca. AD 135), if something new or biblically different were to be introduced by Jesus, we would have expected the opposite of silence on this matter.

Yes, I know the immediate refrain offered: Jesus fulfilled all of those images in His incarnation, life, death, resurrection, and ascension. True. However, fulfillment does not mean abrogation. It means just that: to fulfill, complete, bring to fruition, but we will address that in the next chapter.

Transmission of the Authority of Jesus

Here is one of the overriding challenges within Christianity: the issue of authority. Who speaks for the Church—not a particular denomination, which is an abomination to unity in the Body of Christ anyway, but the Church, the universal Body of Christ. Here, the disagreement will intensify among Christians.

It is tremendously difficult to biblically accept the notion that the Triune God of the universe, the God who meticulously, deliberately, precisely, exactingly, divinely communicated to His people the manner, the structure, the exactitude of the "house" in which He was to be worshiped and the way the worship was to be practiced and executed those who violated those requirements and commandments, would then suddenly and without explanation discard, eliminate, set aside that preciseness derived from His revealed word and go to an anything goes, decide how you want to do it, free-for-all type of understanding of Christianity as the understanding of Jesus fulfilling all that went before. The "Well, that's your interpretation, not mine" mindset of many makes no sense at all.[11]

Consider this: Baptists and non-Baptists (simply as a point of comparison) disagree on the issue of baptism. All parties appeal to the Bible. How does the Church decide which view, if any, is correct? One must be correct because the sacraments were instituted by God; they are not manmade. So who decides? Who has the authority to speak for the Church when the very Church itself is appealing to the same authority and cannot decide?

---

11   I completely realize that there is a middle position called elder rule. My intention is not to directly challenge specific positions *per se*, just the mindset held by some Christians. However, if one follows the argument, any polity that is not covenantally connected to the Old Testament model of high priest, priest, Levite which translates into bishop, priest, deacon, according to this author, fails as a biblical polity.

There has to be a God-given authority, which appeals to the Bible authoritatively, that arbitrates these matters so the Body of Christ stands unified, in its witness to a fallen world, on these important doctrinal questions.

One of the reasons (among many) that the world does not take anything we (Christians) say seriously is because we cannot agree on essential issues, all the while appealing to the same Book concerning what is and isn't the correct understanding of what that Book says.

Don't misunderstand what I am asserting. I am not advocating for some amorphous, mysterious, indescribable type of Roman magisterium. Not at all. I am speaking of apostolic practice, apostolic doctrine, and apostolic authority via succession (which we will address momentarily). All three must be present in order to speak for the Church. If any one of these is absent, you have a group of Christians gathering for something, but it is not a Church.

However, when you wrongly incorporate an incorrect view of polity from the sixteenth or seventeenth century into the early Church, what happens is an imbalance of the three above elements. When the voice of the Church for the previous thousands of years, from the Old Covenant Church to the New Covenant Church, has identified authority as coming directly from divine revelation; maintained that authority in covenant continuity passed on from Jesus to the apostles; then the apostles (all of them, not merely a mentioned few) laid hands directly on their specified disciples, whom we have called bishops; and that authority to speak for the Church has been maintained in a biblical context since formally and divinely revealed at Mt. Sinai, you have a true Church.

Nothing has changed in the blueprint or pattern of polity except it is now Christological rather than Mosaic: three orders divinely instituted then; three orders carried over, divinely sanctioned and endorsed (Matthew 23:1–3), into the New Testament.

Does one, then, seeing this authority bestowed by the Lord Jesus on the apostles in numerous places in scripture, truly believe and want to assert that, after all that the Lord did, all He went through, all that He accomplished for His people—pronounced the transference of the authority over heaven and earth that was His to His apostles[12] to "make disciples of all nations," to "build up" the Church, to "lay hands on others" for the purpose of proclaiming God's word, [13] "to appoint elders" to lead churches[14]—suddenly, abruptly, permanently ended with the apostles? There is now no more designated, specified ecclesiastical authority to defend God's Church and word against error or heresies?[15]

There is now no more a class of clergy to teach the correct meaning of God's word based on the authority transmitted to them from the heirs of the apostles: bishops?[16] Currently, authority to speak for the Church is simply "I have a Bible, you have a Bible, we each interpret texts differ-

---

12   Matthew 28:18: "And Jesus came and said to them, 'All authority in heaven and on earth has been given to me. 19 Go therefore and make disciples of all nations, baptizing them in the name of the Father and of the Son and of the Holy Spirit'"; Matthew 10:1: "And he called to him his twelve disciples and gave them authority over unclean spirits, to cast them out, and to heal every disease and every affliction Matthew 20:25 But Jesus called them to him and said, 'You know that the rulers of the Gentiles lord it over them, and their great ones exercise authority over them. 26 It shall not be so among you. But whoever would be great among you must be your servant, 27 and whoever would be first among you must be your slave, 28 even as the Son of Man came not to be served but to serve, and to give his life as a ransom for many'"; Luke 10:19: "Behold, I have given you authority to tread on serpents and scorpions, and over all the power of the enemy, and nothing shall hurt you" (ESV).

13   Acts 6:6: "These they set before the apostles, and they prayed and laid their hands on them. 7 And the word of God continued to increase, and the number of the disciples multiplied greatly in Jerusalem, and a great many of the priests became obedient to the faith. Acts 8:17 Then they laid their hands on them and they received the Holy Spirit." Acts 19:6–7: 6"And when Paul had laid his hands on them, the Holy Spirit came on them, and they began speaking in tongues and prophesying. 7 There were about twelve men in all" (ESV).

14   Acts 14:23: "And when they had appointed elders for them in every church, with prayer and fasting they committed them to the Lord in whom they had believed" (ESV).

15   2 Corinthians 10:7: "Look at what is before your eyes. If anyone is confident that he is Christ's, let him remind himself that just as he is Christ's, so also are we. 8 For even if I boast a little too much of our authority, which the Lord gave for building you up and not for destroying you, I will not be ashamed" (ESV).
2 Corinthians 13:10: "For this reason I write these things while I am away from you, that when I come I may not have to be severe in my use of the authority that the Lord has given me for building up and not for tearing down." 3 John 1:9: "I have written something to the church, but Diotrephes, who likes to put himself first, does not acknowledge our authority" (ESV).

16   Matt. 8:3–4 (NKJV): 3 "Then Jesus put out His hand and touched him, saying, 'I am willing; be cleansed.' Immediately his leprosy was cleansed. 4 And Jesus said to him, 'See that you tell no one; but go your way, show yourself to the priest, and offer the gift that Moses commanded, as a testimony to them.'"
Matthew 23:1: "Then Jesus said to the crowds and to his disciples, 2 'The scribes and the Pharisees sit on Moses' seat, 3 so do and observe whatever they tell you, but not the works they do. For they preach, but do not practice.'" Titus 2:15: "Declare these things; exhort and rebuke with all authority. Let no one disregard you" (ESV).

ently, sometimes in total contradiction, and that's what the church is." Is that really what our Lord Jesus was doing when He communicated His authority to His apostles? The impression one gets from contemporary Christianity at times is that our Lord taught men to be good, gave them a book (the Bible), and then left them to find out what it meant and do as they please. Or was it a continuation of the Old Testament pattern of ordaining men, by the laying on of hands, to signify the transmission of authority to lead, teach, and rule the Church? Those given that authority would then themselves identify worthy men and lay hands on them, transmitting this Godly authority to them to perpetually lead the Church? Yes, there would be sinful men. Yes, there would be failures. Yes, there would arise apostates and heretics, but that does not mitigate the God-ordained pattern.

Consider this illustration. You have a PhD in political science focusing on the foreign policy relationship between the United States and Great Britain. You have taught this subject for decades. You are considered a noted expert in the field, appearing at numerous speaking engagements on this topic. Your best friend is the ambassador to the Court of St. James, and you are invited to join as they travel to Great Britain to appear before the queen and the prime minister. The two of you enter the chamber to speak to the British dignitaries about US/UK relations in foreign policy. Your friend asserts the policy of the presidential administration under which he/she is working. You, being the expert, pipe up and correct your friend's opinion, claiming, though it accurately represents the administration's position, it is incorrect. Who has the authority to correctly present the administration's position? Your friend. Not you, even if your view is the correct theoretical view on foreign policy. Why? Because he/she is the authorized representative of the president of the United States. You have no authority to speak for the president. This is how biblical authority works.

At this point, one might raise the issue of the right to private interpretation. Any average Christian can say, "If you refuse to hear my teaching, you will not have the right views of Bible truth." But they can never say, "If you refuse to hear my teaching, you oppose my Lord Himself because He authorized (through His chosen apostles and their authorized bishops) and sent me to teach you." The standard refrain, once again, when engaging in theological or doctrinal difference goes something like this: "Well, that is just your interpretation.[17] Christ left no command to belong to any particular Church, or even what one would look like organizationally. He taught no creed. He merely taught men to love their neighbors, have faith in Him, and heed His word. No book but the Bible, no creed but Christ."

If the right to private interpretation of Scripture trumps all other claims, and if all expressions of the Church are valid merely because they are composed by believers who have the right to exercise this private interpretation of scripture, how is it possible for any one Church to critique or criticize another?

a. How is church discipline able to be carried out? All one would need to do is move down the road to another church with similar views as one's own (as happens far too often anyway, at least in the United States). Forget Matthew 18 and Acts 5.

b. Though the belief in the authority of the creeds is rejected (by which is meant the three historic orthodox creeds),[18] why do all Evangelical churches have doctrinal statements or statements of faith or "what we believe" documents? These are the very same things as creeds, carrying in these churches the very same type of creedal authority. So if it was written by a guy named Athanasius in the fourth century, it has no authority, but if I write my own creed for my Church today, it is binding?

c. If the principle of private interpretation means each individual has the right to authoritatively assert that their private interpretation is correct and binding, and this private interpretation is equally as valid as any other private interpretation, how is any adjudication of conflicting doctrinal positions reached? Ultimately, all one is left with is a matter of individual views and personal opinions about the Bible (see Osteen, Hagee, Hickey, Paula White, Hinn, et al.).

---

17   The implication, as the late R. C. Sproul would say, is that this means there is *no one correct interpretation.*

18   The three historical creeds to which I refer are the Apostles Creed, the Nicene Creed, and the Athanasian Creed.

d. Why, then, does scripture, Moses, the prophets, the apostles, and God speak of only one Church, one people, one body, one Bride (" . . . I found it necessary to write appealing to you to contend for the faith that was once for all delivered to the saints" [Jude 1:3, ESV])?" Notice Jude's precise use of the phrase "the faith," not merely "faith."

e. Korah's rebellion is an excellent example of one assuming their private interpretation is authoritative. Numbers 16:1: Korah's rebellion was against Moses's clerical authority to be the sole intercessor and spokesperson before God on behalf of the people. Korah's charge was "The Lord is with the people." They had their private interpretation, and because they rebelled against the authoritative presentation of God's word by Moses, they were judged.

Before moving on to the next natural point, a discussion of apostolic succession, we need to unpack apostolic practice a bit further. When I, as an Anglican, speak of apostolic practice, my primary focus is on what they did, or liturgy.[19] Therefore, when I speak of worship, I am, in this context, speaking of that which occurs in a Church or liturgical setting. First, the word "liturgy," within the broad contemporary Christian culture, is viewed with a jaundiced eye, under great disdain. Unfortunately, it is usually, and in some cases, justifiably identified with Churches (Roman, Eastern Orthodoxy, or Anglo-Papism[20]) that generally rely only on the liturgy as the focus of worship, to the dismissal of solid preaching of God's word, or some other abuse of worship. Second, it has a deep and varied usage in ancient literature. For our purposes, we will concentrate essentially on its religious usage, which has two applications, mentioning its secular usage briefly.

The term is actually a hybrid of two Greek words, one for the word

---

19 λειτουργέω, λειτουργία, ας, ἡ f:: "*Leitourgeo* as a verb, or *Leitourgia*, as a feminine noun."

20 By Anglo-Papism, I mean those Anglican denominations that are so theologically similar to the Roman Church that it is quite difficult to distinguish between them. It is a distinction without a difference in their core doctrines.

for "laity"[21] and the other for "work,"[22] so the combination of the two essentially means the work of the laity. This extends back to its usage in the secular arena.

Nonbiblical Usage

In its secular usage, the word strictly involved public service performed by an individual. It meant to serve, with the implication of more formal or regular service, generally with the idea, "to serve, provide service; for a public office which a citizen undertakes to administer at his own expense."[23] This would also include, when viewed very broadly, a political usage that extended to cover all kinds of services to the body politic, virtually service of any kind, particularly military service.[24] Basically, from the nonreligious view, the term, linked to the national citizenry, meant "concerning the people or national community." It was the direct discharge of specific services to the body politic.

General Religious Usage

From this secular understanding, it was only a matter of time before the term for service, generally speaking, was used in more extended contexts, not being limited to merely the body politic or secular social convention. Eventually the term was appropriated for use in a religious milieu. We see it appear in pagan religions, then in the LXX (Septuagint) translation of the Old Testament, and, finally, it shows up in New Testament usage.[25]

---

21   Λῆϊτος/Λαός or *Laitos/Laos* (H. Strathmann & R. Meyer, 1964). λειτουργέω, λειτουργία, λειτουργός, λειτουργικός (G. Kittel, G. W. Bromiley, & G. Friedrich [eds.], *Theological Dictionary of the New Testament* [electronic ed., vol. 4]. Grand Rapids, MI: Eerdmans: 215–217).

22   ἐργ or *erg*.

23   Ibid., Kittel, vol 4, 216.

24   Ibid., 216–217.

25   The following sections—Pagan Usage, LXX Usage, New Testament Usage—are taken predominately from, *op. cit.*, λειτουργέω, λειτουργία, λειτουργός, λειτουργικός (G. Kittel, electronic ed., vol. 4: 215–231).

Pagan Usage

It is seen used in the cultic sense on inscriptions from Messene concerning the mysteries of Andania (92 BC; these are the so-called basket-bearers and the bearers of secret cultic objects on certain sacral occasions).[26] We then encounter it in the texts about the twins Thaues and Taus in the Serapeum at Memphis (serving Apis, the bull god of Egypt), which give us many examples of the cultic use of the word.[27] One example of such religious service was that these bearers of sacred cultic objects would minister or serve by bringing offerings to the gods Serapis and Isis, in the performance of certain cultic actions.[28] Similar were the cultic acts of the *choachytes* (basically, the name of a position held by one who serves), who had to make regular offerings to the dead (*Anubis*) and participated in the embalming of sacred animals by those called thereto,[29] these were described as liturgists or servers.[30] This sets the all-important stage for our movement into the usage of the term "liturgy" in the Bible.

LXX Usage

The original meaning of *leitourgia* (henceforth, the English transliteration of "liturgy" will be used), though wholly secular, becomes significant in New Testament worship. However, the only way to understand the change in meaning is by way of the LXX[31] and its almost uniform, cultic, and priestly use of the word.

The LXX use of liturgy appears, for the most part, to distance itself from the non-cultic use of *saret*, but it does, however, lean to attaching itself to other words for cultic service.[32] With two exceptions, in Ezek

---

26   Ibid., 218.
27   Ibid., 218.
28   Ibid., 218.
29   Ibid., 218–219.
30   λειτουργίαι.
31   For those unfamiliar with this symbol, LXX is the Roman numeral 70. In the Letter of Aristeas, we read that Ptolemy II Philadelphus (285–247 BC) requested seventy godly men (later seventy-two to account one scholar from each Jewish tribe) to translate the Hebrew Bible into Greek. They did; they produced this Bible independently and found that all seventy versions, miraculously, were identical. This translation is called "The Septuagint" (for 70).
32   *Op. Cit.*, Kittel, 219.

44:12 and 2 Chronicles 15:16,[33] the reference is always to the worship of Yahweh performed by the priests and Levites either in the tabernacle or the temple. Thus, the word becomes a definite technical term for this religious service.[34]

Hence, we find liturgy addressing the priests in the tabernacle (e.g., Nu. 8:22; 16:9; 18:21, 23), service to the Lord or God (e.g., Dt. 18:7; 2 Ch. 11:14; Ez. 45:4), and so forth.[35]

Usage in the New Testament

This, then, brings us to the New Testament usage of the term. The ecclesiastical use of the word "liturgy" is, obviously, quite different from its original meaning and use in the body politic and is the result of the evolution of the term as its usage was transferred to the Christian cultus from Old Testament concepts, of course assuming Greek trappings.[36] This may be seen very clearly in the literature of the fourth century. The role played by the New Testament in this history of signification will have to be determined in what follows.

The New Testament sees liturgy used in essentially (though not exclusively) two senses: the general idea of duty or service and religious activity involving ritual service of priests and ministers before God.

Let us briefly look at the first usage before closing out this section with the second. In the early Church, there are times when individuals, including the apostles themselves, would perform service, or have service on their behalf, that was not directly connected with corporate worship in the Temple or, subsequently, the synagogue.

In Romans 13, the apostle Paul is commending the Christians at Rome to obey the civil authorities because it is God who establishes such governments. He then states, after providing a brief exhortation to be in subjection to the authorities, in verse 6, "For because of this you also pay taxes, for they are God's ministers (*leitourgoi*—the plural form), attending continually to this very thing" (Romans 13:6, NKJ).

The government, then, is providing a service, a "ministry" to God,

---

33   Ibid., 220.
34   Ibid., 219.
35   Ibid., 220.
36   Ibid., 226, 229.

in the broadest, most general sense, by levying taxes. Something to think about during tax time. Then, in II Corinthians 9, the apostle Paul is speaking of the distribution of the offerings and gifts given *in* worship but not the actual worship service. He points out, "For the administration of this service (*leitourgias*) not only supplies the needs of the saints, but also is abounding through many thanksgivings to God (2 Corinthians 9:12, NKJ).

Therefore, our tithes, gifts, and offerings are not only offered to God for the work of worship but also for the Church (i.e., the congregation) to "minister" (do liturgy) to her members. Allow me to offer one more passage to highlight this idea of liturgy or service, not specifically related to a worship service.

As the apostle Paul was writing from his jail cell to his Philippian brethren, he was moved with compassion, not only out of personal concern for the Philippians and their situation but because Epaphroditus was distraught as well because of their state. The apostle writes,

[25] Yet I considered it necessary to send to you Epaphroditus, my brother, fellow worker, and fellow soldier, but your messenger and the one who ministered (*leitourgon*) to my need; [26] since he was longing for you all, and was distressed because you had heard that he was sick. (Philippians 2:25–26, NKJ)

So, because Epaphroditus was so exercised at the circumstances of the Philippian Church and his brethren in that congregation, the apostle Paul sent away the person who was ministering (*leitourgon*) to him while he was incarcerated.[37]

So far, we have seen the term for liturgy or minister used in service to the state or civil community and to specific individuals or a religious community while not necessarily being involved in a worship service directly; therefore, now we move, for our purposes, to what is the most important way to understand the idea of liturgy: to God in worship. One would expect that I would heavily employ material from Hebrews as it is the epistle to Hebrew Christians drawing heavily upon Old Testament concepts; well, Hebrews certainly plays an important part in our dis-

---

37   Other verses dealing with this first usage of *leitourgia* are Romans 15:27; Philippians 2:17; 2:30; Hebrews 1:7; 1:14; and others.

cussion, but it is equally important that we see the concept of liturgical worship is not limited to Hebrews.

Initially, we should quickly examine St. Luke's gospel. We see the first New Testament use of liturgy as the ritual activity of priests or priestly service before the throne of God and the profound act of Christian service and ministry. Specifically, we see its application as the service or ministry of the priests relative to the prayers and sacrifices offered to God, or, to put it another way, the pattern or structure employed in worship. In Luke 1, he is drawing upon the LXX usage of the Old Testament term; speaking of Zacharias, the priest and father of John the Baptist, he writes, "And so it was, as soon as the days of his service (*leitourgias*) were completed, that he departed to his own house" (Lk. 1:23, NKJ).

As King David was nearing the end of his reign, and his eventual death in Israel, he instructed Solomon to set divisions for the Levitical priests. There would be twenty-four divisions, and each division would only serve/perform liturgical functions twice a year. Some priests never had the opportunity to serve in the Temple at all. This moment, the ability to administer his liturgical responsibilities, the burning of incense in front of the veil separating the holy place from the Holy of Holies, would have been the greatest joy of his service to God. Here, Zacharias, old and probably performing liturgically for the final time in his life, experiences the great joy, grace, and honor of worshiping God and receives a vision from the Archangel Gabriel.

The term for liturgy is used in common prayer during a worship service. St. Luke writes in Acts:

> Now in the church that was at Antioch there were certain prophets and teachers: Barnabas, Simeon who was called Niger, Lucius of Cyrene, Manaen who had been brought up with Herod the tetrarch, and Saul. [2] As they ministered (*leitourgountōn*) to the Lord and fasted, the Holy Spirit said, "Now separate to Me Barnabas and Saul for the work to which I have called them." (Acts 13:1–2, NKJ)

Some understand that this passage is specifically identifying the "fellowship of prayer."[38] The assertion goes something along these lines: The messengers of Christ and leaders of individual congregations do not have to fulfill a liturgy for the *secular political* (emphasis added) community.[39] Their task is to proclaim in the word of the crucifixion of Christ the *leitourgia* that has been fulfilled once and for all,[40] the liturgy of the Old Testament sacrificial system having been fulfilled in the once-for-all sacrifice of Jesus Christ. But the cultic terms could not be applied specifically to Christian offices as such.[41] The new community had no priests, for it consisted of priests.[42] Here is the idea of the priesthood of all believers.

There are a few points to make concerning this line of argumentation. Initially, the idea that Acts 13:1–2 is exclusively speaking of the fellowship of prayer is merely an assertion based on the Hellenistic presuppositions read into the text. There is nothing in the text itself or the historical context that does not admit that what was happening in Acts 13 was anything other than a full-fledged worship service, in which case, liturgy, in this passage, means just that: liturgical worship. Secondly, the claim that there are no priests in the early Christian Church belies, once again, a failure to recognize the covenantal continuity that the apostles would have understood; additionally, it does not consider that, while not at this time specifically using that term "priest," the concept of one leading worship, as understood in the Old Covenant, would fit quite naturally in the new Jewish Christian worshiping community. In other words, those leading New Testament worship (some might actually have been priests; see Acts 6) would have been drawn from the category of elder or presbyter, which, we have seen, would eventually become a clerical order itself in the later third and early fourth centuries. Finally, while there is a natural change from Old Testament to New Testament usage, especially as it relates to the transition from the Old Testament sacrificial priesthood to the New Testament Christological priesthood, the term is still employed for the function of specific service, either indirectly or directly, related to God. That Old Testament ministry or liturgy

---

38   *Op. Cit.*, Kittel, 226.
39   Ibid., 226.
40   Ibid., 226. Λειτουργία.
41   Ibid., 228.
42   Ibid., 228.

has been fulfilled and now transfers to the new ministry or liturgy of service to Christ Jesus.

In Romans 15, the apostle Paul makes a remarkable statement concerning his ministry and service for Christ. He puts it this way, " . . . that I might be a minister (*leitourgŏn*) of Jesus Christ to the Gentiles, ministering (priest) the gospel of God, that the offering of the Gentiles might be acceptable, sanctified by the Holy Spirit" (Romans 15:16, NKJ).

This must be understood as a definitive understanding of liturgy being worship. The ministry of which the apostle Paul is speaking of to the Gentiles is to present the Lord Jesus to them and, as an apostle, and following Acts 2:42ff, this would have included communion, thus, a worship service or liturgy. One of the unintended effects of this text is it certainly appears to contradict the idea that the apostles did not involve themselves in a formal type or pattern or structure of liturgy. With the connection to the temple/synagogue pattern of worship, the idea that mere fellowship of prayer, as the dominant type of service, is vastly overstated. Also, the apostle Paul speaks not only of being a minister (liturgist) of Jesus Christ, but he specifically connects this with the concept of being a priest of the gospel. This connection is generally overlooked and critically important. And the word he uses for priest is the Jewish understanding, *heriourgounta*.[43] This term unites the words for priest and work. In other words, the apostle is saying, he is performing priestly work or work of priests. The significance of the apostle Paul's use of "priest" linked with "liturgy" in this verse cannot be overstated. The apostle Paul, the former rabbi, virtually draws a straight-line connection to his current ministry (functioning as liturgist) and the sacred responsibilities of the Jewish priesthood. There is no disputing what the Old Testament priesthood was doing in the tabernacle and temple; they were the leaders of liturgy, corporate worship, for the people. The apostle Paul is using "liturgy" in the sense of an Old Testament priest. He consciously connected "liturgy" with "priestly functions," not, and it is crucial to note this, as one performing ritual sacrifices but as one engaging in priestly work and service in the temple. He is discharging

---

43   Minister in sacred service, serve as priest (Walter Bauer, William F. Arndt, F. Wilbur Gingrich, and Frederick W. Danker, *A Greek-English Lexicon of the New Testament and Other Early Christian Literature*. Chicago: The University of Chicago Press, 1979: 373).

a priestly ministry in relation to the gospel. By bringing the Gentiles to Christ, through the gospel, the apostle Paul offers them to God. All the overtones of priestly sacrifice are here without the actual physical sacrifice. Liturgy, for the apostle Paul, in this verse, has an overshadowing sacred ring.

If he is not referring to his work as a minister in the sense of a peculiar and unique function, in comparison to all Christians, one would have expected to see his use of the generic term for service: deacon.

Here, we now turn to Hebrews. The use of the term liturgy in Hebrews cannot be seen as an accidental insertion by the author of Hebrews.[44] The author of Hebrews is immersed in the perspective and language of Old Testament worship, and he uses this background to exposit the meaning of the Lord Jesus's person and work. In the context of the Old Testament understanding of functioning in the tabernacle and temple, liturgy emblazons itself in our understanding of what was taking place.[45] If the author had not used the term in his epistle, given its strong bonding with Old Testament themes and their juxtaposition with Jesus Christ, we would have thought it an odd omission.[46] Herein, then, we see the author's understanding, dependence on, framework, and usage of the LXX usage.[47]

Let us examine Hebrews 8 and 10. The author states,

> Now this is the main point of the things we are saying: We have such a High Priest, who is seated at the right hand of the throne of the Majesty in the heavens, [2] a Minister (*leitourgos*) of the sanctuary and of the true tabernacle which the Lord erected, and not man. (Heb. 8:1–2, NKJ)

> But now He has obtained a more excellent ministry (*leitourgias*), inasmuch as He is also Mediator of a better covenant, which was established on better promises. (Hebrews 8:6, NKJ)

---

44   *Op. Cit.*, Kittel, 226.
45   Ibid., 226.
46   Ibid., 226.
47   Ibid., 226.

And every priest stands ministering (*leitourgōn*) daily and offering repeatedly the same sacrifices, which can never take away
sins. [12] But this Man, after He had offered one sacrifice for sins
forever, sat down at the right hand of God. (Hebrews 10: 11–
12, NKJ)

There is much that we could discuss in these passages; however,
I want to focus on four elements of these passages. The first point of
significance for our purposes is that the author immediately makes it
clear that he is drawing upon Old Testament patterns and imagery. His
audience would have instantaneously identified with the concept of the
ministry (liturgical responsibility) of the high priest. So he is setting up
another comparison between the Lord Jesus and His Old Testament ty-
pological counterparts. Second, the ministry (liturgical responsibility)
of this High Priest does not need to be continually repeated because
Jesus Christ presented, offered, and accomplished the final sacrifice for
sin never to be offered again. The Old Testament high priest, in offering the sacrifice for either himself or the nation of Israel, had to quickly
depart the Holy of Holies when he was done. He then would repeat the
process yearly. This High Priest, Jesus Christ, not only did not need to
vacate the Holy of Holies, but He sat down there, at the Father's right
hand. Third, though the sacrificial element of the ministry of this High
Priest has ended, never to be repeated, He is still leading liturgical worship in the heavenly sanctuary, created by God, for all eternity. As we
celebrate worship here on earth, our Lord and Savior Jesus Christ is the
transcendent, divine, eternal liturgist leading worship in heaven. Lastly,
in verse 6, not only is His liturgical practice superior to that of the Old
Testament high priest, but it is also never ending. Each Old Testament
high priest at some point would have to cease their liturgical responsibilities. As long as the Lord Jesus is the fulfillment of the Old Testament
priesthood and leading worship in heaven, that worship will continue.
Since His priesthood is eternal, His liturgical ministry is also eternal.
Whereas the continuation of the Old Testament high priestly ministry,
in that the sacrifice, whichever variety it was, would only cover sin for a
day, week, month, or year, our Lord Jesus's liturgical sacrifice took place
once, and He now leads, and we now participate and receive the benefits

of that once-for-all perfect sacrifice as He continually functions in His capacity as divine liturgist.

Also, pay close attention to the concepts of sacrifice and liturgy that are present in Hebrews 10:11–12. Sacrifice is intimately connected to and linked with liturgy. In the Old Testament, we read that it was the constant sacrifice of animals to perpetually cover and atone for sin until, of course, the final one true sacrifice arrived, Jesus Christ. In Hebrews, this one true sacrifice is linked to our Lord Jesus's liturgy in heaven, but it is His once-for-all, perfect sacrifice that is in view. This is the "remembrance" of which He spoke when He said, "Do *this* . . . ": remember, re-enact, participate in my sacrificial atoning work, not in a re-sacrifice of the Lord Jesus but in a repetition of the ceremony He instituted the night prior to His sacrifice. This is an aspect of the where, how, and why we receive the grace of Christ in the Eucharist in communion. The where is in the House of God, church, where the ceremony is celebrated; the how is through our being grafted into Christ and the ongoing ministry (liturgy) of the Holy Spirit, where, through the instrumental means, the bread and wine, we receive His grace; and the why is because He said receiving Him, His Body and Blood in the whole person of Christ, divine and human, in that very bread and wine is the reason for communion. The liturgy in which we participate is, in the final analysis, a participation in the full drama of the life, death, burial, resurrection, and ascension of the Lord Jesus Christ. The sacrifice made the Old Covenant effectual. The Lord Jesus's sacrifice made the New Covenant effectual. This then provides the profound reality that His liturgical work is superior because His liturgical work in heaven is alone eternally effectual and perfect so as to be unrepeatable (in comparison with the Old Testament liturgy).

Finally, in our brief discussion of liturgy, we come to the early Church and the witness of the Church fathers and their use of the term.

Usage of the Church Fathers

As the transition from secular to religious (as represented in the Old Testament via the LXX usage) to the New Testament occurred, the solidifying of the ecclesiastical usage and meaning of the term is in place. The natural development is hardly a surprise; as we have seen earlier in this treatment, the early Church would have been earnestly seeking an identity of her own once the breach with Judaism became official and permanent.

This specific, ecclesiastical understanding and usage of the term liturgy is unquestionably clear in the writings of the Church fathers. Rather than going through the entire patristic corpus, I will use Clement (AD 35–AD 99) as the principle representative of the fathers and their general usage of the term "liturgy" in an ecclesiastical context.[48]

The first thing we notice about the concept of liturgy is Clement utilizes the concepts from the Old Testament priesthood, maintaining the previously established link between LXX and New Testament. He states in his First Epistle to the Corinthians 32:2: "For from him have sprung the priests and all the Levites who minister at the altar of God."[49]

The "him" to which he is referring is the Patriarch Isaac; however, the significance of the passage is that Clement is linking the priesthood with liturgy or service at the sacrificial altar of God. Liturgy then, according to Clement, is in connection with the sacrificial ministry to God. He continues the liturgical connection to service to God around the altar of sacrifice but makes an interesting distinction. In the same epistle, 40:2, he says:

> Those, therefore, who present their offerings at the appointed times, are accepted and blessed; for inasmuch as they follow the laws of the Lord, they sin not. For his own peculiar services are assigned to the high priest, and their own proper place is prescribed to the priests, and their own special ministrations devolve on the Levites. The layman is bound by the laws that pertain to laymen.[50]

---

48 If one is interested in the full body of sub- or post-apostolic treatment of this topic, the work by Schaff and Wace, *Ante-Nicene, Nicene,* and *Post-Nicene Fathers,* is the place to begin. If one is versed in Greek and Latin, the *Patrologia Graeca* and *Patrologia Latina* (also known as the *Patrologia Cursus Completus*), edited by J. P. Migne, are the most exhaustive treatments on the works of the fathers.

49 Clement of Rome (1885), *Ante-Nicene Fathers (ANF). The First Epistle of Clement to the Corinthians*. In A. Roberts, J. Donaldson, & A. C. Coxe (eds.), *The Apostolic Fathers with Justin Martyr and Irenaeus* (vol. 1, 13). Buffalo, NY: Christian Literature Company.

50 *Ibid.,* vol. 1, 16.

Here, he not only continues to indicate the liturgical function of the priesthood in presenting sacrifice, which in this case was offered by the priests on their own behalf to cleanse them from sin, but he points out that laymen also have responsibilities to the law of God, in worship, that pertain to them. Liturgy, the work of the people in their worship of God, carries with it multiple applications, clergy, and laity.

In a frequently overlooked passage concerning the connection between those who have the authority to minister (i.e., perform liturgical duties in an official capacity before God), Clement offers this extremely important and insightful comparison and link between those to whom the Lord Jesus specifically entrusted and transferred His authority to speak for the Church (and, by extension, perform liturgically) and the rebellion of Korah against Moses and Aaron and the subsequent events. We have discussed the Korah rebellion elsewhere, but as a reminder, Korah complained that Moses was assuming too much authority and responsibility before God and that the people of Israel (i.e., the Church in general) were "holy."

> They gathered together against Moses and Aaron, and said to them, "You take too much upon yourselves, for all the congregation is holy, every one of them, and the LORD is among them. Why then do you exalt yourselves above the assembly of the LORD?" (Numbers 16:3, NKJ)

Of course, the profound irony here is Korah was a Levite from the tribe of the Kohathites, the priests who handled all the holy vessels in the tabernacle and temple. Yet for whatever reason—jealously, pride, hubris—he was essentially arguing for an early form of congregational polity. Clement's take is illuminating as it relates to who should have the authority to lead or perform officially sanctioned liturgical functions before God. Pay close attention to the very first sentence because the remainder of the citation is linking the two concepts. In 43ff, he writes,

> And what wonder is it if those in Christ who were entrusted with such a duty by God, appointed those [ministers] before mentioned, when the blessed Moses also, "a faithful servant

in all his house," noted down in the sacred books all the injunctions which were given him, and when the other prophets also followed him, bearing witness with one consent to the ordinances which he had appointed? For, when rivalry arose concerning the priesthood, and the tribes were contending among themselves as to which of them should be adorned with that glorious title, he commanded the twelve princes of the tribes to bring him their rods, each one being inscribed with the name of the tribe. And he took them and bound them [together], and sealed them with the rings of the princes of the tribes, and laid them up in the tabernacle of witness on the table of God. And having shut the doors of the tabernacle, he sealed the keys, as he had done the rods, and said to them, Men and brethren, the tribe whose rod shall blossom has God chosen to fulfil the office of the priesthood, and to minister unto Him. And when the morning was come, he assembled all Israel, six hundred thousand men, and showed the seals to the princes of the tribes, and opened the tabernacle of witness, and brought forth the rods. And the rod of Aaron was found not only to have blossomed, but to bear fruit upon it. What think ye, beloved? Did not Moses know beforehand that this would happen? Undoubtedly he knew; but he acted thus, that there might be no sedition in Israel, and that the name of the true and only God might be glorified; to whom be glory for ever and ever. Amen.[51]

So even though one might be qualified, have all the right training, and so on, it is only when one has the requisite authority that one is able to perform liturgical duties before God, whether in the Old Testament or the New Testament. The Christian community, with its own liturgical responsibilities, cannot count as one of those duties leading worship on a Sunday. Their priesthood is activated once they leave the sanctuary and become a nation of "priests" to a fallen world. This specifically transmitted authority of office in the Christian community is

---

51 Ibid., vol. 1, 16–17.

to be safeguarded and protected, as was Moses and Aaron's authority in the Old Testament. The tasks of the high priest, priests, Levites, and the *laikos Anthropos*,[52] work of man, are all prescribed by specific regulations.[53] Should one continue to assert that the laity has equal spiritual authority to conduct liturgical duties, compare 41:5 and 44: 2–6 to that assertion: Ye see, brethren, that the greater the knowledge that has been vouchsafed to us, the greater also is the danger to which we are exposed.[54]

As the holder of an episcopal office, bishop of Rome, Clement is clearly stating that the doctrine taught by the Lord and Savior Jesus Christ and the apostles was the doctrine taught to "us" (those to whom episcopal authority was given). They are the only ones with that authority, authority to lead worship (in a Church setting, of course), the authority to speak for the Church at large. To put a fine point on this argument,

Our apostles also knew, through our Lord Jesus Christ, and there would be strife on account of the office of the episcopate. For this reason, therefore, inasmuch as they had obtained a perfect fore-knowledge of this, they appointed those [ministers] already mentioned, and afterwards gave instructions, that when these should fall asleep, other approved men should succeed them in their ministry. We are of opinion, therefore, that those appointed by them, or afterwards by other eminent men, with the consent of the whole Church, and who have blamelessly served the flock of Christ in a humble, peaceable, and disinterested spirit, and have for a long time possessed the good opinion of all, cannot be justly dismissed from the ministry. For our sin will not be small, if we eject from the episcopate those who have blamelessly and holily fulfilled its duties. Blessed are those presbyters who, having finished their course before now, have obtained a fruitful and perfect departure [from this world]; for they have no fear lest any one deprive them of the place now appointed them. But we see that ye have removed some men

---

52 λαϊκὸς ἄνθρωπος.
53 *Op. Cit.*, Kittel, 228.
54 *Op. Cit.*, ANF, vol. 1, 16.

of excellent behaviour from the ministry, which they fulfilled blamelessly and with honour.[55]

There is great honor for the sacrifice of bishops and priests (presbyters)—note the two distinct offices—and shame on those who do not recognize their Godly service, liturgically or otherwise.

This connection between bishop and liturgy (priests [presbyters] as a separate office are also connected to this function) is confirmed by the Church historian Eusebius (bk III, chapter 13.2): "In the second year of his reign, Linus, who had been bishop of the church of Rome for twelve years, delivered his office to Anencletus."[56] In the Greek translation, Eusebius states that Linus handed the "office" (liturgy) off to Anacletus (this is merely an alternate spelling of the same name).

In the *Constitution of the Holy Apostles*, "liturgy" is used in the offices of bishops, priests (presbyters), and deacons (VIII, 4, 5; 18, 3; 47, 28, and 36):[57]

> Wherefore we, the twelve apostles of the Lord, who are now together, give you in charge those divine constitutions concerning every ecclesiastical form, there being present with us Paul the chosen vessel, our fellow-apostle, and James the bishop, and the rest of the presbyters, and the seven deacons.[58]

The result, therefore, is a thoroughgoing transfer of the Old Testament concept of the priest to the Christian clergy.[59] The terms used for liturgy, then, are thus used to denote important religious actions, es-

---

55   Ibid., vol. 1, 17.

56   Eusebius of Caesaria (1890), *Nicene and Post-Nicene Fathers (NPNF): The Church History of Eusebius*. In P. Schaff & H. Wace (eds.), A. C. McGiffert (trans.), *Eusebius: Church History, Life of Constantine the Great, and Oration in Praise of Constantine* (vol. 1, 147). New York: Christian Literature Company.

57   *Op. Cit.*, Kittel, 228.

58   A. Roberts, J. Donaldson, & A. C .Coxe (eds.). (1886). *Nicene and Post-Nicene Fathers (NPNF). Constitutions of the Holy Apostles*. In J. Donaldson (trans.), *Fathers of the Third and Fourth Centuries: Lactantius, Venantius, Asterius, Victorinus, Dionysius, Apostolic Teaching and Constitutions, Homily, and Liturgies* (vol. 7, 481). Buffalo, NY: Christian Literature Company.

59   *Op. Cit.*, Kittel, 229.

pecially the eucharist. The link to the Old Testament concepts is quite powerful and overwhelming.

So much more documentation could be presented, but I fear I have gone on too long as it is. But why? Why was it necessary to be so laborious with this presentation? Could it not have been summed up in one or two sentences? Well, yes. But there are a few reasons that would not have been satisfactory. First, anyone can state anything as being the case. It was important to ensure a proper understanding of what we were talking about at the beginning. Second, given the pervasive antipathy, negative connections to Rome, and simply a profound misunderstanding of the term and how it applies to worship, it was crucial to attempt to eliminate as many of those misconceptions as possible. Lastly, there was concerted effort on my part to apply the term "liturgy" to its customary usage, "worship," and correct the widespread false impression of what worship is.

If one followed the development of the term and its usage from secular to Old Testament to New Testament to early Church, one would immediately see that it was active participation. Worship is something "we," clergy and laity, each with our own duties and responsibilities as members of a congregation, do. It is that in which we are to be involved; we are to act; we are to realize that what is taking place is giving something to God by our actions because He is absolutely worthy of it. Worship or liturgy, if one was following along, is not sitting in a pew, or on a bench, or in a folding chair and having someone else do virtually everything. Sitting for prayer, then standing for singing, then sitting for a forty-five-minute or one-hour talk (sermon), then standing to sing, and so on is not Church worship in any sense of what that term means. Christians doing those things are more akin to attending some religious seminar, not offering worship to the transcendent God of the universe. Worship, then, is performed or accomplished according to a set, God-established pattern prosecuted by the clergy: priests. I am sure there will be some who will be upset or downright offended by that. But my challenge to them is examine the term used; examine scripture. Then present an argument that anywhere in scripture, in the time of the ministry of the Lord Jesus, the apostles, or the early Church, can one find anything that remotely resembles what goes on today.

We are commanded by God, not asked, not begged, not politely requested, but *commanded* by the God of the universe to meet Him on a specific day, at a specific place, at a specific time to give Him the glory, honor, praise, thanksgiving, and the humility He deserves. Not to sit for an extended period of time to be entertained by a really great band. One can experience that at a Christian concert.

The Old Testament priests were forbidden to enter the Holy of Holies and approach God. The high priest only had the privilege once a year. The Savior Jesus Christ not only tore down that veil that separates us from that holy place, not only entered Himself and sat down in the holy place, but He brings us *into* that most holy of holy places to worship at the very throne of God. We are privileged to do what no one before us could do: unrestrainedly enter God's most holy of sanctuaries and approach Him without fear of death, all because we are in Christ: "Therefore, brethren, having boldness to enter the Holiest by the blood of Jesus" (Hebrews 10:19, NKJ).

Christian worship is something incomparably revolutionary in that, by actually being united with the deity we are worshiping, He brings us spiritually into His very presence in His heavenly realm. Prior to Christianity, worshiping a deity was more of an us/them understanding. The union, if there was one, was totally dissimilar to what we have in Christ Jesus. Our participation in it should be the same. How does anything that counts for worship today resemble anything that took place in the tabernacle/temple, synagogue, or early Church?

This naturally brings us to the question of "apostolic succession."

Apostolic Succession

Apostolic succession, or the successive and continuous transmission and transference of ecclesiastical authority, began in the Old Testament (it simply was not called that);[60] it was continued by our Lord Jesus in the New Testament as He passed His authority on to His apostles, and then His apostles passed this authority on to the bishops, and is the only biblically mandated and sanctioned manner to correctly and

---

60 Look at Numbers 27:20 where Moses confers, transfers, passes on "some of his authority" to Joshua.

authoritatively speak for the Church. Please note that last part: only biblically mandated and sanctioned manner to correctly and authoritatively speak for the Church. I reiterate this point mentioned above so as not to leave any doubt as to what I am *not* claiming. I am not stating that Christians do not have the right to read, interpret, discuss scripture. What I am saying is there is a divinely ordained class, clergy in apostolic succession, and only they have the right to speak for the Church; they are called bishops.

Apostolic succession must be maintained by apostolic practice, apostolic doctrine, and apostolic authority; all three must be present for there to be true ecclesiological authority, even for bishops; otherwise, whatever else is going on, one does not have the authority to speak for the Church. The mere laying on of hands is necessary but not sufficient for the transmission of authority.

If there is no correct apostolic succession (as listed in these three elements), there is no real church. All you have are a group of Christians meeting on Sundays for, well, whatever they choose to call it: prayer meeting, Bible study, whatever. But it isn't a true Church.

Here is the key to the argument of authority in the Church. Begin with a consistent application of covenant continuity and only part from that when it is clearly in violation or opposition to changing Mosaic content to Christological content.

The issue is not a problem or deficiency or failure or fault with the God-revealed blueprint divinely communicated to Moses. The problem lay within the human, depraved, fallen heart, rejecting God's established and divinely revealed pattern of authority (among other elements), which necessitated the one true, final, eschatological fulfillment, Jesus Christ, who transformed the Mosaic content into its fulfilled reality, Christologic. No, I am not advocating in any way, shape, or form a continuation of the Mosaic economy or Mosaic theology. Absolutely not. What went before, the pattern given to Moses, is perfectly fine; we simply need to change the content from Old Testament, Mosaic theological content to New Testament Christological content.

Once that is accomplished, there will be tweaks to the content (i.e., the priesthood is no longer genetically inherited but passed on through divinely communicated authoritative functions and commands; ministry is no longer limited to a genetic component but to those in Christ), but the structure, the pattern, the blueprint, copy, or shadow is intact.[61]

One must keep in mind a proper understanding of type/antitype.[62] Too many people think that type is eliminated once antitype is present. That is an incorrect understanding that will become clearly evident when we address the question of pleroma or fulfillment in the next chapter.

Apostolic succession is not, as some might assume, a straight linear movement. That is a straw man fallacy. Apostolic succession is more like a spider web with the various threads connecting in a multi-varied combination. In other words, apostolic succession was not from apostles A, B, and C to individuals 1, 2, and 3. No, it would've been Apostles A, D, F ordaining or consecrating individual 1; then Apostles B, C, E ordaining or consecrating individual 2; and, finally, Apostles C, D, F ordaining or consecrating individual 3. There is advancement, but the succession is holistic, not linear. This is addressed in Canon 4 of the Council of Nicaea, AD 325, where the number of bishops needed to consecrate another man to the bisphoric is preferably three (though two is considered valid). This is what we mean when we discuss apostolic authority based upon apostolic succession.

This becomes a critical matter when individuals claim they have begun a new church plant. For the sake of illustration, suppose a group of people attempt to start a church (an imprecise use of the term "church" at that):

a. That does not make it a church simply because they have the desire and effort.

b. If they disagree on any point of doctrine, all appealing to the Bible, who has the authority to arbitrate between positions? Matthew 18, if read carefully in context, concerns the authority to exercise church discipline in an already established church. The point of arbitration in doctrinal disputes is to be a bishop in apostolic succession, with apostolic authority, articulating apostolic doctrine.

---

61   The Greek terms used here are *hypodegmati* (ὑποδείγματι) and *skia* (σκιᾷ).
62   See chapter 2, Vos.

The idea of a group of people gathering together to worship is a very plausible scenario. However, that scenario is simply a conditional situation. It is not a church until proper biblically ordained clergy in apostolic succession arrive with the authority to lead them in proper church worship. That group of individuals has no biblical authority to administer the sacraments. Baptism will only be conditional, and there is no case where they can administer the Eucharist.

This situation is quite common in missionary endeavors. Indigenous peoples, compelled by the Holy Spirit, drawn in their divine election, suddenly experience regeneration and conversion, are then given faith, and they gather together, pray, and petition God for a minister, someone to properly lead, train, catechize, educate, and, in all manner, exercise ecclesiastical leadership, authority, and so forth.

In I Corinthians 11:26, in the Upper Room, our Lord Jesus institutes and celebrates the Eucharist, the sacrament of holy communion, and during this celebration He says, "For as often as you eat this bread and drink the cup, you proclaim the Lord's death until he comes" (ESV).

Now, obviously, the apostles were not going to live thousands of years until the Lord's return. So if the Eucharist is to be celebrated until the Lord's return, the order or office to which they belonged, with the authority transferred by the Lord to administer the sacrament, must last until the Lord returns. Here is a direct promise of the perpetuity of the apostolic order or office (see Acts 1:20, where the word used for "office" is the Greek term for "bishopric") only with apostolic authority in view. It was a commission to them to celebrate the constant memorial of His passion; their authority would then transition to bishops. The actual biblical continuation of apostles would be impossible today because no one can meet the trifold requirements of being an apostle, especially given no one alive currently has seen the resurrected Lord Jesus.

Our Lord ensures they have the ability and power to execute this office, telling them three times He is bestowing the Holy Spirit upon them for this ministry (John 14:26; 16:13; and 20:21). This cannot be to them exclusively as individuals because individuals die and pass from the scene, but the authority of this office and ministry is to exist in perpetuity or at least until the Lord's return. What is then transmitted to the bishops is the perpetuity of apostolic authority (Matt 18:17–18).

He establishes a unique relationship with them and them alone (think Yahweh and Moses). Look at the power of Luke 22:29 in this context: "And I bestow (*diatithami*)[63] upon you a kingdom, just as My Father bestowed one upon Me" (NKJ).

He grants to them the same possession, the same authority, that the Father granted to Him: the power to dispose a will, the power to exercise authority in His Kingdom, this New Covenant.

Consider the issue addressed earlier in the book; if the Church is exclusively invisible, a collection of disconnected groups as is claimed, how, in unity, could there be an address of the issue of something akin to the Jerusalem Council? How can anything be settled when there is no recognized final authority to which to appeal on earth? Again, not some magisterium but authority through apostolic succession.

A consistent problem for Christians is this: in subscribing to the four visible bonds of catholic unity,[64] how can they, without sinking into pure, abject subjectivism, prove that they actually, truly possess and teach Apostolic Doctrine? Without an appeal to the Church and her authority, even if it is not infallible, they have no certainty or even genuine confidence of being in possession of apostolic doctrine, to say nothing of succession or authority.

Additionally, how in the world can the Church, as a Kingdom, being an organism, even an organization, organize itself or serve any function of a Church, teach men, convert them, and support its ministry, without becoming instantly and necessarily visible? What, really, is an invisible Church? How would one find it? Where would it exist? How can one join a Church that is invisible? Be taught by it? Receive grace from it? One must join a denomination, and that just creates the problem with which we began: is that denomination a true Church? I refer all back to Vos.

This, of course, returns us to the dilemma of asserting that there is no physical, visible Kingdom/Church, with recognized ministers, laws, sacraments, as we observed earlier.

A modern gathering of Christians may teach total, complete ab-

---

63 διατίθεμαι.
64 "One, Holy, catholic, and apostolic" Church. Catholic meaning whole, unified, undivided, not Roman.

solute truth. Their teaching may convert scores of individuals; it may flourish as an organization (i.e., as Scientology or the Mormons) and do a tremendous amount of good. Whatever its effects, it cannot assume the authority or identity of the New Testament Church or claim its life unless they have a minister in apostolic succession. Quite bluntly, as a matter of fact, it is not the New Testament Church. It has no organic connection with it; it has no share in the unity that is the Body of Christ, the Church, which is a necessary and essential characteristic of the original organism.

Besides, no matter how strenuous the claim, no currently defined orthodox group existed prior to the Reformation, except those within an episcopal form of government. As a matter of fact, the refrain is always that, in the Reformation, the attempt was to purify the Church and return it to its original state in the New Testament. But if the Church was corrupted immediately after the death of the apostles (as some have claimed), and there were no explicit instructions by the Lord Jesus as to what the Church was to look like (especially in terms of polity), how would any of the Reformers have been able to claim that they had achieved the desired purity? To what were they appealing? There is little to demonstrate that their purified model resembles anything that looked like the trifold offices passed on from the Old Covenant. This matter is magnified especially considering the differences in understanding, say, of the sacraments and very nature of the Church that exists among them all. The painful interaction between Luther and Zwingli at Marburg has left the Church unnecessarily divided ever since the Reformation.

And what if the assertion that the Church, immediately following the death of the apostles, became corrupt is true? Was not the Church in the Old Testament corrupt? The Jews did not say, "Hey, let's purify the Church by starting a new nation, a new Israel!" No, they attempted to purify what God had established. When we arrive in the New Testament, in the first three chapters of the Book of Revelation, we see the same situation. To whom is the Lord Jesus speaking here? In His revelation to the apostle John,[65] He was addressing the seven Churches of Asia Minor. Was He not dealing with disobedience? Sin? Rebellion? Apathy?

---

65   Written between A.D. 70 and 95 (depending on how it is dated).

Corruption? What does the Lord Jesus do? Does He tell them to leave, withdraw, flee these corrupt Churches and create a new Church, like the Church of the Invisible Holy Purified Body of Christ? No, He tells them, "Hold fast," "Repent," "Return to your first love," the Body of Christ, the Church. The Old Testament Church, as she dealt with sin and impurity, looked to the coming Messiah; the New Testament Church, as she deals with sin and impurity, looks for the return of the Messiah. The pattern is the same.

Also, there were Jewish conflicts during the time of the Lord's own ministry. There existed the competing Houses of Hillel and Shammai, one liberal and one conservative. Does that mean there was no true expression of God's remnant of Israel?

One assertion is the Jerusalem Council arises in contrast to an episcopal polity. Is this as cut and dried as supposed? The Council of Jerusalem (Acts 15) is where the question of Gentile inclusion into the Church (which would have still been the Temple/synagogues at this juncture) comes into play. The Gentile question, as well as the Jerusalem Council itself, would be odd if the force and predominance of the Jewish character and structure of worship and polity were not preeminent. After all, if after the Ascension of the Lord Jesus, the apostles immediately rejected their Jewish liturgical heritage, especially as it manifested itself in worship and polity, why would there have been any difficulty? Why would a council need to be called at all? Judaism is over; circumcision is done away; why the fuss about a couple of Gentiles?

Why was St. James addressed with episcopal prominence? In Acts 15:13, James asserts his authority, not like a moderator but like a monarchial bishop:[66] "Listen to me . . ." He heard all sides, with the elders present, and then he pronounced a final decision. He did not go into chambers, conference with others, and after hearing all the arguments, then a consensus was reached; no, it was his decision that was levied. Look at Acts 15:19, where St. James utters, "I judge." Then, in Acts 12:17 and 21:17, the apostles Peter and Paul, and associates, say they are re-

---

66   Without opening the debate about the various views on what type of bishops there were in the early Church, a monarchial bishop was an individual bishop who essentially ruled, either a region or city, alone. Some have argued that in the early Church, the office of bishop functioned in a more collegial manner.

turning to Jerusalem to report their activities to "James." He did not report before a presbytery or classis to give a report.

Why, if episcopacy is so egregiously wrong, as alluded to earlier, is
there:

a. No alternative form of Church government found anywhere in
    the early Church extended throughout Church history, until
    the time of the Reformation (unless you import back into the
    early record a type of elder rule)?

b. No concentrated or even superficial argument found opposing
    episcopacy in the early Church?

c. How could such an erroneous form of Church government have
    gone unchallenged by the apostle John (who was, at the time of
    the ascendency of episcopacy, still living), especially since two
    of the most prominent voices of monarchial episcopacy, Ignati-
    us and Polycarp, were his direct disciples?

In chapter nine, I specifically address the issue of the relationship
between bishop and presbyter, so for the purposes of the discussion
dealing with apostolic succession, I want to introduce Irenaeus (c. AD
130–202), who was a disciple of Polycarp (who was a disciple of the
apostle John), and his comments on the nature of succession. What is
important to realize in these comments from the revered bishop is that
Irenaeus was battling the heresy of Gnosticism. As an argument against
the authority of the Gnostic teachers and their doctrine, he invoked the
succession of bishops and their authority and teaching, received directly
from the apostles, as the defenders of the truth of the gospel that they
had received from the apostles, in opposition to the Gnostic teaching.

It is within the power of all, therefore, in every Church, who
may wish to see the truth, to contemplate clearly the tradition
of the apostles manifested throughout the whole world; and we
are in a position to reckon up those who were by the apostles instituted bishops in the Churches, and [to demonstrate] the *succession* (emphasis mine) of these men to our own times; those

who neither taught nor knew of anything like what these [heretics] rave about. For if the apostles had known hidden mysteries, which they were in the habit of imparting to the perfect apart and privily from the rest, they would have delivered them especially to those to whom they were also committing the Churches themselves. For they were desirous that these men should be very perfect and blameless in all things, whom also they were leaving behind as *their successors* (emphasis mine), delivering up their own place of government to these men; which men, if they discharged their functions honestly, would be a great boon [to the Church], but if they should fall away, the direst calamity.[67]

In this next citation, Irenaeus presents the apostles Peter and Paul as the foundational sources of the authority of orthodox bishops. Regardless of whether you accept that the apostle Peter was involved in founding the Church at Rome or not (I do not hold to this position), the apostle Paul certainly was.

Since, however, it would be very tedious, in such a volume as this, to reckon up the successions of all the Churches, we do put to confusion all those who, in whatever manner, whether by an evil self-pleasing, by vainglory, or by blindness and perverse opinion, assemble in unauthorized meetings; [we do this, I say,] by indicating that tradition derived from the apostles, of the very great, the very ancient, and universally known Church founded and organized at Rome by the two most glorious apostles, Peter and Paul; as also [by pointing out] the faith preached to men, which comes down to our time by means of the successions of the bishops. For it is a matter of necessity that every Church should agree with this Church, on account of its preeminent authority, that is, the faithful everywhere, inasmuch as the apostolical tradition has been preserved continuously by those [faithful men] who exist everywhere.[68]

---

67 Irenaeus, *Adversus Haereses* (Book III, chapter 3.1).
68 Ibid., Bk III, chapter 3.2.

In a powerful argument in favor of apostolic succession of the bishops, Irenaeus actually names the first twelve bishops of Rome in his argument against the Gnostics.

> The blessed apostles, then, having founded and built up the Church, committed into the hands of Linus the office of the episcopate. Of this Linus, Paul makes mention in the Epistles to Timothy. To him succeeded Anacletus; and after him, in the third place from the apostles, Clement was allotted the bishopric . . . To this Clement there succeeded Evaristus. Alexander followed Evaristus; then, sixth from the apostles, Sixtus was appointed; after him, Telephorus, who was gloriously martyred; then Hyginus; after him, Pius; then after him, Anicetus. Soter having succeeded Anicetus, Eleutherius does now, in the twelfth place from the apostles, hold the inheritance of the episcopate. In this order, and by this succession, the ecclesiastical tradition from the apostles, and the preaching of the truth, have come down to us. And this is most abundant proof that there is one and the same vivifying faith, which has been preserved in the Church from the apostles until now, and handed down in truth.[69]

Of course, he would not omit his mentor from the pantheon of apostolically appointed bishops:

> But Polycarp also was not only instructed by apostles, and conversed with many who had seen Christ, but was also, by apostles in Asia, appointed bishop of the Church in Smyrna, whom I also saw in my early youth, for he tarried [on earth] a very long time . . . [70]

Finally, Irenaeus makes it abundantly clear that if one is not in apostolic succession, one is to be considered suspect in his teaching:

---

69 Ibid., Bk. III, chapter 3.3.
70 Ibid., Bk. III, chapter 3.4.

Wherefore we must obey the priests of the Church who have succession from the Apostles, as we have shown, who, together with succession in the episcopate, have received the certain mark of truth according to the will of the Father; all others, however, are to be suspected, who separated themselves from the principal succession.[71]

There are many more examples that could be cited, but this should suffice as a representation of the argument used in support of orthodoxy against heresy. Even though there are some who will argue that episcopacy arose merely as a response to heresy, Irenaeus's quotes show that to be false. He is quite clear as to the link from apostle to bishop in the Church.

People reject hierarchical forms of leadership or authority, in this case episcopacy, due to abuse, especially in the church. But abuse of something never invalidates or repudiates the ultimate legitimacy of a thing, no matter what it is. There can be abuse (and, I dare say, there has been) in all forms of ecclesiastical authority, to say nothing of secular authority. However, though an obvious point, without some sort of hierarchical structure or leadership, what one is left with is anarchy.

One final point. Based on what has just been argued, the questions arise: What happens if indeed there is a bishop with apostolic authority, in apostolic succession, and who is incorrect on apostolic doctrine? What happens if there is a parishioner who is, in fact, correct? Are we stuck with the bishop's false doctrine?

This is an excellent point and requires much more space than we can devote to it here. The short answer is: a. By virtue of his departure from apostolic doctrine, he loses his authority. Remember what was said above: all three are needed—apostolic practice, doctrine, authority in succession—for one to represent the Church; and b. There is supposed to be a visible, known group of bishops, the college of bishops or house of bishops, with one head bishop, presiding/archbishop, to which any and all can appeal in such cases. This creates the proper biblical checks and balances; think of the apostle Paul rebuking the apostle Peter in order to avoid division and schism.

---

71   Ibid., Bk. IV, chapter 26.

Obviously, we have not seen this since the Reformation, and each current iteration, especially within orthodox conservative Anglicanism, has its own house of bishops and presiding/archbishop, which I am sure grieves our Lord. However, that is the quick answer; it is our current situation, and must be left there for now. At least, though, conservative Anglicans are attempting to retain the divinely ordained polity found in scripture.

8

Christom Fulfills the Old Testament

"Do not think that I came to destroy the Law or the Prophets. I did not come to destroy but to fulfil."

—*Matthew 5:17 (NKJ)*

WHEN DISCUSSING THE RELATIONSHIP BETWEEN THE Old Covenant and the New Covenant, the issue of fulfillment becomes a necessary factor in the exchange. There are many obvious reasons for this: the avoidance of heterodox theology, a proper understanding of the ministry of Jesus, sidestepping the Judaizer error found in the apostle Paul's Epistle to the Galatians, and others.

Through utilizing an understanding of the biblical context, proper exegesis, and so forth, the most forceful point used to articulate the contemporary understanding of what fulfillment means theologically is defining the Greek[1] term from which we derive our term "fulfillment." We will look at several linguistic aids to determine what the meaning of the word is. The difficulty is that there is a significant and seriously incorrect interpretation of that word that has overwhelmed and dominated Christian circles for years. When one arrives at Matthew 5:17, though the word is translated correctly as "fulfilled," the meaning of "fulfilled," in contemporary Christian circles, becomes something more closely aligned with "to end," "abrogate," "terminate," or "eradicate," specifically being connected to the ceremonial law as that which is fulfilled. This is

---

1 The word *plhroow*, πληρόω.

the impression that one gets when engaging in a discussion about Matthew 5:17.[2]

Instead of dealing with the meaning of the term in its lexical form first, I'm going to show the theological challenges of understanding it in terms of how it is currently understood in theological parlance and then move to a number of lexical citations. I believe I am correct, given the linguistic data I provide, in this assessment of how the word "fulfill" or "fulfillment" is being used currently, so I will dismiss immediately the notion that I have erected a straw man fallacy.

Theological Application

The primary challenge I see for those who advocate for the abrogation, termination, or end of the ceremonial law due to Christ's fulfillment of it is not only an error in linguistic understanding and interpretation but a myopic view of the theological understanding due to a forcing of ideology upon the text. I say this as one who formerly argued for such an understanding of this question. My argument proceeds something like this:

Part I

1. We are commanded to worship God.

2. Scripture presents the requirements of that worship as being very specific, detailed, and precise commands from God. So specific, in fact, that deviation from God's instructed way to worship (i.e., approach) Him led to, in one case, banishment (Cain, of course connected with murder) and, in another case, execution (Nadab and Abihu, Aaron's sons, on the day of their ordination, I might add).

3. This scriptural requirement is a general principle; by that it is meant that, regardless of the who, when, or where, the com-

---

2   Matthew 5:17: "Do not think that I came to destroy the Law or the Prophets. I did not come to destroy but to fulfill" (NKJ).

manded way to approach God has not changed or been terminated. He still demands to be approached as He commanded.

4. These commands, alluded to prior to the Sinai covenant, were formalized there, in Yahweh's infallible revelation to Moses.

5. This specific way to approach God, worship Him, involves a certain ritual that forms the core of what is called ceremony or ceremonial worship.

6. Therefore, ceremony is nothing more than a way to worship or approach God, which we have already seen He has delineated quite clearly and explicitly.

7. Any form of worship is intrinsically ceremonial in nature. It involves rites, actions, sacraments, and the like. Therefore, if a Baptist, Presbyterian, Methodist, or so-called nondenominational Christian engages in worship, they must incorporate ritual acts or actions that lead to a particular ceremony or ceremonial acts of some form in their worship. In other words, every Christian, regardless of their denomination, practices ceremony when they worship.

8. So the questions then become: Since worship is ceremonial, what is the proper ceremony to be performed? Where does one find instructions for this type of ceremony?

Part 2

Given that the foundational principles have been identified (in the Old Covenant), now it is imperative to properly interpret ceremony in the context of worship. Since ceremony and worship are intrinsically connected, and every church practices worship/ceremony, whatever the fulfillment of the ceremonial law means, it simply cannot mean there is no pattern as to how we worship or that there is no practice of ceremony. The corollary to that is that since there must be ceremony/worship of God, because He commanded us to worship Him, we already have a pattern given to us by God on Mt. Sinai.

In other words, fulfillment of the ceremonial law does not mean the end of ceremony/worship. If it is not the end of ceremony/worship, what type of ceremony, then, is to be practiced in worship, particularly given the precise and specific instructions God previously gave His people, the Old Testament Church, in worshiping Him? God's character and nature do not change; His immutability is in relation to His nature, His character, His person, and that is why His commands are so exacting. Accommodations or modifications will necessarily be made as cultures change and the gospel is introduced into those cultures. We already have seen that in the early Church. The Church necessarily modified her temple-influenced synagogue worship to inculcate her new Christological theology, but the precision, specificity, and exactitude in how He is approached or worshiped will never change as it derives from His eternal character.

God does change how He interacts with man but only in response to man's actions with respect to Him. Consider the case of Jonah and Nineveh. Nineveh was to be judged; God's holy character and righteousness demanded their sin be judged. Jonah goes to pronounce God's judgment upon Nineveh. However, they repent, so God does not judge them. Hence, in worship, since God's character is the focal point, and that character has not changed and will not change regardless of what man does in the context of worshiping Him, the exactitude of His requirements to worship Him remains intact.

That is why, though the Old Testament Mosaic content is no longer binding on man, how we worship, approach, and offer ceremony to God (i.e., the patterns He established) are still binding. As I have mentioned multiple times in this book, we see the endorsement of this form/pattern of ceremony or worship by our Lord Jesus, the apostles, and many of the Church fathers. The difference is now these patterns are informed by Christ and Christological content and not Mosaic content; that is the correct concept of fulfillment of the ceremonial law.

There are a number of other factors that do come into play, such as the change from the strict rabbinic manner of practicing this ceremony in the New Testament, the inclusion of Gentiles in this worship, and the differences between worship in Gentile Christian Churches and Jewish Christian Churches in the New Testament, but all of these are easily explainable when one comprehends the progressive understanding of

Christological theology in worship as it replaced Mosaic theology in worship. The Holy Spirit did not reveal everything to man all at once in the Old Testament, and He did not do it in the New Testament. With that, let us consider the destruction of the Temple in the context of fulfillment.

In reference to the destruction of the Temple, one must ask:

1. How does Jesus Christ, being the true eschatological Temple and fulfilling that typology, eliminate a specified place to worship or practice ceremony? Especially since our Lord Jesus commanded the Eucharist and baptism to continue as sacramental elements of His Kingdom, His Church.

2. Since, as we have presented earlier, the Temple influenced, and the synagogue borrowed, the Temple liturgy, how does Our Lord fulfilling the Temple imagery eliminate what was practiced in the synagogue by way of Temple influence? Where is the repudiation from either the Lord Jesus or the apostles of either Temple worship or synagogue services predicated upon that Temple worship?

The Lord Jesus Christ never replaced worship in the Temple; He fulfilled it. Remember, the temple was where liturgy took place. The temple was where forgiveness of sins took place for the Jew. The temple was where sacrifice took place. The synagogue was where scripture reading, sermons, prayer, and teaching took place but not sacrifice. Yet for His entire earthly life, the Lord participated in these forms of ceremony and worship. The apostles, upon the Lord Jesus's arrival, followed Him in that worship. After His ascension, they continued to worship in the Temple (see Acts) and the synagogue. After the Temple's destruction, are we to assume or attempt to assert that suddenly everything they had been practicing for their entire lives, and now properly interpreted for them by the Lord Jesus, changed? Where is the biblical proof of that? What text demonstrates that?

If the Lord Jesus, in fulfilling the "Law and Prophets," intended to correct centuries of Jewish liturgical error, where is the command to practice something new? If He replaced the Temple with something new to occur someplace new, where is it? Would we not expect that the God of the universe, who originally instituted the ceremony and form of worship revealed to Moses on Mt. Sinai and practiced for hundreds of years by His people, would give us something telling us to move on to something different? Especially since this would be undoing centuries of Jewish liturgical worship, ceremony, and practice by orthodox Jews. But we see none of this in scripture. And if, as the argument is stated, we are to practice something in worship or the Church only if it is directly commanded in Scripture or can, from reasonable biblical inference, be supported, should we not keep what God has already originally commanded and Jesus Christ explained by His fulfillment?

If our Lord Jesus was going to disavow all that had gone before by the assertion of His fulfilling all of the law and prophets, where is the new pattern of worship, the new order of ministers, and the explication of a new form of government indicated by Our Lord? His orthodox monotheistic Jewish followers would have at least expected such. Though it should be an obvious point, if one is going to make the argument that fulfillment means elimination, one must explain why Jesus didn't offer an alternative for what went before. That Jesus was silent on the issue of clerical orders and Church government isn't an argument against the continuation of the Old Testament Church structure, it is actually a confirmation that that structure is continued, with the obvious theological changes, in the New Testament Church structure. In contemporary vernacular it could be likened to version 1.0 being upgraded to version 1.1. There is no need to duplicate every single idea from the previous to the subsequent. All one needs is the very specific, clearly articulated updated information; i.e., from Mosaic theology to Christologic theology. The fact that He is, in reality, the more glorious Temple, rather than eliminating the Temple, confirmed its importance, confirmed the importance of a place to express this Temple worship.

I will repeat what has been previously stated. Our Lord Jesus worshiped in the Temple and synagogue. The apostles worshiped in the temple (until its destruction) and synagogue. The disciples of the apostles worshiped in the synagogue (after the Temple's destruction). They were Jews. They thought of themselves as the true Israel, true Jews; they would never have substituted something different for the Temple or synagogue unless commanded to do so. They would never have replaced it, especially since that is where the Lord Jesus sanctioned worship (can you imagine orthodox, monotheistic Jews even suggesting it?). The fact that the Temple's destruction, foretold by our Savior, ended the last element of Jewish theological content did not mean it ended the concept of a place where worship was to be conducted. A place to worship God, the Triune God, was still required. Here is where the connection between old and new, Old Covenant and New Covenant, comes into play. The Old Testament Church and its structure and ministers becomes the New Testament Church, only with a more full, robust, and complete theological understanding, the understanding that now the Messiah has come, and He has come in the person of Jesus Christ to fulfill, fill up, complete the pattern or sketch. Consider Romans 13:8: "Owe no one anything except to love one another, for he who loves another has fulfilled the law" (NKJ).

Apply the definition of fulfill, meaning "to abrogate" or "end," to this verse. All one must do is to love one's brethren, and the law is "abrogated." No one anywhere in the history of orthodoxy would espouse this type of "anti-nominianism." Now compare with this understanding "fill," "fulfill," "bring to completion," "to finish something already begun." Which better fits the biblical text? There is a decided difference. To complete something already begun does not necessitate it being eliminated. One can complete a jigsaw puzzle already begun; does one get rid of the puzzle?

Lexical Understanding

Below, I give the proper lexical definition of "fulfill" from several different sources. This was done so as not to be accused of cherry picking my definition from only sources with which I agree or that agree with my understanding. If one truly desired to dig deep, I commend *The Theological Dictionary of New Testament Words*, by Gerhard Kittel. It is the definitive source on the theological meaning of New Testament words. Spoiler alert: my definition comes from Kittel; I simply cited these others because, for the layman, they are easier to negotiate than Kittel, which can be a handful.

The only modification I made to these definitions was to remove the textual apparatus cited (various long Greek phrases from antiquity so as not to confuse you), but here are the sources so one can look them up if they so choose. This might strike you as ungainly or superfluous and that they should be placed in a footnote, but given the lengthy historical misunderstanding of how this term is understood, I wanted to present the information in the body of the book so the reader is immediately exposed to it.

Frieberg Lexicon[3]

Literally, with an idea of totality *make full, fill (up) completely*

Louw and Nida[4]

πληρόω (plhrowo): to cause something to become full—"to fill." "(The net) was full" (Matthew 13.48).

Liddell–Scott:[5]

πληρόω, (plhrowo): to *make full:*
I. *to fill full of,* pass. *to be filled full of.*
2. *to fill full* of food, *to gorge, satiate,*
II. *to fill with,*
2. *to make full* or *complete,* or in the passive: *to be completed.*
3. *to fill* it.
4. *to fulfil, pay in full, make up;* Passive, *having poured* wine into the vessel *till it was full,* Passive, *to crowd into* a place.

Bauer, Arndt, Gingrich[6]

πληρόω, (plhrowo): 1. *fill, make full* (Matthew 13:48; Luke 3:5; John 12:3; 16:6; Acts 2:2, 28; 5:28; Romans 1:29; Ephesians 5:18; Philippians 4:18; 2 Timothy 1:4). 2. of time *fill up, complete, reach its end* passive (Mark 1:15; John 7:8; Acts 7:23, 30; 9:23; 24:27). 3. *bring to completion, finish* something already begun (John 3:29; 17:13; 2 Corinthians 10:6;

---

3 Bible Works 10 software program.
4 *Ibid.*
5 *Ibid.*
6 *Ibid.*

Philippians 2:2; Colossians 1:25). Galatians 5:14 may be classed here or under 4 below.**4.** *fulfill* a prophecy, promise, etc. (Matthew 1:22; 5:17).

Colin Brown, *The New International Dictionary of New Testament Theology*[7]

πληρόω *Full or fullness. Also, to fill a vessel, so that the result can be described as (plhrwma.) plhrwma. It is also significant in that it is used in regards to those fulfillment-quotations which have their origin in the Church's understanding of its faith or, episodes in the life of Jesus which were seen as the fulfillment of the divine plan of salvation revealed in the O.T.*

Therefore, when you consider the definition of "fulfill" as given, it becomes clear that it does not mean end, abrogate, or finish with a view to erase what has gone before. Hopefully, then, you can see how I understand that the end of the ceremonial law and Christ fulfilling the law has more to do with content than pattern. Imagine you have a child's coloring book in front of you. You see the outline of the various figures, but there is no content. You fill in the content by using the various colors in your box of crayons. This is essentially what it means when the Bible tells us Jesus fulfilled the Old Testament. He filled in or completed with new content the sketch of the Old Testament.

If you separate the pattern or ceremony from the content, you are left with God's specific instructions on how to worship Him. Instructions He revealed infallibly and eternally from heaven. Instructions given in order for the earthly worship of Him to mimic the heavenly worship of Him. Instructions that are now fulfilled (completed, started then and finished now, filled up, made full) in Christ and understood via the prism of Christological theology.

Think of the Lord Jesus's statement of fulfilling the law and the prophets in this manner. At the risk of stepping on some toes, this is essentially what He was saying, and I'll close with this: "I have not come to put an end to what the law and prophets taught, because they expressed the full nature, character, and person of God; no, what I am doing is taking their outline and completely filling in all of the missing elements that they could not communicate because it was not revealed to them.

---

7   Colin Brown, *The New International Theological Dictionary of New Testament Theology Vol. 1.* Grand Rapids, MI: Zondervan Publishing, 1967. Entry on πληρόω: 733–744.

I am, if you will, taking a cup and totally filling it up with Me. You see, this is why I'm not 'destroying' or 'utterly ending' the law and prophets, because they were telling you, to the best of their ability, given the knowledge My Father revealed to them, about Me."

I pray that helps clear up some misunderstandings.

9

"Bishop/Elder" or "Bishop and Elder"?

For a bishop must be blameless, as a steward of God, not self-willed, not quick-tempered, not given to wine, not violent, not greedy for money

—Titus 1:7 (NKJ)

For ye were as sheep going astray; but are now returned unto the Shepherd and Bishop of your souls

—1 Peter 2:25 (KJV)

FOR THE BETTER PART OF THE past half millennium, Christianity has been instructed and led by those who advance elder rule as the primary and biblical form of polity. The support for this can be briefly summarized by claiming that the early Church was weened in the synagogue; the synagogue was led by elders; therefore, the biblical form of Church government is elder[1] rule. When challenged by the claim that bishops[2] are also mentioned in the Bible, specifically Acts 20:28, I Timothy 3:1–2, Titus 1:7, and I Peter 2:25; 5:2–4; the reply is, "The word in Greek is 'overseer' and is a synonym of and used interchangeably with the Greek word for 'elder.'" The question is: is this accurate linguistically, contextually (does it interpretatively make sense in the context of scripture), and theologically? These are the issues we address in this chapter.

---

1 The Greek word is presbuteros (πρεσβύτερος), from which we derive our word "elder." The term "priest" is a contracted form of this word.

2 The Greek word is episkopos (ἐπίσκοπος), from which we derive our words "overseer" and "bishop," as translated in the King James Bible.

It would be easy for me at this point to simply provide my definition of the terms with which we will deal and allow the reader to follow up and research their meanings in order to ensure I'm not offering merely my opinion as to what these terms mean. Instead, I will once again provide various citations from a few Bible dictionaries as well as from two of the most respected tools dealing with the theological meaning of words, Botterweck and Ringgren's *Theological Dictionary of the Old Testament* and its New Testament counterpart, Kittel's *Theological Dictionary of New Testament*.

Elder

Let us begin first by examining what standard Bible dictionaries say about the term "elder." As you read these citations, look closely at how each of the contributors defines the term. There is a very subtle move that they make that manifests a certain presuppositional bias. They are not just providing an etymological or lexical definition; they are inserting their own theological bent. This is not unusual per se, but it does cloud the discussion. It is difficult to rest on a dictionary's definition if an author's bias becomes a part of the definition. For example, I am theologically Reformed, which means I have a very specific understanding of the meaning of atonement. The basic lexical meaning of "atonement" from a Bible dictionary should be "to cover over," "to make right," "to bring together," or the trite phrase that used to be used in certain circles, "to make at-one-ment." This is a very rich biblical term with a broad range of meanings depending on context. Now that is a straightforward, simple presentation of the term belying no particular theological bent, save possibly a conservative theological position. However, if I define atonement by stating, "Atonement is the payment of the sins of the elect by Jesus Christ on the cross, whereby He took the place of only His elect," I would not be advancing a workable definition for anyone but Reformed Christians. This is a theological view that must be defended and simply cannot be stated as I have stated it as the biblical definition of atonement.

With that said, I will begin with *Easton's Bible Dictionary*.[3] Initially, *Easton's* begins by defining an Old Testament "elder" in the standard way a dictionary would define a term, as a "person clothed with authority, and entitled to respect and reverence," "a political office," "a rank among the people indicative of authority."[4] This is exactly what we would expect and want. The entry continues by pointing out other important ways "elder" is used in the Old Testament by providing examples within context in scripture: "elders appear as governors (Deuteronomy 31:28); local magistrates (Deuteronomy 16:18); administers of justice (Deuteronomy 19:12)," and so on.

Easton, in transitioning to the discussion of elders in the New Testament, says, "The Jewish eldership was transferred from the old dispensation to the new." So far, so good. Then comes this statement,

> The creation of the office of elder is nowhere recorded in the New Testament, as in the case of deacons and apostles, because the latter offices were created to meet new and special emergencies, while the former was transmitted from the earliest times. In other words, the office of elder was the only permanent essential office of the church under either dispensation.

How is it possible for him to include in his definition the assumptions he provides in the final two sentences? How does he know that elder was an office in the New Testament identical to what he described in the Old Testament? Where did that element of the term suddenly import itself into its lexical meaning? I ask this because he then goes on to say that the "elders in the New Testament were pastors." All of them? One is perfectly within one's right to draw theological conclusions based on terms in scripture, but one first must have an accurate definition of the term without theological baggage as a part of the lexical meaning. We will leave Easton at this juncture and move to our next source, *Holman's Bible Dictionary*.[5] The contributor for this entry in *Holman's* begins by

---

3   Bible Works 10 software program, the entry on "elder" in *Easton's Bible Dictionary*. The following references come from that source.

4   The entry 1146, under "elder" in *Easton's Bible Dictionary*.

5   Logos Bible Software 8, entry on "elder," in *Holman's Bible Dictionary*.

stating, "In the Old Testament, 'elder' usually translates the Hebrew word *zaqen* from a root which means 'beard' or 'chin.'" And then, "In the New Testament, the Greek word is *presbuteros*, which is transliterated in English as 'presbyter' and from which the word 'priest' was derived." A good beginning. The contributor of this article then reiterates what Easton mentioned concerning the types of usage we see in the Old Testament, delving into a slightly more extensive historical accounting in the various books but not straying from usage as identified by the text.

When we arrive in the New Testament, we see another interesting conceptual move by a contributor. The article makes this application of the term "elder" in New Testament usage:

> In the New Testament, frequent reference is made to the elders of the Jews, usually in conjunction with the chief priests or scribes (for example, Matthew 21:23; Mark 14:43). *In this context the elders, apparently members of leading families, had some authority but were not the principal leaders in either religious or political affairs. Elders did have leading roles in the government of synagogues and after the fall of the Temple became even more central to Jewish religious life.* (Emphasis mine.)

Notice what happens in this quote in the second full sentence: "elders were not principle leaders in either religious or political affairs." And then, in the final sentence, see the prominent religious position elders gain in this definition. Again, that is a theological assessment. How did we get from "beard" or "chin" in the Old Testament, which is referring to an older man, to "elder" referring to a religious office? ("Elder" as an ordained ecclesiastical office or order didn't arise until the late third or early forth century in Judaism! Which will be addressed in a moment.) You will notice that, much as is done in the citations of the Old Testament passages in identifying how the term "elder" is used in those passages, both Easton and Holman, in claiming New Testament dependence on the Old Testament term, have followed the same prescription in identifying usage in the New Testament except they insert a theological component that was neither included in the Old Testament meaning of the term nor explained in its derivation. This pattern is repeated in virtually every Bible dictionary or encyclopedia. Numerous biblical passages will be cited in support of their theological use of the term, but that is question begging because that is the issue we are trying to determine. What does the word mean? Not the theological meaning a particular author imports into the term and how they then use it. The usual procedure is first you define what a word means, and then you use it in a theological context.

Shortly, we will look at representative passages and see if what has been asserted so far has another interpretation, but let us move on to the first of the two heavyweights, Botterweck/Ringgren, before we get to Kittel. It is critical to observe, before moving to Botterweck/Ringgren and Kittel, that we are traversing into texts that do, in fact, deal with the theological meanings of the words they are describing.

Botterweck/Ringgren begins by looking directly at the etymology of the Hebrew word for elder, *zāqēn*. The author of this article, J. Conrad, says the Hebrew word for elder means "beard."[6] He continues by stating that in the "OT . . . it always refers to old men . . . or elders or officials."[7] It can also mean "be old, grow old."[8] Interestingly, in the very next section, Botterweck adds, "In the LXX, *zāqēn* is rendered 127 times by *presbuteros*, 23 times by *presbytēs* . . . "[9] This is a significant addition in attempting to determine what "elder" means. For the next two entire pages, Conrad picks up the argument and emphasizes that *zāqēn*, "elder," refers to or deals with age in some direct manner.[10] The import of this for the purposes of our examination cannot be overemphasized. There is, etymologically, no understanding of the term in any way other than having to do with a man's age. An elder, then, was simply "a wise old man, probably with a beard, of good repute."

I want to conclude with a few final additions from Botterweck/Ringgren. The article continues following the understanding of elder, dealing primarily with the respect and authority of an individual due to his age.

---

6   J. Conrad and G. J. Botterweck, , H. Ringgren (ed.), D. E. Green (trans.), זקן (zaqen), *Theological Dictionary of the Old Testament* (Revised Edition, vol. 4, 122). Grand Rapids, MI; Cambridge, UK: William B. Eerdmans Publishing Company, 1980.
7   Ibid., 122.
8   Ibid., 123.
9   Ibid., 124.
10   Ibid., 124–126.

Elders are seen as "the guardians of the internal order of their community, and therefore exercise local jurisdiction (Ruth 4:1–12)";[11] "They
have considerable political importance as representing the community
to the outside world (Judges 8:14, 16; 1 S. 11:3; cf. 1 S. 16:4, and, for a
non-Israelite city, Josh. 9:11)."[12] They become "representatives of major
tribal territories."[13] They chose leaders[14] and are even courted by King
David.[15] "Concretely, their primary activity is to furnish counsel . . . "[16]

To truly grasp the inconsistency of how this term is used defini-
tionally to determine a theological meaning, it is critical to establish the
baseline lexical meaning in the Old Testament since all recognize the
New Testament's reliance on the Old Testament's meaning.

This brings us to the New Testament and Kittel. As a spoiler alert,
Kittel will essentially agree with the imposition of the theological meaning of "elder" as found in both Easton and Holman; subsequently, I will
not be torturing you with Kittel's understanding of "elder" because there
isn't any substantive difference between what they present and the previous dictionary treatments. If one has the wherewithal and overbur-
dening interest to see how Kittel handles "elder," I leave the reference information in the footnote below.[17] The real significant information, the
information that hints at a difference and, therefore, lack of synonymity
between "elder" and "overseer," is in the term "overseer" or "bishop."

---

11   Ibid., 127.

12   Ibid., 127.

13   Ibid., 127.

14   Ibid., 127. Jephthah in Judges 15:5–11; David is anointed by the elders of the northern
tribes, II Samuel 5:3; cf., 3:17; then back to Absalom, II Samuel 17:4.

15   Ibid., 127.

16   Ibid., 127.

17   G. Bornkamm (1964–). πρέσβυς, πρεσβύτερος, πρεσβύτης, συμπρεσβύτερος, πρεσβυτέριον,
πρεσβεύω. G. Kittel, G. W. Bromiley, & G. Friedrich (eds.), *Theological Dictionary of the New Testament* (electronic ed., vol. 6, 651). Grand Rapids, MI: Eerdmans. It must be pointed out before
delving any deeper that Bornkamm was a Lutheran scholar, and the Lutheran view of bishops
is quite different from the traditional, historical "episcopal" position. This does not mean that
Bornkamm's presentation is automatically wrong—that would be a fallacious assertion—but
one must be aware of the presuppositions of anyone presenting a specific view. That is one of the
reasons I have stated in a couple of places that I come at this entire discussion from a Reformed
Anglican view.

Bishop

The first breadcrumb offered by Kittel comes almost at the beginning of the entry for "bishop" or "overseer," where German Lutheran theologian H. W. Beyer says, "The LXX gives to the common word ἐπισκέπτομαι . . . the occasional suggestion given when used of the looking down of the gods."[18]

Beyer sharpens his previous statement by adding, "ἐπισκέπτομαι has a religious content in the LXX *only* (emphasis mine) when God is the Subject of the action."[19] He adds, "In Deuteronomy 11:12 Canaan is described as a land ἣν Κύριος ὁ θεός σου ἐπισκοπεῖται,"[20] "upon which God looks down in grace," "upon which His eyes rest from the beginning of the year to the end, and which is therefore very fruitful."[21] Then there is the following illuminating comment by Beyer, "It is worth noting that this sense does not occur in secular Greek but only in the context of the Old Testament history of salvation, from which it passes into the New Testament."[22] So at the outset of the etymological discussion of the roots of "overseer" or "bishop," we find that it originally had divine relation and connotation and that, from the LXX, this is passed from the Old Testament to the New Testament.

From this platform, Beyer points out that one of the characteristics of "overseer" or "bishop" is "to appoint, to commission, to install someone,"[23] and he cites Numbers 27:16: "Let God the Lord . . . set a man over the congregation . . . that the congregation of the Lord be not as sheep which have no shepherd."[24] What makes this so striking is that in this root meaning of the term, Beyer is actually anticipating some of the primary ministries, roles, and functions that are reserved

---

18   H. W. Beyer (1964–). ἐπισκέπτομαι, ἐπισκοπέω, ἐπισκοπή, ἐπίσκοπος, ἀλλοτριεπίσκοπος. G. Kittel, G. W. Bromiley, & G. Friedrich (eds.), *Theological Dictionary of the New Testament* (electronic ed., vol. 2, 601). Grand Rapids, MI: Eerdmans.
19   Ibid., 601. ἐπισκέπτομαι and ἐπισκοπεῖται are cognates of the term ἐπίσκοπος," "bishop" or "overseer."
20   Translation: ". . . which the Lord your God oversees."
21   Ibid., 601.
22   Ibid., 602.
23   Ibid, 602. See Numbers 4:27 and 32.
24   Ibid., 602–603.

for a bishop, ordination and consecration. To this he adds, "This saying may well have played a part in the *installation of leaders in the early Christian Church*, and possibly in the selection of the title ὠπίσκοπος[25] for the leaders of the congregation"[26] (emphasis mine). Beyer, while obviously not advocating for a distinct separation between the terms for "elder" and "bishop" or "overseer," is at least providing the lexical meaning of the word such that a separation of the two terms is most plausible—not only plausible, but as I will show shortly, a clear reality.

Though Beyer wants to argue that *episkopos* is a "community function"[27] where the "episcopal" function would later be assumed by one individual,[28] he pivots slightly by making the following statement: "At 1 Pt. 5:2, . . . Here the terms ποιμὴν[29] and ἐπίσκοπος[30] are brought into close interconnection."[31] What makes this terminological connection so eye-opening is that the Greek word he identifies here, "ποιμὴν" (*poiman*) or "flock," is Peter's obvious allusion to the Lord Jesus's ministry (for which even Beyer refers back to 1 Peter 2:25, where Peter identifies the Lord as the "Bishop," per the KJV, "of our souls"). There is even the interplay of the word for "flock" and the related word for "shepherd" (*poimanate*). Taken with John 10, the Lord Jesus's revelation of Himself as "The Good Shepherd," it becomes interpretatively strained to think that there are multiple representations of *the* Good Shepherd in this context because this verse is generally regarded to refer to the episcopal office of archbishop. Whether one is unwaveringly convinced of my connection here, the fact is Beyer opens the door for this link to be postulated. Lest anyone think I am grasping at straws or going out on a limb, Beyer follows the above comment concerning 1 Peter 5:2 with this gem:

> The official work of presbyters, who are obviously the same as the ἐπίσκοποι καὶ διάκονοι[32] of communities in the Gk. world (→

25 *Opiskopos* is a cognate of *episkopos*.

26 Ibid., 602–603.

27 Ibid., 604.

28 Ibid., 604.

29 "Flock."

30 "Bishop" or "overseer."

31 Ibid., 604.

32 Episkopoi kai diakonoi, or "bishop and minister," or, alternate translation, "overseer even

615 f.), is thus to follow the pattern of the ποιμὴν καὶ ἐπίσκοπος Jesus Christ, consisting in ποιμαίνειν and ἐπισκοπεῖν, in feeding the community and in responsible care for it, in watching over its eternal welfare.[33]

As mentioned numerous times, the connection of "presbyters" with "episcopos" or "Bishops/overseers" is to be expected, but read closely, one again sees a slight pivot in his statement. The "shepherd"/"overseer" connection is linked to Christ as the pattern, yet he is defining the "function" of a bishop, "feeding the *community*," being "responsible" for its care and eternal welfare. Given that his previous understanding of community is not merely the local parish or congregation, he once again subtly separates the "presbyter" from the "episkopos" and describes a bishop here.

The next move Beyer makes is one that every advocate of "episcopacy" would applaud. While reiterating the New Testament's dependence on the LXX's rendering of "episkopos" in the Old Testament,[34] he makes the revealing statement, "No less notable from the standpoint of the history of the term are the two passages where it has the sense of *office*" (emphasis mine).[35] With this almost benign comment, Beyer begins to describe "episkopos" as an official office. This has been an argument those who advocate for an episcopal polity have been making for centuries and has been rebuffed by non-Episcopalians. Yet here is an affirmation that it is an *office* in some sense, by a non-Episcopalian:

> The first is Nu. 4:16, where we read of the ἐπισκοπὴ ὅλης τῆς σκηνῆς[36] which is committed to Eleazar, the son of Aaron. Here we can see clearly how the Heb.[37] פְּקֻדַּת and the Gk. ἐπισκοπή lead from the literal sense of oversight to that of official responsibility.[38]

---

minister."
33   Ibid., 604.
34   Ibid., 605.
35   Ibid., 607.
36   "Oversight of the whole tent (i.e., tabernacle)."
37   The Hebrew for "oversight or visitation."
38   Ibid.,607.

To further buttress his point, Beyer states, "The NT uses ἐπισκοπή in the sense of 'office' as well as 'visitation.'"[39] And again,

> According to Ac. 1:16 ff. Peter saw in the fate of Judas the ful-
> filment of OT prophecy. He grounded the need to choose a
> substitute on (Psalm) ψ 108:8: "His office let another take".
> Here, then, the apostolic office is described as ἐπισκοπή. When
> we know that in 1 Tm. 3:1 the Christian office of bishop is also
> called ἐπισκοπή, we are tempted to see connections and with
> their help to explain the development of Christian titles. It
> should be noted, however, that the term is used for the apostolic
> office in Ac. 1:16 ff. only because the selection of a replacement
> was seen to be a fulfilment of the prophecy in ψ[40] 108:8. We can-
> not deduce from this any closer relationship between the apos-
> tolate and the episcopate. On the contrary, early Christianity
> had a clear sense of the distinction between the two. The term
> ἐπισκοπή in 1 Tm. 3:1 does not derive from Ac. 1:20 or its OT
> original. It is newly coined on the basis of the title ἐπίσκοπος
> which had meantime established itself in the early Church. This
> is the more easily possible, of course, because ἐπισκοπή is al-
> ready used for "office" in the language of the LXX.[41]

In this quote we find, arguably, the most blatant instance of import-
ing theological presuppositions into a meaning. Granted, this is a theological dictionary, so I only point it out so that the reader will understand that his theological position is not a part of the lexical meaning of
the term.

First, citing the apostle Peter, Beyer correctly points out that there
was a biblical, prophetic need to find a replacement for Judas's *office*,
where the apostolic office is defined by the term "episkopos." Second,
citing the apostle Paul in I Timothy, he once again defines "episkopos"
as an office but a "bishop's" office. Third, what Beyer gives, Beyer takes

---

39   Ibid., 608.
40   I.e., Psalm 108.
41   Ibid., 608. It is important to note that Beyer here cites the verse to which Peter is referring
in Acts 1:20, as Ps 108:8, which is the LXX version.

away, and he attempts to mitigate the force of the meaning that he has just given by stating that because it was applied directly to the apostolic office, it cannot be inferred to transfer that meaning in any other context, particularly the episcopate. Why? How about the transfer of apostolic authority rather than the full gamut of apostolic office? Fourth, and here is the egregious case of forcing your views on a term, he asserts that the meaning of "episkopos" does not derive from Acts 1:20 and I Timothy 3, because, and I quote from above, "It is newly coined on the basis of the title ἐπίσκοπος which had meantime established itself in the early Church. This is the more easily possible, of course, because ἐπισκοπή is already used for 'office' in the language of the LXX."

Read that again; reread it. This is a horrendous imposition of Hellenistic thinking into this concept. One of the reasons I waited to deal with this issue, at this point, near the end of the book, was to lay out the historical, biblical, and, yes, theological connections required to support my argument. My position rests on the clearly presented link between the Old Testament Church and its Jewish nature and the fact that the early Church in the New Testament believed they were the fulfillment of Old Testament Judaism. He completely repudiates that idea.

Fifth, he then, in the very next sentence, contradicts his previous point by saying, "This is the more easily possible, of course, because ἐπισκοπή is already used for 'office' in the language of the LXX." Well, what is it? This newly coined understanding belies his dependence on Hellenistic presuppositions (i.e., the term is more a Greek concept than a Hebrew one). Are we not allowed to make the connection between "episkopos" and the Old Testament, or are we? I refer to his original lexical description that "episkopos" has overt religious connotations. "Elder" or "presbuteros" does not.

Sixth, eventually the New Testament mentions men as "leaders" of the Church. For Beyer,

This raises two important questions in the history of Church government: a. Who is called ἐπίσκοπος and b. From what period does ἐπίσκοπος cease to be a description of the free action of members of the community and become the designation of bearers of a specific office to which they and they alone are called?[42]

He answers the first question quite provocatively by arguing that the title (which he doesn't immediately supply) is given only in the context of, and this is critical, "settled local congregations in which regular acts are performed."[43] In other words, formal liturgy. Interestingly, he excludes traveling, nomadic charismatic gospel preachers, and even the apostles, prophets, and teachers.[44] He claims these are never identified as "episkopos."

He answers the second question as we would expect: that it was a long, protracted process where the "elder" and the "episkopos" slowly separated and resulted in two distinct offices.[45] You can surmise from his statements his dissatisfaction with this historical development (if it actually transpired as such).

The late Ronald S. Wallace makes a curious but revealing observation about all this back and forth between "elder" and "bishop." In his article on "Elder" in the *Evangelical Dictionary of Theology*, the late Scotsman makes this comment:

> It is often asserted that in the Gentile churches the name *episkopos* is used as a substitute for *presbyteros*[46] with identical meaning. The words seem to be interchangeable in Acts 20:17 and Titus 1:5-9. But though all *episkopoi* are undoubtedly *presbyteroi*, it is not clear whether the reverse is always true. The word *presbyteros* denotes rather the status of eldership while *episkopos* denotes the function of at least some elders. But there may have been elders who were not *episkopoi*.[47]

What a starkly honest observation by a Scot Presbyterian. Look

---

42   Ibid., 615.
43   Ibid., 615.
44   Ibid., 615.
45   Ibid., 615–627.
46   Alternate spelling of "presbuteros."
47   Ronald S. Wallace, "Elder," *Evangelical Dictionary of Theology.* Edited by Walter A. Elwell. Grand Rapids, MI: Baker Book House, 1984: 347.

closely at the statements in Dr. Wallace's quote. The meaning of the term only goes one way, and some elders may not have been "episkopoi" (which is merely the plural form of "episkopos"). How, then, can they be interchangeable? This assessment by Wallace reveals that "elder" (*presbuteros*) is not an office at all but a category from which others are taken. As a former marine, I was in the US military, but not all military members were marines. This is the same principle at work here. When we keep in mind what elder or *zāqēn* in the Old Testament meant, this makes perfect sense. All "old, wise, bearded" men were "elders" or were to be "elders," but not all "old, wise, bearded" men were "episkopoi." To be an *episkopos*, one must be an elder, but simply because one is an elder does not make him an *episkopos*. Or to put it another way, *presbuteros* describes the qualities, attributes, and character of an *episkopos* (or bishop), those characteristics one needs to be a bishop, but *prebuteros* itself is not an office from which *episkopoi* (bishops) arise.

It is from this perspective that I will conclude this chapter by critiquing the assertion that "presbuteros" (elder) and "episkopos" (bishop or overseer) are synonymous or interchangeable in three points: lexical challenges, historical observations, and textual analysis.

Lexical Challenges

As has been argued in various ways throughout this treatment, I believe the case for hard and fast synonymity of the two terms in question is not merely vastly overstated but incorrect as it is applied. I know I stand against the majority opinion; however, I am not dissuaded. In reference to the question of the alleged synonymity of these terms:

a. First, Baptist New Testament scholar D. A. Carson, writes:[48]

    i.   "I am not saying that any word can mean anything. Normally we observe that any individual word has a certain

---

48   D. A. Carson, *Exegetical Fallacies*. Grand Rapids, MI: Baker Book House, 1984: 30–49. I have the greatest respect for Dr. Carson's scholarship, and I have attempted to be gracious, cautious, and circumspect but direct and honest. One must be very aware of his excellent reputation and work. He still, however, can be mistaken, as I believe he is here at the points I will identify.

limited semantic range, and the context may therefore modify or shape the meaning of a word only within certain boundaries . . . I am not saying words are infinitely plastic" (30–31).

ii. Problems Surrounding Synonyms and Componential Analysis: "Hyponymic relations . . . pairs of items do not have the same semantic values: they do not mean exactly the same things, but they have the same referents (they make reference to the same realities, even though their meaning is different)" (p. 49).

What Dr. Carson cautions is that words should also be understood in context; they are not so malleable that they are virtually plastic and can mean anything, and even though words might have the same reference, their meaning is different.

He, at one point, makes a telling statement:

Semantic Anachronism: This fallacy occurs when the late use of a word is read back into earlier literature. At the simplest level, it occurs within the same language, as when the Greek early church fathers use a word in a manner not demonstrably envisioned by the New Testament writers. It is not obvious, for instance, that the use of episkopos (bishop) to designate a church leader [has any New Testament warrant].[49]

Now here is a New Testament scholar chiding some for "reading back" into the New Testament, from a later time, the exact thing he does as a Baptist. He reads "back" into the New Testament his understanding of "elder rule" in the Baptist Church to define elder (*presbuteros*) in New Testament texts. I have already shown what the lexical definition of *presbuteros* is; in a moment, I'll show it is not an ordained office, and yet here we have an example of practicing the very thing against which we are being warned. Much to the chagrin of Prof. Carson, there is more than sufficient biblical warrant for *episkopos* to designate a bishop over

---

49   Ibid., 32.

both a local parish and a region. In addition, as has been mentioned, even if they were synonymous, usage and context would then have to be considered, where questions of meaning arise. In the case of these two terms, usage is different.

It is essential at this juncture that I acknowledge that language develops over time; changes do occur in the meaning of terms. I'm an old man; I grew up in the '60s (1960s, not 1860s), and during that time, I recall the term "bad" meaning, well, bad, something not good or wrong. Then, toward the end of the '60s and the early '70s, it came to mean something was cool, far out, or radical (I told you I am old). In today's social climate, I have no idea what it means anymore.

My point is, while I recognize linguistic changes, etymology still plays an important role in understanding language. The term "erg" is still used in engineering and physics circles. However, rather than merely being used as a unit of work or energy, it now can mean anything from "ergonomics," the study of "workplace efficiency," to "employee resource group."

Historical Observations

Of all the arguments that can be marshalled against the alleged synonymity of the two terms in question, the historical material is probably the most damaging and cherry picked of all sources available. I can only speculate as to why this is, but what follows is only some of the historical material that stands in opposition to the claim that *presbuteros* and *episkopos* are synonymous.

We have already seen, from the Old Testament usage, that, apart from the question of age, an elder was a governmental or administrative position (Joshua 24:31; 1 Kings 12:6). From the divine revelation on Sinai to Moses, administrators were prominent in the Mosaic economy. It was apparent that even while in bondage in Egypt, there were national elders who represented the people (Exodus 3:16; 4:29; Joshua 24:1, 2). Arriving in Canaan, they were named "elders of Israel," "of the land" (1 Samuel 4:3; 1 Kings 20:7), "of the tribes" (Deuteronomy 31:28), or "of the city," (Deuteronomy 19:12; compare Deuteronomy 16:18 and Ruth 4:9, 11). There were elders during the period of the judges (Judges

2:7), the period of the kings (2 Samuel 17:4), under Babylonian captivity (Jeremiah 29:1), and on the return (Ezra 5:5).

The force of this historical observation is clear: grown, mature, wise, old men were considered elders, and they held various governmental positions. They were not ordained as priests were. It cannot be stressed or reiterated enough that the New Testament dependence upon Old Testament meaning of this term establishes its etymological heredity and, therefore, New Testament meaning. The constant reference to the New Testament elders as ministers in some sense of ordained clergy is pure fiction at this point in biblical history.

At this point, I'm going to cut the so-called Gordian knot and momentarily bypass the New Testament texts (we will deal with that in our next section) and examine the definitive blow to this five-hundred-year-old false assertion of interchangeability between the terms.

German Protestant scholar Emil Schürer, in his classic work *A History of the Jewish People in the Time of Jesus Christ*, which has been modernized by Geza Vermes and others, knocks all the pegs of the synonym claim off their moorings. Schürer begins with:

> In view of this fact it is highly instructive to find, that upon the Roman inscriptions we nowhere meet with the title πρεσβύτερος[50] (or any other like it, by which to denote the member of the γερουσία[51] as such; for the ἄρχοντες[52] were certainly not ordinary members, but the committee of the γερουσία). This fact can only be accounted for from the circumstance that it is only the offices properly so called that are mentioned by name upon the epitaphs, whereas the "elders" were not looked upon as officials in the technical sense of the word. They were the representatives and advisers of their community, but not officials with specific functions entrusted to them.[53]

---

50   *Presbuteros*: elder.
51   *Gerousia*: the Council of Elders in Judaism.
52   *Archontes*: ruler of the synagogue.
53   E. Schürer, *A History of the Jewish People in the Time of Jesus Christ, Second Division*. Edinburgh: T&T Clark, 1890: vol. 4, 249.

Initially, we must notice that he introduces two new terms: "council of elders" (*Gerousia*) and "ruler" (*archontes*). So Schürer is informing us that, in archaeological discoveries, the inscriptions found on Roman buildings indicate that "elders" are not "officials" in the technical sense but merely community representatives and advisors with no specific functions. This certainly would make it difficult to identify the term *elder* with any sense in which *elder* is used by contemporary Christianity (i.e., minister in a church). If this were the total of Schürer's contribution, that "elders" were "not officials in a technical sense," it would be enough to cause a cautious supporter of the "presbyter"/"bishop" interchangeability to pause. He continues, "Besides the elders who had the general direction of the affairs of the congregation, special officers were appointed for special purposes."[54] Elders, according to Schürer, during the time of our Lord Jesus, had no special function. Theirs was a general administrative duty. This is obviously a carryover from the Old Testament understanding of the purpose of an elder, in distinction from an ordained position such as priest. He makes mention of an oddity within generic ministry of a synagogue and that is that there are no specific duties of any kind assigned.[55] So the reading of scripture, public prayer, and preaching were open to anyone.[56] This explains why the Lord Jesus could walk into a synagogue, take the Isaiah scroll, read it, and then preach from it (Luke 4:21). This explains much in the development of both liturgy and polity, which we will explain momentarily, particularly if elders had only general duties. Carefully consider the next statement by Schürer:

> But though no official readers, preachers and liturgists were appointed, it was above all necessary that: (1) An official should be nominated, who should have the care of external order in public worship and the supervision of the concerns of the synagogue in general. This was the Ruler of the synagogue. Such ἀρχισυνάγωγοι are met with in the entire sphere of Judaism, not only in Palestine, but also in Egypt, Asia Minor, Greece, Italy,

---

54   Ibid., 62.
55   Ibid., 62.
56   Ibid., 62.

and the Roman Empire in general. The office and title were also
transferred from the Jews to the Judeo-Christian churches of
Palestine, nay it is also found occasionally in Christian churches
beyond Palestine.[57]

With this type of loose structure, modifications would occur naturally; an elder would be elected to be the ruler of the synagogue (sometimes called the president of the synagogue). Historically, this ruler of
the synagogue or president of the synagogue has been seen as the highest of the three synagogue orders and the role the *episkopos* would assume at the time the Church and synagogue become intertwined. Note
that he points out that this office and title were transferred from the Jews
to Jewish-Christian Churches. Quite a natural move, I might add.

The next series of statements by Schürer draws this entire argument
of the interchangeability of *presbuteros* and *episkopos* to a head. Schürer,
in comparing the elder (*presbuteros*) with the ruler of the synagogue
(eventual bishop), makes the following devastating comment regarding
the ruler of the synagogue, the *archisynagoges*: "That this office differed
from that of an elder of the congregation is proved by the joint occur-
rence of the titles πρεσβύτεροι and ἀρχισυνάγωγοι."[58]

First, the *presbuteroi* and *archisynagogoi* differed because both titles
were used concurrently, together, jointly for different functions. There is
no interchangeability here: "But it is most instructive, that according to
the evidence of the inscriptions one and the same person could fill the
offices of both ἄρχων and ἀρχισυνάγωγος."[59]

However, a ruler or *archon* could fill both offices of ruler and ruler
of the synagogue. In other words, a "ruler" could become a "bishop"
(*archisynagoges*). Yet these two offices were distinct:

The ἄρχοντες were in the Dispersion the "chiefs" of the congregation, in whose hands lay the direction in general. The office

---

57   Ibid., 62.
58   Ibid., 64–65.
59   Ibid., 64–65.

therefore of the Archisynagogos was at all events distinct from theirs.[60]

Nor can he have been the chief of the archontes, who was called γερουσιάρχης. He had therefore nothing to do with the direction of the community in general. His office was, on the contrary, that of specially caring for public worship.[61]

Once the individual became a chief ruler or ruler of the synagogue (*archon*), that was his primary duty. He could not become the ruler of the council (*Gerousia*). His specific responsibility was pastoral care.

He was called "archisynagogus," not as head of the community, but as conductor of their assembly for public worship. As a rule he was indeed taken out of the number of the elders of the congregation. Among his functions is specially mentioned e.g. that of appointing who should read the Scriptures and the prayer and summoning fit persons to preach.[62]

Here is a powerful argument against terms being synonymous. The primary role of a ruler of the synagogue (*archon*) was being the leader of a Church's public worship (as conductor of their assembly for public worship). He might be taken from the elders of the congregation, meaning his office was distinct from their duties and they were not interchangeable. He had the duty that every bishop had and has today: being a leader; appointing readers, those to pray, and preachers. Jewish elders were not responsible for worship in the synagogue (or Temple), though they enjoyed seats of honor at the synagogue assemblies. Doubtless, the synagogue rulers were frequently elected from among their number.

I think this presents more than an adequate refutation of the idea of the interchangeability of the terms *presbyter* and *episkopos*. If one has followed the argument from New Testament dependence upon the Old Testament meaning of "elder" that the early Church, considering themselves the fulfillment of Israel, worshiped in the Temple and then the

---

60   Ibid., 64–65.
61   Ibid., 64–65. Gerousiarchas.
62   Ibid., 64–65

synagogue and understood temple worship to involve three ordained clerical offices, which eventually would be assimilated into the synagogue and begin to inform and shape that worship there (the fact that the bishop, "episkopos," is identified with the "ruler of the synagogue"), one would be hard pressed to refute the argument that "presbyter" and "episkopos" are not interchangeable.

The fact that the synagogue had numerous individuals with varying duties doesn't mitigate against the position of the ruler of the synagogue being a bishop because, as I've asserted earlier, there would've been a period of transition from Mosaic theological content to Christological content. On the contrary, the fact that there were numerous ministries in the early Church, up to twelve different ones, only supports the tight connection between the synagogue and the Church. God not only progressively revealed His word to His people; He progressively revealed how to understand it, via the ministry of the Holy Spirit, to His people.

One final historical inclusion must be a limited sampling of the earliest documentary support for episcopacy. These are given to us by Bishop Thomas Shank.[63]

St. Ignatius of Antioch (AD 30–AD 117)

Where the Bishop appears, there let the people be; as where Christ Jesus is, there is the catholic Church (Smyrnaeans, Ch. VIII).

He who is within the sanctuary is pure, he who is outside is impure; that is to say, he who does anything apart from Bishop, presbytery, and deacons, is not pure in his conscience. If one follow a separatist, he does not inherit the Kingdom of God (Trallians, Ch. VII).

For everyone whom the Master of His household sendeth to be His steward over His own house, we ought to receive as Him that sent Him. Plainly then we ought to regard the Bishop as the Lord Himself (Ephesians, Ch. III). For even Jesus Christ, our

---

63   Rt. Rev. Thomas Shank, *Apostolic Succession: The Continuing Ministry of Christ Among Us.*

inseparable life is the manifest will of the Father, so also Bishops settled everywhere to the uttermost bounds of the Earth as so by the will of Jesus Christ.

Let all reverence the deacons, as the appointment of Jesus Christ, and the Bishops, as Jesus Christ, who is the Son of the Father, and the Presbyters as the Sanhedrin of God and assembly of the Apostles. Apart from these there is no Church (Trallians, Ch. III).

Hippolytus (c. AD 212):

With the Agreement of all let the Bishops lay their hands on him and the presbytery stand by in silence . . . (the prayer followed), . . . And now pour forth that power which is from Thee, of the princely Spirit which Thou didst deliver to Thy beloved child Jesus Christ, which He bestowed on Thy Holy Apostles who established the Church (Apostolic Tradition 4).

We could even mention Tertullian's chiding of heretics in *De Praescriptione Haereticorum*, 20, 21, and 32, when he stated, "Let them produce the original records of their churches; let them unfold the roll of their bishops, running down in due succession from the beginning."

We now turn to actual texts.

Textual Analysis

One of the best critiques of the failure to link the terms "presbuteros" and "episkopos" is the exegetical argument from Titus 1:5–9, made by former Presbyterian minister Bishop Ray Sutton, where he analyzes Titus 1:5–9:[64]

---

64 This excellent argument is from Bishop Ray Sutton of the Reformed Episcopal Church. Bishop Sutton presents this argument, among others, in his online work entitled *Captains and Courts: A Biblical Defense of Episcopal Government*. The following argument is found on 68–84. The paper can be found here: https://stevemacias.com/wp-content/uploads/2013/12/captains_and_courts.pdf. I am not convinced by all his arguments, but there is much here from which to benefit.

⁵ For this reason I left you in Crete, that you should set in order the things that are lacking, and appoint elders in every city as I commanded you—

⁶ if a man is blameless, the husband of one wife, having faithful children not accused of dissipation or insubordination.

⁷ For a bishop must be blameless, as a steward of God, not self-willed, not quick-tempered, not given to wine, not violent, not greedy for money,

⁸ but hospitable, a lover of what is good, sober-minded, just, holy, self-controlled,

⁹ holding fast the faithful word as he has been taught, that he may be able, by sound doctrine, both to exhort and convict those who contradict. (NKJ)

Look at how Paul words this section:

A. "For this reason . . . " Why did Paul leave Titus in Crete?

    1. That he should set in order the things that are lacking;

        a. That he (not as an apostle but with apostolic authority as a bishop) should appoint presbyters in every city;

        b. That he should determine who are qualified to be in ministry and what that ministry should be.

    2. Let us examine verses 5 and 6 and 7–9:

        a. According to what Paul tells Titus in verses 5 and 6, a *presbuteros* (a priest) or elder should have the following qualities:

        b. Blamelessness (anegklatos),[65] be the husband of one wife, have faithful children, and not be unruly or accused of riot.

Now, compare this with verses 7–9 as Paul presents Titus the qualifications of what:

---

65 ἀνέγκλητος.

3. An *episkopos* should be

    a. Blameless

    b. Not self-willed, not soon angry, not given to wine, no
        striker, not given to filthy lucre, a lover of hospitality, a
        lover of good men, sober, just, holy, temperate, holding
        fast the faithful word as he hath been taught that he may
        be able, by sound doctrine both to exhort and to con-
        vince the gainsayers.

This is the sum of Bishop Sutton's treatment. If the terms *presbuteros*
and *episkopos* (elder and bishop) are synonyms, if they are interchangeable, why the repetition? And then why the subtle difference, why the
more extensive list for an *episkopos*/bishop? If they are essentially the
same, all Paul is saying by the repetition of the term "blameless" is, "Appoint elders who are blameless because an elder must be blameless." That
is called a tautology, something that is true by definition and merely repeated. For instance, "A round baseball is a baseball that is round." One
is merely repeating the same idea, in the same proposition, by slightly
rearranging the words used.

But if the apostle Paul is instructing Titus as a bishop, he is advising
him to appoint (ordain) elders who are pure because the bishop is to be
pure. The purity element in Church leadership is to be reproduced all
the way from deacons to bishops. The standard is the Lord Jesus, exemplified in the ecclesiastical standard, and the bishop, who is supposed to
emulate our Lord, who then is to appoint leaders (priests) who are to be
as both he and the Lord Jesus are: blameless leaders (not sinless—only
the Lord can claim that).

In Acts 4:5, we have rulers, ἄρχοντας (*archontas*) elders, πρεσβυτέρους
(*presbuteros*), and teachers. Then in verse 23, we have chief priests and
elders. If, as argued, the model is the Old Testament, trifold office, upon
which the New Testament trifold office is based, we see here, plainly,
two separate offices, an office of chief priests and elders (presupposing
"elders" in this context even means an ordained position, which it does

not). So the office of chief priest and that of an elder cannot be the same "office"[66] because "elder" was not an office yet.

Acts 14:23 and 20:17–38. There were multiple churches in Acts to whom Paul was speaking ("elders in every Church"). In other words, the tendency to deal with these texts where the apostle Paul is speaking to multiple elders is to function on the principle that there is a body of ruling elders that Paul is either addressing or ordaining to care for the church at Ephesus. On its surface, that assumption is question begging. The issue of an office (clergy) of ruler elders is what they must prove; it cannot simply be assumed that is the context in which the apostle is addressing these men. The implied assumption is there is only one church in Ephesus. If he is speaking to one church in Ephesus, with all these elders, we have the equivalent essentially of a modern-day megachurch. The persecution from either the Jews or the Romans would have made something of this nature a very large church, highly unlikely at this moment historically. This is not a repetition of Pentecost, which was set in the context of the mandatory Jewish festivals so there would have been large caravans of pilgrims from all over in Jerusalem. I know that will not be acknowledged, but that is the sense one gets in these discussions.

Yet we know that both the Epistles to the Ephesians and Colossians were circular epistles, meaning they were sent not to a church in Ephesus but the "churches" in Ephesus. This point is clearly seen in Revelation 1:4, where Apostle John is writing to the "seven Churches in Asia." However, upon careful reading of the context, one sees that these are "sees," or what we would identify as cathedral churches in Asia with various smaller churches or parishes under their care and authority. This understanding changes the dynamic of the argument. With multiple churches, there would have to be multiple bishops and/or priests to minister to those congregations. This (along with Acts 20) is not a matter of ordaining men to the office of elder, as if it were an ordained office—we've already seen that's not what elder means; this is a matter of Paul, either setting up administrators to govern the churches or or-

---

66   Twenty-two times in the New Testament, the terms "elders" and "chief priests" are used together; twice, the term "scribe" is added. One becomes hard pressed to maintain the connection between the terms as the same offices, given this amount of biblical and historical support for the opposing position.

daining men out of the category of "mature, grown men," "elders," to either the office of bishop (which would explain verse 28) or priest. He is leaving these bishops among them with the *episcopal* authority to ordain and exercise church discipline.

What is happening is that the apostle Paul is speaking to multiple individuals of various churches in the region of Asia Minor. Something akin to a man per church, so to speak. Otherwise, the context requires that elders here, not being an office, is referring to a group of mature, wise men who hold the office of bishop. In other words, once again, one can be an elder and not be a bishop, but one cannot be a bishop without first being an elder. Just as one can be a man without being a father, but one cannot be a father without being a man.

In Acts 15: 2–23, we see the apostles and elders. Again, they cannot be the same office. Once again, if the Old Testament model is followed, the apostles are passing their authority (here is where Beyer erred) on to the bishops who took their place. We have the clear distinction between bishop and elder.

What about the ordinations of Saints Timothy and Titus? If the pattern of episcopacy is wrong and elder rule is the correct biblical pattern, why didn't the apostle Paul instruct Timothy and Titus to present all those to be ordained to be brought before the "elders" or "classis" or "presbytery"? Why did he not instruct Timothy and Titus to bring all who were to be ordained "back to the Church" in Jerusalem, where all the apostles, functioning as a presbytery, classis, or group of elders could collectively examine the respective candidate/s? Rather, he gave them each individually the authority and instructed them to ordain *presbyters*, as priests, as a bishop, would.

For that matter, why did the apostle Paul not require Saints Timothy and Titus to appear before the "presbytery" in Jerusalem? Isn't that what happened to Judas's replacement, Matthias (Acts 1:20–26)?[67] This establishes a pattern of authority. Though the apostles held a special or unique office, their ability to ordain (lay hands on) those considered for leadership derives not exclusively from their apostolic uniqueness but from their connection with the Old Testament patterns established. The

---

67 Also note, once again, the use of *episkopos* as "office" in verse 20.

question also must be asked, why, given their unique apostolic office, did they function in an episcopal rather than elder rule or presbyterian? They all appear before or appeal to St. James as the bishop of the Jerusalem Church with specific, individual authority.

Revelation 4:4. There is no question there is more than one interpretation of this verse; however, given the context of the first three chapters and the dialogue with the various churches in view, I believe the most applicable interpretation of the twenty-four Elders is to see them as archetypal representations: twelve Old Testament patriarchs, twelve New Testament apostles.

Let us conclude by quickly looking at two verses from St. Paul's Epistles to Timothy.

1 Timothy 4:14: "Do not neglect the gift that is in you, which was given to you by prophecy with the laying on of the hands of the eldership" (NKJ).

Initially, this appears to be a simple, straightforward explanation of an ordination setting. The eldership got together, laid hands on, in this case, Timothy, and ordained him. However, we once again run into the issue of what a term means in the boarder context. Much of what has already been written concerning the term "presbuteros" or "elder" applies here; therefore, I will only make a few observations.[68]

First, all of what has been previously stated concerning the definition of "presbuteros" applies directly to this text. Second, it would not be unusual for a group or body of elders to lay hands on a man at his ordination as a means of recognition, confirmation, and support. This practice is seen in the Old Testament, even though the elders did not ordain anyone. They did, however, lay hands on individuals as a sign of the office about to be assumed and the gift imparted by God, confirmed by the laying on of hands. This practice continues today in Anglican, Roman Catholic, and Greek Orthodox churches, where the bishop ordains the priests and then has fellow clergy come forward and lay hands on the newly ordained priest. They obviously are not the ones doing the or-

---

68   Felix Cirlot, in his work *Apostolic Succession: Is It True?*, deals a thorough refutation, beginning particularly in part IV, 383ff, to the question as to whether this was a "presbyterian" form of a group of elders *(presbyters)* ordaining Timothy. This text can be ordered only directly through his brother (R.A. Cirlot, 3006 Wheeling Street, El Paso, TX).

daining. Third, if one compares this with II Timothy 1:6, it is quite clear in that text, where he says the gift Timothy received was by the "laying on of *my hands.*" It was the apostle Paul who ordained Timothy and laid his hands on Timothy just as bishops do today. The elders or presbyters, whether clergy or not, would have been laying on their hands in much the same way it is done today, as acknowledging and endorsing this one as a new member of clergy. Lastly, in the chapter dealing with St. Jerome and the assertions made concerning his views on the subject, this question of who ordains is mentioned in slightly more detail.

The classic theory of Lightfoot that the episcopate arose out of the presbyterate by a gradual process, whereby one of the elders of a local church was elevated to the position of monarchical bishop, has won many supporters. There is also the argument from St. Jerome, around the fifth century, that is in concert with Bishop Lightfoot, which will be dealt with in a separate chapter.

What is unfortunate is that most people merely regurgitate arguments from three hundred years ago (and earlier, in some cases) from Lightfoot and others. With all due respect to the good bishop, Lightfoot didn't have access to the linguistic tools we have today, and even though St. Jerome is an ancient source, there are more ancient sources, much closer to the apostles, having been taught by the apostles (Ignatius, for one), that I believe offset St. Jerome's claims if they are indeed to be understood as has been claimed. Again, I will deal with St. Jerome's statements concerning *presbuteros* in a subsequent chapter.

To summarize:

a. The term *presbuteros,* as seen in both its Old and New Testament usage, simply means "a bearded old man with dignity."

b. When examining the term in its biblical, historical, and theological context, there is no linguistic identity, etymologically speaking, between *presbuteros* (elder) and *episkopos* (bishop). While there is a connection, that connection is determined by usage in context and cannot merely be asserted as proof of virtual interchangeability.

c. Schürer has conclusively shown that *presbuteros,* from the Hebrew *zaqen*, was distinct from and not at all synonymous with *archisynagoges*. In other words, while the synagogue utilized the "office" of *archisynagoges*, it did not identify that office with a lower or equal office called *presbuteros*.

d. Schürer has also shown that even given the most favorable development, *presbuteros* did not evolve into an ordained office until the third century, and then only in the Jewish or synagogue community.

e. When one then considers the New Testament usage of *presbuteros*, all the previous elements must be factored into the understanding of the term. Therefore, even if, and that is a significant if, *presbuteros* was used in the New Testament to speak of clergy in some manner, it was speaking of them as having the quality of being a *presbuteros*, "a distinguished, bearded old man with integrity." Therefore, there is a *presbuteros* out of which comes an office, say, priest. But no case can be made for the term being an office at this time in the Church.

f. What has not been extensively discussed is the way in which language practically develops in the context of usage. A more perspicuous manner to identify New Testament clergy would have been to use the phrase "the priest who is presbuteros" or "the presbuteros priest." Yet, as one can see, this is a bit cumbersome. It would only be natural to conflate the two terms for brevity, even though they are not speaking of the same thing, an ordained office. The writers and their audience would have naturally understood this shorthand manner of speaking, which would be lost to us today due to time and linguistic change. For them, to say "Brother Saul is a *presbuteros*" would have meant that they understood that to mean that Brother Saul was "a distinguished bearded old man with dignity" who *now* holds an ordained position. Language is strange at times in how it develops.

g. The fact that *presbuteros* is distinct from *episkopos* is clear from a proper understanding of the etymological, linguistic, historical, theological, and biblical data. We are not speaking of identical offices but of the quality and characteristics a man must possess in order to hold an ordained office. The fact that the New Testament possibly or potentially uses a contextual shorthand in no way mitigates or eliminates the distinct and separate meaning of the two terms. So when the New Testament speaks of *presbuteros* in Acts and other places, what is being identified is a man or group of men who are old, dignified, and of sufficient character to be clergy. That man or some in the group could possibly be ordained, most in the group probably are not, but in no way does the mere utterance of the term *presbuteros* mean that we are speaking of an office of ordained men in the context of the church of the first three centuries. The data is very clear: men were chosen for ministerial office because they had the qualities necessary to be ordained; they had the qualities of being *presbuteros*.

h. Finally, the reason this is such a significant issue is due to the manner in which *presbuteros* is identified in today's ecclesiastical discussions. The assertion is made that the manner in which *presbuteros* is used today is taken directly from scripture; hence, all biblical and theological arguments are alleged to bear the authoritative weight of the word of God. In other words, *presbuteros* and *episkopos* are synonymous terms and therefore interchangeable. Since they are interchangeable, so the argument goes, we are not talking about different offices but merely different functions. However, we have seen, I believe, rather convincingly that this is not the case at all but that we are in fact talking about two separate terms with markedly different meanings.

There also is the matter of the development of episcopal offices arriving virtually immediately in the Church in its historical context. If the office of bishop (*episkopos*) is not synonymous with the office of elder (*presbuteros*), because no such office existed, then by the sheer logic of the historical account, the office of bishop stands alone and in primacy as the highest office of clerical orders. The fact that the office of elder was not an ordained office within the first three or more centuries of the

Church—and when it is finally seen as an ordained office, it is within Judaism not Christianity—ends the discussion of synonymity between the terms.

Consequently, if the current contention that the way both terms are used today cannot be supported from scripture or history, how the term is used today must be brought into conformity with the correct biblical, theological, lexical, historical usage. Plainly put, it must be acknowledged that elder rule as a biblical form of church polity is, in fact, wrong and not at all a biblical form of church polity but a much later fabrication to suit a particular agenda. *Episkopoi*, bishops, then are most certainly *presbutero*, elder or better, "distinguished old men with beards"; but *presbuteroi*, elders, are not always *episkopoi*, bishops.

Before bringing this chapter to a close, a word about dissent. I realize that this view is unique, to say the least, in contemporary Christianity, and I expect disagreement. I hope, however, that as one reviews this treatment, one will notice that the majority of sources I have cited are not Anglicans. I have chosen to reference those whom I knew would not agree with my position, generally speaking. On the contrary, almost all my citations are from people with whom I would disagree on one or more topics. Yet, as you can see, the general theological material for my view is there for anyone to research. It took me over thirty years to come to this position; may the Lord expedite your journey.

Conclusion

THE QUESTION OF THE NATURE OF the Church or ecclesiology, if not the most important challenge Christianity faces internally, in my opinion, must rank in the top two. As we have seen over these chapters, when discussing the nature of the Church, we address heaven and its relationship to earth, worship, kingdom, authority, Church government or polity, covenants, sacraments, and so much more.

In covering these topics, I have honestly attempted to present my position in a fair manner without singling out any one group. I hope I have achieved that intent. In any event, my purpose was not to go after anyone but to offer a comprehensive exposition of a particular view of the Church. I made no secret that I am an Anglican, I am Reformed, and I would be identified as "high church" (for my purposes, I define high church as the belief that formal ceremony and ritual is thoroughly biblical), without any affinity for Roman theology. While I am utterly convinced of this, I realize I should probably address some anticipated objections.

1. *The Bible does not specifically command any form of Church government.* I believe I have more than adequately refuted this, but let's do it once more before we depart. The covenantal connection makes this a vacuous statement. New Testament Jews would utilize Old Testament Jewish practices. Also, if there was no specified biblical form of worship or Church government commanded between the period of the destruction of the Tem-

ple and the irrefutable very early establishment of episcopacy, how could episcopacy have ascended to the fore and gained prominence, then priority, without challenge? In other words, one would expect a rebuttal of the kind that would state, "What gives you, who demand we function with an episcopal polity, the right to claim that that is the biblical polity for everyone?" That is, if there was no one form of polity commanded in scripture, or even if there were, alternate forms existed.

2. *Continuing the above objection, the Bible does not specifically command a particular style of worship.* One would have to ignore the Lord Jesus's earthly ministry and where He worshiped. One would have to ignore the apostles' ministry and where they worshiped. Finally, one would have to ignore the Church fathers (disciples of the apostles) and where they worshiped. It must be answered, then, what type of worship was occurring between the Temple's destruction and the preeminence of episcopacy. One cannot merely say "synagogue" worship without considering the trifold-office arrangement of said synagogue (modeled upon the Temple). Additionally, one would have to ignore Schürer's compelling arguments.

Also, where is the proof that anything other than synagogue worship (heavily influenced by Temple theology and worship), with its three primary official offices, took place until the bar Kochba rebellion, circa AD 135?

Questions to Consider in Review

How could devout, orthodox Jews, who had worshiped with Jesus in the Temple and synagogue, suddenly abandon that form or pattern of worship and move to a "however the spirit moves you" type of worship, especially given the precise manner in which God commands to be approached in worship? See Exodus 19:6 and I Peter 2:5, 9. Reference the apostle Paul's teaching in Romans 3–4. What benefit is it, then, to be a Jew? We confidently know the following:

1. Where the apostles and their disciples (the Church fathers) worshiped. They worshiped in the Temple and synagogue, continuing that pattern after the Temple's destruction.

2. They learned the structure (liturgy) of worship in the Temple and synagogue.

3. They attempted to understand and modify Temple/synagogue worship to comport with New Covenant theology.

4. They applied this combination of understanding, structure, and modification to the Church.

5. They would have naturally been influenced by priests and Levites as these groups were converted to Christianity and migrated into, first, the Jewish-Christian synagogue then the church (Acts 6). The office of high priest would be replaced by the office of bishop as the extension of the apostolic office.

We can deduce from scripture:

1. The Church would have naturally concluded that trifold offices of the Temple (high priest, priest, Levites), with the three primary offices of the synagogue (archisynagogues, elders, minister), would become their ecclesiastical offices.

2. These would come to be known as three primary Episcopal holy orders (bishop, priest, and deacon).

Therefore, as has been stated earlier, those of us from traditional Church communities accept that, just as in the case of infant baptism, neither the Lord nor the apostles would have had any reason to inscripturate a specific, written biblical defense because none was needed. For them, it would have been understood to be an obvious continuation of the covenantal principle. The three orders of Episcopal ministry would be accepted as a natural extension of Temple orders, as well as the fact that there was no historically contemporary argument opposing the assumption of the Old Testament three-order structure into the New Testament.

What we see as silence in the question of a specifically command-ed New Testament form of polity is the progressive working out of the question: how do we reconcile Temple officers and synagogue officers with the development of the nascent Church and its Christological em-phasis (e.g., the issue before the Jerusalem Council in Acts 15)? Here is where the Covenant of Grace becomes critical in our understanding of the connected issues of worship and polity. If the true Church is of the seed of Abraham, and the disciples were reared, as devout, Ortho-dox Jews, in their Jewish heritage, they would have seen themselves as fulfilling the Messiah's establishment of His Jewish Kingdom as, them-selves, true Jews. Therefore, though theologically adhering to the Lord Jesus's teaching, they would have implemented and presented that new teaching in the context of their Jewish worship patterns. Hence, no oth-er form of worship would be discussed (or needed) because Jews wor-shiped in one specific way.

This raises additional questions that must be addressed by those opposing primitive episcopal primacy:

1. *The matter before the Jerusalem Council:* the question of au-thority and the Council of Jerusalem (Acts 15), where the question of Gentile inclusion into the "Church" (which would have still been the Temple and synagogue at this junc-ture) comes into play. The Gentile question, as well as the Jerusalem Council itself, would be odd if the force and pre-dominance of the Jewish character of worship and structure of worship were not preeminent. After all, *if* after the ascen-sion of the Lord Jesus, the apostles immediately rejected their Jewish liturgical heritage, especially as it manifested itself in worship and polity or understood it to be a different form of polity other than episcopacy, why would there have been any difficulty? Why would a council need to be called at all to allow Gentiles in this new Church? That would have been a Jewish concern.

2. *Why was James addressed with episcopal prominence?* As dis-cussed earlier, when we examine Acts 15:13; Acts 15:19; Acts 21:17 James's authority is more representative of a bishop, with

his various official pronouncements, than any other type of ecclesiastical office.

3. *If episcopacy is so egregiously wrong:*

    a. Why is there no alternative form of Church government to be found anywhere in the early Church extending throughout Church history until the time of the Reformation (unless you import back into the early record a type of elder rule)?

    b. Why is there no concentrated or even superficial argument found opposing episcopacy in the early Church?

    c. As I pointed out in chapter 8, how could such an erroneous form of Church government have gone unchallenged by the apostle John, especially since the most prominent voice and advocate of monarchial episcopacy, Ignatius, and two prominent advocates of episcopacy in general, Papias and Polycarp, were the apostle John's direct disciples? One would have expected him to correct his pupils.

    d. Again, to borrow from chapter 8, to argue that Ignatius, Papias, and Polycarp, disciples of the apostle John, would teach a form of Church polity that would differ from what they learned at the feet of their beloved "father" and then intentionally deviate from what he taught them, creating a new form of polity, would require very heavy support from numerous sources, especially given the respect and honor bestowed upon Ignatius by all, not to mention the reverential status the apostle John had even among Romans. The elderly, living Apostle John, around when these men wrote, would have been an imposing and intimidating figure from which to depart. Can one dogmatically and with complete confidence claim that these men would have challenged their apostolic father, while he was alive, with some false view of polity?

    e. And, of course, we have dispelled the notion that *presbyteros* (elder) and *episkopos* (bishop) are interchangeable as synonyms.

Remember, abuse of something never invalidates or repudiates the ultimate legitimacy of a thing, no matter what it is. Try to consistently apply this principle to all our responsibilities in scripture. If we apply the principle that abuse requires rejection, what do you think will be the results? There is a quote inscribed on the wall of the Department of Justice building that reads, "Where law ends, tyranny begins." If law is the written or verbal extension of authority, without authority, we have a form of tyranny.

I would also refer the reader to reexamine the apostle Paul's presentation in Galatians that the law was a schoolmaster, intended to bring, drive, force men to Christ and my connecting this passage to covenant continuity.

We assert that a Church, as previously mentioned, already existed. There was no need to give specific instructions for a New Church because of the continuity that existed between Old and New. There was a simple carryover.

Recall the first thing that our Lord did after making His proclamation in the New Testament Church that the Kingdom of God was at hand. He established its structure:

1. He ordained twelve men to preach to this Kingdom now at hand and gave them a technical name, apostles (Mark 3:14; Matt 10:7).

2. He established a unique relationship with them and them alone (think Yahweh and Moses).

Remember what we presented in Luke 22:29 and its force in this context: "And I bestow[1] upon you a kingdom, just as My Father bestowed one upon Me" (Luke 22:29, NKJ). By bestowing this right, the Lord grants to them the same possession, the same authority, that the

---

1   *Diatithami* (διατίθεμαι).

Father granted to Him: the power to dispose a will, the power to exercise authority in this New Covenant.

1. This Kingdom, the Church, is the work of Jesus Christ (Matthew 16:18–19), not man.

2. He chose those who would lead and build His Church (John 15:16). In other words, simply because Christians get together as Christians does not mean they get to create their own church. Christ preached that His Kingdom[2] was at hand. Kingdoms do not merely exist because we feel that they do in our hearts. Remember our British subject. The triumphal entry of the Lord Jesus is a perfect example of a King coming to His Kingdom and throne. That is what we celebrate on Palm Sunday. He came to assume His throne, in His house, in His holy city. He was the true Ark of the Covenant, coming to, once again, fill the Holy of Holies, because, during His lifetime, the Holy of Holies was empty.

    Not only this, but Jesus emphatically and vigorously upheld the authority of the Church to everyone, especially His apostles and disciples.[3]

So did the Lord Jesus, in fact, build a Church? No, because He did not need to. One already existed. He simply, by fulfilling the Old Testament Mosaic theological foundation, made what was always His, His in New Covenant theological content, as the second person of the Triune Godhead, as the God-Man. It had a particular structure and order. It was an extension of and modeled after the Church He built in the Old Covenant. This is the Church against which the gates of hell will never prevail.

But if, as has been argued, there was an early Church, which was "hopelessly corrupt" immediately after the death of the apostles, this proves little in relation to polity. Israel also was corrupt but never completely abandoned by God. Therefore, if the argument for rejecting this early Church is impurity, and the Reformation was an attempt to return

---

2   Matthew 3:2; 4:17; Matthew 12:28 (NKJ).
3   Matthew 8:3–4; Matthew 23:2–3; and Matthew 28:18–20; et al.

to a pure Church, haven't they failed miserably as well? Covenant conti-nuity must be properly understood to rectify this faulty view.

There is a woeful failure to understand that those patterns we see in the Old Testament Church, which are divinely created and mandated and which inform our worship, polity, and ministry, are eternal. What must change between the covenants is a Mosaic theological foreshad-owing (type) of the theology of these patterns and the Christological fulfillment (antitype) of those theological patterns.

I have belabored the point (and many others, I know) that the Greek word for "fulfill" or "fulfillment" doesn't mean to abolish or eradicate or abrogate; it means to complete with a view to "fill in what is missing." If the Mosaic Covenant is a "shadow," as the writer of Hebrews informs us, then it is an outline, a stencil, a tracing of what provides the form that the Lord fulfills. When the fullness of light is cast upon the object, the shadow, rather than disappearing, becomes fully realized and is seen in full clarity for what it is.

The stencil or tracing is not erased; it is completed. One of the He-brew terms for what Moses received on Mt. Sinai is "blueprint." What is missed, apparently, is that this divinely revealed, infallibly eternal blue-print, given by God to Moses (to *us*), is not limited to the tabernacle but the entire law. The law, which is the revealed character and nature of God, is completed in Christ Jesus. Therefore, any discussion of covenant must incorporate all these elements equally, or one's view of all of these elements will be flawed.

Now consider how detailed and precise God's instructions were in reference to the purity codes in Leviticus. We all remember how God required any member of the Nation of Israel to be free from any issue, whether blood or any other fluid. God's character is flawless, perfect, and in order to fellowship with Him, be in a relationship with Him, so must His people be flawless, perfect. The slightest imperfection sepa-rated the individual from God. Recall the offerings God mandated in Leviticus 1–4.

This, of course, is where the sacrificial system comes into play. Rest easy; I am not going to recapitulate the entire sacrificial system. I do, however, want you to notice something about God's requirements. Look at Numbers 28 and 29. Begin with the first day of the month in

Numbers 28:11–15. Look at how precise the specifications are. Two young bulls, one ram, seven lambs, all blameless, all were in their first year of life. Then note the exact measure of the materials to be offered with these sacrifices: three-tenths of an ephah, mixed with olive oil for each bull; two-tenths of an ephah, mixed with olive oil for each lamb; and so on. And this was merely the first day of each month.

Then there were the daily offerings: two lambs in the first year of life without blemish and, of course, the attendant ephah. At the end of the week, there was the sabbath offerings on top of the daily offerings: two more lambs (four in all on the sabbath) with the ephah.

If this were not daunting enough to comprehend, we have the respective festivals that required sacrifices. Passover, where we have two bulls, one ram, seven lambs. The Feast of Weeks, with two bulls, one ram, seven lambs. The Feast of Trumpets, on the first day of the seventh month: again two bulls, one ram, seven lambs. The Day of Atonement, the tenth day of the seventh month: one bull, one ram, seven lambs. The Feast of Tabernacles, the fifteenth day of the seventh month: thirteen bulls, two rams, and fourteen lambs.

Plus the Feast of Tabernacles was a monumental celebration all by itself. For eight consecutive days, there would be sacrifices of the above listed animals in descending numbers. On day one, thirteen bulls, two rams, fourteen lambs, of course with the ephahs. Day two, twelve bulls, two rams, fourteen lambs. Day three, eleven bulls, two rams, fourteen lambs, and so on until the eighth day, when one bull, one ram, seven lambs, plus all the ephahs were added to the animal sacrifice. Additionally, don't overlook the frequent appearance of the number seven in this allocation, the number representing perfection.

Of course, we know that the primary point of all of this was to drive us to Jesus Christ and to recognize the horrendous effects of sin and what it takes to propitiate a holy, righteous, and sovereign God. We are utterly helpless, which is why we run to and cling to the Lord Jesus. But the reason for listing the sacrificial requirements is to emphasize that it is all, it was all, directly related to the nature and character of God. One cannot help but notice how precisely, how meticulously, God specified He be placated through sacrifice in order for fellowship to be restored, sins forgiven, celebration to commence.

The fact is God's character and nature never change. Hebrews 13:8 states that He is the same, "yesterday, today, and forever." All of what I just presented was to point out that it was commanded by God because His character and nature are such that it demands this type of exactitude. Although Jesus Christ fulfilled, completed, the sacrificial system, He never changed God's character and nature. How is an argument possible that, with such a demand for perfection in how He is to be worshiped and approached that it required our Lord Jesus's perfect sacrifice to complete it once for all, suddenly God no longer cares about how He is to be worshiped and approached? That it does not matter as far as God is concerned? That is a very, very difficult position to maintain given the biblical record.

God spent thousands of years, prophets gave their lives, not to eliminate ceremony and ritual from Jewish worship but to bring the Jews back to proper faithful worship. In scripture, there is no such animal as a pure Church, Old Testament or New Testament, save the triumphant, glorified Church in Revelation.

So, if I understand correctly, the contrary argument goes something like: God establishes His Kingdom on earth, in nascent form in Eden and then more fully presented on Mt. Sinai. In that presentation, He divinely institutes polity to fallen, sinful, depraved men.

The high priest was a sinner and, at times, expressed his depravity, violating God's commands. *Wow, stop the presses! I cannot believe depraved, fallen, sinful men sin. Holy mackerel, am I surprised!*

These priests continually violated God's established pattern of obedience, and He did not state, "Hmm, you know, these people simply sin all the time; let's chuck this polity and move on to something else." *No!* For thousands of years, this divinely established, God-given and sanctified form of polity—three orders of high priest, priest, and Levite in the Old Testament and then bishop, priest, and deacon in the New Testament—existed all the way up until the sixteenth century, and then, suddenly, the miraculous, the perfect form of polity, where no one violates God's commands. Where all the ministers are perfectly sinless and never abuse their offices. Elder rule has arrived. Gee, what a relief that it took God all those centuries to finally get it right. Sometimes sarcasm is the best way to highlight difficulties in some arguments.

Sola Scriptura is just that: *sola,* the only infallible authority but not the only authority. It is not "*Solo* Scriptura." The late J. I. Packer wrote a follow-up book to *Knowing God* called *God Has Spoken,* which, in many ways, is even more important than *Knowing God,* and almost no one refers to it. It addresses some of these issues, and he wrote it over forty years ago! What is so sad is that it appears as if almost no one has picked up on it.

I will repeat this assertion until it is seared in every reader's mind; if the Lord Jesus was going to disavow all that had gone before and claim that His *fulfillment* of all of the law and prophets completely set aside and eradicated what had gone before in the Old Testament Church, where is the strenuous, pronounced, clear renunciation of the Old Testament? Where is the Church that replaced it? To cite the New Testament Church begs the question.

All discussions of polity, in my estimation, have either strongly minimized or totally omitted the strongest argument for a specific and direct establishment of a particular form of government that is right there in scripture, hiding in plain sight as it were: covenant continuity.

I began this journey as a young man in a Charismatic Baptist Church in Italy. I arrived at this position as a middle-aged graduate student attending a Presbyterian seminary. To state the obvious, a lot has transpired in between.

I have been blessed to have some of the most gifted, Godly Christian scholars as my teachers and friends, all who have taught me something of value.

I am firmly convinced that if those of us who are committed to the inerrancy and absolute infallibility of God's word would begin this exploration into the Church in general and worship and polity in particular, following the example I have presented here, much common ground could be reached.

To understand that, if we begin with what takes place in the Kingdom of heaven is what God inserted in the earthly realm, all the way back in Genesis, we would start to unravel the question of what the Church on earth is to be. It was this Kingdom of heaven, and all that it contained, that was communicated to Moses on Mt. Sinai. It was this divine, inerrant, infallible revelation of this heavenly Kingdom to Moses that was to be not only the model for the earthly Kingdom but its virtual duplicate.

To recognize that this heavenly Kingdom would have to be interpreted in such a way as to make all of what takes place in heaven understandable to a fallen, finite race of humans opens an important key to interpreting all that God revealed in the previous covenant.

The exact way He was to be approached, the exact way He was to be worshiped, the exact way His earthly dwelling with man was to be constructed tell us how serious He is about His character and His word.

That there would be administrators, rules, laws, physical structures, sacraments, clergy was what was given to Moses on Mt. Sinai, and all of those elements, in a manner that is a mystery to us, in some way explains and is patterned on the heavenly Kingdom.

Through all the trials, failures, accomplishments, and victories; through all of the sin, repentance, redemption, and salvation; through prophetic judgments and prophetic hope, this is what God instituted on earth and how He interacted with His people.

At their bleakest moment, at the height of their disobedience, when His people were convinced that Ichabod (the "Spirit of the Lord has departed") was permanent, that the Spirit of the Lord had departed *never* to return, a child is born. He would bear the government, the Kingdom of heaven, on His shoulders and would be called Wonderful Counselor, Mighty God, Everlasting Father, the Prince of Peace, Jesus Christ.

He would come to God's people and assume His rightful place in God's dwelling, His dwelling, and live not only as the perfect example of how to worship the Father, but He would be the perfect Lamb to reconcile us with the Father.

The Temple was His Temple. Its worship was His worship. Its ministers, high priest, priests, and Levites, were His ministers. He would train His disciples that this was the biblical place and the biblical manner in which one was to worship God. Because this Temple, His Temple, represented Him.

He completed the pattern and taught His followers to do the same. And when the time came for Him to depart, He made sure they knew that this is what was to continue. This is the way it is to continue, to worship the Father, Son, and Holy Spirit in this manner.

There was never a repudiation of the beauty, the glory, the majesty of what God had previously revealed because God never errs! God's Kingdom of heaven, intruded in the earthly realm, became His earthly Kingdom, and upon the arrival of His Son, the Son brought with Him *His kingdom.*

This is what He left His disciples. This is what He left us. One day, He will return and gather His people together to ascend and begin an eternity of worshiping the Triune Godhead, in the fulfillment of the Kingdom on earth, the Kingdom of heaven, where it all began.

Allow me to conclude by saying, as a theologian and philosopher, one sometimes experiences moments, visions of grandeur, where we come to the conclusion that what we say or teach or write will actually make an impact on someone, somewhere, and change the world. A bit self-aggrandizing, I realize. Many important subjects which could add to the discussion had to be left to a later time to avoid becoming more pedantic than this "popular" treatment already is. Therefore, rather than entertaining such flights of fancy, my prayer for this book would be that it would contribute to the discussion of the Church in all her elements. That, in that contribution, it would be received not as a stick in someone's eye but as an open invitation to consider an ancient (the most ancient?) form of Church government and worship. That it would be understood and recognized as the pattern of the Church that was divinely revealed from heaven and that Church government and worship, then, are not optional practices in the Church, secondary issues left up to individual conscience, but are divinely commanded practices to be conducted in this manner. For if that is the conclusion, we have our first step in discussing true ecclesiastical unity in the Body of Christ, to eliminate many divisions among us, and to present to a fallen world that we worship one Lord, have one faith via one Baptism, and the world will know that we are His disciples because we keep His commandments and have love for one another. Because if what is presented here is accurate, any failure to implement these ideas is a failure to properly worship God. One then does not have a true Church.

Soli Deo Gloria   *Advent 2020*

Appendix A

The Curious Case of St. Jerome

I BELIEVE THAT I HAVE MADE more than a solid case for the arguments I have presented thus far. Since the majority opinion is the opposite of my view expressed in these pages, I have only cited representative examples of that position to try to avoid turning this into a polemical debate. After all, my intention was to offer a positive, more traditional view on the matters of worship, polity, and the like.

So, given that I hold that position (three episcopal offices and emphasizing the distinction between *presbuteros* and *episkopos*), what do I do with the following citations from one of the best-known and, arguably, most well-renowned Church fathers, Jerome? A Roman Catholic to boot, who appears to offer a position that contradicts my position. I quote:

> Indeed with the ancients these names [bishops and presbyters; my inclusion] were synonymous, one alluding to the office, the other to the age of the clergy.[1]

Or this,

> For when the apostle clearly teaches that presbyters are the same as bishops, must not a mere server of tables and of widows

---

1 Jerome, "The Letters of St. Jerome." In P. Schaff & H. Wace (eds.), W. H. Fremantle, G. Lewis, & W. G. Martley (trans.), *St. Jerome: Letters and Select Works* (vol. 6, Epistle 69, 143). New York: Christian Literature Company, 1893.

be insane to set himself up arrogantly over men through whose prayers the body and blood of Christ are produced? Do you ask for proof of what I say? Listen to this passage: "Paul and Timotheus, the servants of Jesus Christ, to all the saints in Christ Jesus which are at Philippi with the bishops and deacons." Do you wish for another instance? In the Acts of the Apostles Paul thus speaks to the priests of a single church: "Take heed unto yourselves and to all the flock, in the which the Holy Ghost hath made you bishops, to feed the church of God which He purchased with His own blood." And lest any should in a spirit of contention argue that there must then have been more bishops than one in a single church, there is the following passage which clearly proves a bishop and a presbyter to be the same.[2]

Lastly, and I include this citation even though I cannot find the source, in order to avoid any assertion that I'm omitting statements that count against my position, St. Jerome is cited as stating, "If anyone thinks the opinion that bishops and presbyters are the same, to be not the view of the Scriptures but my own, let him study the words of the Apostle to the Philippians."[3]

The venerable bishop appears to be arguing the opposite of what I am claiming. While this is not a treatment on the thought of the great Church father, it is important to address his contention as it is used by opponents of the position I espouse to "allegedly" refute my view. There will be three lines of response to St. Jerome's position: first, the context in which he presented these statements; second, the writings of a few contemporaries of his, St. John Chrysostom (AD 349–AD 407), Ambrosiaster (active AD 366–AD 384), and, of course, St. Augustine of Hippo (AD 354–AD 430); and, finally, the underlying presupposition often either ignored or merely left unaddressed when evaluating St. Jerome's comments.

---

2   Ibid., 288.
3   The closest I came to discovering the source for this quote is St. Jerome's *Commentary on Titus* 1:5, attributed to J. B. Lightfoot.

The Context of St. Jerome's Discussion

There is virtually no contention that the majority consensus opinion concerning St. Jerome's view is that bishops and presbyters are one and the same office, that St. Jerome held this position in order to avoid schism, and that some among the "presbyters" were elevated to rank above their presbyter brethren. If not the lengthiest sustained argument, Epistle 146 to Evangelus, cited above in the second quote, is certainly the most apparently unambiguous at face value. It is there where St. Jerome not only makes the previously cited statement but links the term "elder" to bishop by citing the apostle John's epistles.

What is one to make of this apparently uncontroverted and clear case made by one of the most eminent Roman Catholic saints in history? According to St. Jerome, there is really no discussion; bishops and presbyters are the same.

Let us first look at the context in which St. Jerome makes one of these statements. In the first citation, Epistle 69, St. Jerome was responding to a request from Oceanus to issue a formal protest against a bishop of Spain named Carterius, who apparently violated the apostolic prohibition in I Timothy 3 and Titus 1 of being "a husband of one wife," for Carterius had just remarried. St. Jerome counseled Oceanus to let the matter go because Carterius's first marriage was prior to his being baptized a Christian and, therefore, according to St. Jerome, didn't count as a violation of the prohibition. So the question is, what does this have to do with the identification of the offices of bishops and presbyters? If one reads those passages closely and then reads St. Jerome's counsel to Oceanus, one will see that his focus is on "moral qualifications," not specifically attempting to define ecclesiastical offices. What he is basically saying to Oceanus is, "Look, the moral qualifications of a bishop and presbyter are the same."

Now I will grant immediately that what we are engaging in is nothing more or less than the interpretation of a Church father interpreting a passage of scripture sixteen hundred years after the fact, and that is a very challenging venture indeed. However, given the context of Epistle 69, my interpretation is equally as valid as any other and preserves the position that St. Jerome was, in fact, not opposed to the trifold office of bishop, priest (presbyter), and deacon.

In the second citation, Epistle 146, St. Jerome is writing to a person called Evangelus regarding the stated dignity of the office of presbyter. It appears that some were trying to argue that a deacon could ordain presbyters! St. Jerome vehemently rejects this assertion, going so far as to say, in the same epistle, "For function, excepting that of ordination, belongs to a bishop that does not also belong to a presbyter?" Notice there are two actual arguments by St. Jerome, the second of which is often completely ignored. In the first place, what he is arguing is that a deacon cannot ordain a presbyter because one must rise from the office of deacon to presbyter to bishop. For he states, again in Epistle 146, " . . . must not a mere server of tables and of widows be insane to set himself up arrogantly over men through whose prayers the body and blood of Christ are produced?" In other words, since one must arise from a lower office, how can the lower office ordain the higher office, especially when ordination is reserved for bishops? And it is this last statement that is the often overlooked strength of the trifold ministry. St. Jerome specifically states that ordination is the province of the episcopacy, bishops, alone. This is one of the core functions of a bishop and separates that office from the priesthood (presbyter). The question of the offices being one and the same he explains in the very initial citation, Epistle 69, where he states quite clearly, " . . . (bishops and presbyters) were synonymous, one alluding to the office, the other to the age." This is essentially the same argument, albeit less detailed, that I made in chapter 10. In fact, at the end of Epistle 146, St. Jerome makes the following statement,

> Of the names presbyter and bishop the first denotes age, the second rank. In writing both to Titus and to Timothy the apostle speaks of the ordination of bishops and of deacons, but says not a word of the ordination of presbyters; for the fact is that the word bishops includes presbyters also. Again when a man is promoted it is from a lower place to a higher. Either then a presbyter should be ordained a deacon, from the lesser office, that is, to the more important, to prove that a presbyter is inferior to a deacon; or if on the other hand it is the deacon that is ordained

presbyter, this latter should recognize that, although he may be less highly paid than a deacon, he is superior to him in virtue of his priesthood. In fact as if to tell us that the traditions handed down by the apostles were taken by them from the old testament, bishops, presbyters and deacons occupy in the church the same positions as those which were occupied by Aaron, his sons, and the Levites in the temple.[4]

Once again, St. Jerome makes essentially the same arguments, also without the detail or force, that I have made previously in this book. It is the issue of whether or not, when discussing "presbuteros," one is arguing for that term to mean office (such as priest) or age (which is the strict lexical definition). Combine this with the connection to the Levitical trifold ministry, which he endorses but does not fully drive home for a reason that I will mention in a moment, and it presents the traditional understanding of three separate offices within episcopacy.

Now, do these arguments directly and irrefutably settle the issue? Probably not, but they do offer a plausible alternative understanding, which keeps St. Jerome in the fold of espousing a trifold ministry.

Comparison of St. Jerome's Views with Contemporaries

My second response to the apparent distancing of St. Jerome from the trifold ministry position is his contemporaries. Let us, simply for the sake of argument, grant that St. Jerome actually is presenting a position that is contrary to the trifold ministry (and St.'s Ignatius, Polycarp, Papias, etc., the entire early Church for the first three hundred years, and his own heritage down to today, the Roman Church). Where does he stand in relation to his rather famous and respected colleagues? Is his view new? Unique to him? Or can it be understood to be in harmony with their views on the subject?

Initially, I will present a well-respected scholar, Professor William Tighe, of Muhlenburg College. I offer Professor Tighe's brief statement

---

4   *Op. Cit.*, Jerome, 289.

because it acts as a sort of middle ground between two opposites, that all of St. Jerome's contemporaries either were in agreement with him or in opposition to him.

Professor William Tighe, in "Energetic Processions," November 2009, argues that Theodore of Mopsuestia, in his commentary on the Epistles to Timothy and Titus, while asserting that the terms "bishop" and "presbyter" were men holding the same office, they did not essentially mean that they were the same. He states that Theodore's argument is that when the apostles began to appoint men as successors to their own ministry, these men, deeming themselves unworthy of the title *apostolos*, took for themselves the name *episkopos*, leaving the old "presbyter/*episkopoi*" with the sole title of "presbyter." While not finding this fully satisfactory, he believes it more plausible than what some attribute as St. Jerome's view.

While certainly a mediating view, I am not thoroughly persuaded by either the professor's interpretation of Theodore's position or his unmitigated acceptance (and, thereby, rejection) of St. Jerome's alleged parting from the trifold ministry position.

What I prefer to do is present a few citations from each of the Church fathers addressed earlier and allow the readers to make their own determination. We will begin with the venerable St. John Chrysostom.

In his commentary on Titus 1:5, St. John Chrysostom says,

> Here he is speaking of *episkopoi* [bishops] . . . He did not wish the whole island to be entrusted to one elder, but that each one should have his own charge and care, for thus he would have less labor himself, and those under his rule would receive greater attention. The teacher would not then be required to hold the presidency of many churches but was left to be occupied with one only, and to bring that into order.[5]

At first glance, it appears that St. John Chrysostom is agreeing with St. Jerome's position. However, when taken with this comment from his commentary on I Timothy 3:6, we have a bit more context.

---

5   P. Gorday (ed.), *Ancient Christian Commentary on Scripture (ACCS): Colossians, 1–2 Thessalonians, 1–2 Timothy, Titus, Philemon*, Vol IX. (p. 285). Downers Grove, IL: InterVarsity Press, 2000.

The point is not that the bishop cannot be a young man but that he must not be a new convert . . . For if youth only was an objection, why did he himself appoint Timothy, a young man? . . . But since there were many then who came over from heathen cultures to be baptized, Paul says, "Do not immediately advance to a station of dignity a novice, that is, one of these new converts." For, if even before he has proved himself as a disciple he is made a teacher, he will soon be lifted up into insolence.[6]

When taken together, once again the issue is office and then age. If taken as a cohesive expression of his St. John's thought, it would present an argument along the lines of "A bishop, one of age, experience, and wisdom, should be in charge of one large region, while other men of age, experience, and wisdom should rule cities." If arguing against anything, one would say this is an argument *against* localized (city) bishops but not monarchial bishops. Also, in his commentary on I Timothy, he says, "For it was necessary to appoint one to preside in every city, as he writes to Titus, 'That thou shouldest ordain elders in every city, as I had appointed thee'" (Tit. 1:5.).[7]

The key point to note, in concert with the previous quotes, is that Titus was consecrated a bishop in order to ordain elders. A point with which, by the way, St. Jerome completely concurs: "Paul is speaking here of bishops who have the power of placing presbyters in the individual towns . . . "[8] So if St. John Chrysostom doesn't advance a trifold ministry, as I contend, and St. Jerome agrees with St. John on the issue of only bishops having the authority to ordain presbyters, does St. Jerome, in fact, reject a trifold ministry? One final quote from St. John before we move to the next Church father, Ambrosiaster. In the same commentary on Titus 1, St. John is discussing the moral qualifications of a bishop, and we read,

---

6   Ibid., 172.

7   John Chrysostom, *Nicene and Post-Nicene Fathers (NPNF): Homilies of St. John Chrysostom, Archbishop of Constantinople, on the First Epistle of St. Paul the Apostle to Timothy.* In P. Schaff (ed.), J. Tweed & P. Schaff (trans.), Saint Chrysostom: Homilies on Galatians, Ephesians, Philippians, Colossians, Thessalonians, Timothy, Titus, and Philemon (vol. 13, 439). New York: Christian Literature Company, 1889.

8   Ibid., ACCS, vol. IX., 285.

For if when nature prompted, he was so void of affection or so senseless, that he thought more of his wealth than of his children, how should he be raised to the Episcopal throne, and so great rule?[9]

One would be hard pressed to link the idea of an "episcopal throne" to any usage ever of an "elder" or "presbyter." These forms of titular address have always been limited to and identified with the episcopacy. And if that is the historical case, the idea that both offices are in some way identical becomes extremely problematic and quite difficult for those adherents.

I am including Ambrosiaster because he was an opponent of St. Jerome, possibly because of the latter's heavy dependence upon Origen, but in any case, there is no ambiguity in his position on the concept of the trifold ministry. In his commentary on I Timothy 3:8, he states, in a lengthy quote,

Paul gives instruction that deacons are to be chosen with great care because it is clear that they are the servants of the priests. He wants them to be just like bishops, as he himself says, men who are irreproachable and conduct their affairs in public, with no shady dealings . . . After dealing with bishops, Paul goes on to talk about the ordination of deacons. Why does he do this, except that bishops and presbyters are the same? Both are priests, but the bishop comes first, so that while every bishop is a presbyter, not every presbyter is a bishop. The bishop is the one who is first among the presbyters . . . for it is neither right nor permissible for an inferior to ordain a superior. No one can give what he has not received.[10]

Charles Gore, the nineteenth-century Anglo-Catholic Bishop of Oxford, states in reference to Ambrosiaster's position, in comparison of St. Jerome and Ambrosiaster,

---

9   Op. Cit., NPNF, vol. 13, 525.
10   Gerald Bray (trans & ed.), *Ambrosiaster. Ancient Christian Texts (ACT): Commentaries on Galatians—Philemon.* (p. 128). Downers Grove, IL: InterVarsity Press, 2009.

... neither of these writers disputes the present authority of the threefold ministry or the limitation to bishops of the power of ordination. They do not maintain that, even in the extremest circumstances, a presbyter—a presbyter of the existing Church— could validly ordain . . . "What does a bishop do," says St. Jerome, even when he is minimizing the episcopate, "that a presbyter does not do, except ordination?" The bishop and the presbyter are to one another as the high priest and priest of the old covenant.[11]

Gore goes on to say,

Once more, they do not regard the present three-fold arrangement of the ministry as an innovation of the post-apostolic Church, so that it should lack the authority of the Apostles. The present constitution [of ministerial order, my addition] represents their ordering . . . [12]

There is no question of the presence of the trifold view of ministry in Ambrosiaster's statement. While his interpretation that Timothy was the only presbyter in Lystra is odd, to say the least, his view of what the trifold ministry is fits perfectly in line with the position of the Church and Church fathers prior to him.

Gore once again, in responding to the view that St. Jerome held a twofold view of ministry, states,

Now when we have clearly considered this view, we shall see surely that it is not what is sometimes represented as being. It is not a "Presbyterian" view. It does indeed carry with it the conception of the great Church order being the priesthood; it emphasizes the distinction of presbyter and bishop is nothing compared to the distinction of deacon and priest. Moreover, it involves a certain tentativeness in the process by which the

11   Charles Gore, *The Church the Ministry*. London: Longmans, Green, and Co., 1900: 157–161.
12   Ibid.

Apostles are held to have established the church ministry; it admits a survival of an older constitution into the late life of the Church. But it does not carry with it the idea that the presbyter, pure and simple, the presbyter of the settled church constitution, has the power under any circumstances to assume episcopal functions. It teaches something quite different, viz. that the earliest presbyters were ordained with episcopal functions— were, in fact, bishops as well as presbyters—till the subsequent ordination of presbyters without Episcopal functions put an end to the old arrangement and brought about—not episcopacy—but what we have called nonepiscopacy.[13]

Before leaving our brief interaction with Ambrosiaster and moving on to the Great St. Augustine, one final citation from Ambrosiaster, because not only does it relate to this particular point, but it also sets up the third point I want to mention. In his commentary on Titus 1:5, Ambrosiaster makes this sharp comment,

What we read here is clear. Paul wants someone who is holy in his deeds and wise in his words to be ordained bishop, so that he can encourage the brethren and persuade opponents, especially those from among the Jews, who under cover of the name of Christ were teaching Judaism and whom he elsewhere calls false brethren. Though they had been born again in Christ they were not pure Christians, because they wanted to worship the law on one side and Christ on the other.[14]

There are two aspects of this comment that bear reflection. First, the traditional role of the bishop as "the defender of the faith," the one in whom the truth of Christian doctrine is upheld, is immediately apparent. This goes to the core of the trifold ministry concept. The second is the historical situation between Christians and Jews by the fourth century. I only mention it here as it will be expanded upon in my final point. Before that, however, St. Augustine.

---

13 Ibid., 157–161.
14 Ibid., 155–156.

There is so much material from which to draw in St. Augustine that one has to be careful not to bury his readers in citations; therefore, I will provide the reference and pick a representative sample or two of St. Augustine's position on our topic.

In his classic work, *The City of God*, at the end of commenting on I Timothy 3:1, St. Augustine makes this concluding remark about the apostle Paul: "He wanted to make clear that the office of bishop, episcopatus, implies work rather than dignity."[15]

Clearly, St. Augustine sees the episcopacy as an office to hold. It is important to recognize that point here, especially because in his letter, 173.2, to Donatus of early Church heresy fame, St. Augustine specifically address Donatus as a "presbyter" in distinction from his office as "bishop." There, in an attempt to initially provide irenic, fatherly counsel to the presbyter, he says, "If a man desire the office of a bishop, he desireth a good work, and yet, in order to make the office of a bishop be accepted by many men, they are seized against their will . . . "[16]

In an attempt to head off the impending doctrinal conflict, St. Augustine appeals to Donatus, from bishop to presbyter, in order to reason with him, again indicating a contemporary of St. Jerome appears to be in opposition to his rejection of a trifold ministry.

So what can be concluded from this comparison? Why expend the effort given that, at the start of this point, I indicated how difficult it would be to interpret multiple Church fathers as they interpret various texts of Scripture in order to arrive at some understanding of a contested doctrine some sixteen hundred years later? Especially since no one wants to get into the "your father versus my father" game.

Initially, this comparison requires us to ask, "Are we, in fact, accurately understanding St. Jerome in his historical context?" It certainly appears that his contemporaries advocate a trifold ministerial position. It also "appears" that, while some have interpreted St. Jerome as rejecting that position, his statements seem to line up, quite favorably, with those of his contemporaries on this issue. Now, there is definitely the

---

15   Cited in, *Op. Cit.*, ACCS, *The City of God 19.19*, vol. IX. (169).

16   Augustine of Hippo, *Nicene and Post-Nicene Fathers (NPNF): Letters of St. Augustin*. In P. Schaff (ed.), J. G. Cunningham (trans.), *The Confessions and Letters of St. Augustin with a Sketch of His Life and Work* (vol. 1, 544). Buffalo, NY: Christian Literature Company, 1886.

possibility that I could be incorrectly interpreting his contemporaries. However, with the material presented prior to this chapter, I think my position is more in accord with biblical, theological, lexical, and historical data than the alternative view.

Let us, though, consider that there is a parting of the ways on this topic among contemporaries, that St. Jerome *is* rejecting a trifold ministry, presenting an opposing position to his esteemed contemporaries. Since I have laid out the biblical, theological, and so forth argument earlier, and since that argument also includes the three hundred years of the early Church prior to St. Jerome's assertions, is it not possible that, if indeed this is St. Jerome's view—that presbyter and bishop are the same—he is merely an outlier? That he is not representative of the Church's established position for three centuries, and therefore, his view, while advanced by some, is simply incorrect?

Before moving on, it is important to realize that if St. Jerome had rejected the trifold ministerial model, why is he still considered one of the fathers of Rome? Whether you agree with Roman doctrine or not, and I don't, you have to concede that if he was found to espouse a position that was diametrically opposed to the dogma of the Roman Church, we would have expected him to be at least censured at best, as Aerius was in the fourth century for holding a twofold view of ministry, or excommunicated. He has not had either of these pronouncements levied against him.

The Underlying Assumptions That Contribute to the Popular Interpretation of St. Jerome

Now to my final of the three points to be made, the presuppositions involved in the rejection of separate and distinct offices of presbyter and bishop. If you will recall, I mentioned that the final quote from Ambrosiaster was a clue to this point. In that quote, he posited that the bishop was "to encourage the brethren and persuade opponents"; the bishop was the defender of the faith. It is vital to remember that, at this point in the history of the Church, the animosity between Judaism and Christianity was entrenched. To avow or support too many elements of Judaism at this point made one suspect. No one wanted to be identified with the Judaizer heresy identified by the apostle Paul in Galatians, nor, still, experience the "episcopal" indictment Paul leveled against Peter. No, what started to influence the thought of thinkers of this time was the overarching draw of Hellenism. So, with a few exceptions, Justin Martyr, to state the most obvious, the later Church fathers would more and more subtly begin to identify elements of Christianity with Hellenistic, Greek ideas than overtly Jewish concepts. There are exceptions here and there, but the influence of Greek modes of thought was incredibly powerful. St. Augustine, in the early days of his ministry, was a clear Neo-Platonist, and as already mentioned, St. Jerome was a devoted follower of the Greek father Origen, raising the ire of Ambrosiaster.

With the significance of Greek modes of thought in the Church, the idea that a trifold ministry was clearly the biblical view, due to its dependence on the Old Testament Levitical model of three offices, would naturally be challenged. The two concepts, Greek versus Hebrew, would be in natural opposition; therefore, the understanding of certain doctrines (many?) would be understood via Greek modes of thought, such as leadership in the Church, based upon the Greek terms used.

Additionally, in contemporary scholarship,[17] the understanding of the early Christian world is heavily dependent on Hellenistic concepts, some actually citing the Gnostic heresy as a legitimate, alternative "orthodoxy" to the Christianity received by us today. There are many fine "orthodox" teachers who, in advocating this specific line of argumentation against the trifold ministry position, have incorporated a Hellenistic understanding of this doctrine, and that is unfortunate and wrong.

So while an interesting interpretation of St. Jerome, it would appear to me that, when everything is taken into consideration, though he might be challenging to understand for us today, being so far removed from his context, that he probably would fall well within the bounds of espousing a trifold view of ministerial offices, making quotes of his cited by those rejecting a trifold ministry amusing but not compelling.

---

17   There are a number of players in this field; currently the most notable is the German professor at the University of Heidelberg, Peter Lampe, and the many who follow his lead. One could also cite Margaret Barker, Elaine Pagels, John Behr, and John Zizioulas.

Appendix B

Example of an Anglican Worship Service

The Order for the Administration of the Lord's Supper for Holy Communion

And let us consider one another in order to stir up love and good works, 25 not forsaking the assembling of ourselves together, as is the manner of some, but exhorting one another, and so much the more as you see the Day approaching (Heb. 10:24–25 NKJ).

When I began writing this book, my intention was to present an argument for a comprehensive biblical understanding of traditional liturgical worship and the Church from a Reformed perspective. As I worked through the material, however, I thought it would be helpful to those not familiar with the structure of a traditional liturgical worship service to have something to which they could refer.

Upon reflection, I came to the conclusion that the simplest and most direct way do to this was to take an available online version of the 1928 Book of Common Prayer, which is what we use for worship, and merely insert some pictures to complement an explanation of the service. Here is the result. I pray it is of use.

I must, once again, reiterate the fact that this is the way we worshiped at St. Patrick's Anglican Church.[1] Ninety-five percent of this is what is done in orthodox Anglican churches that use the Book of Com-

---

1   St. Patrick's Anglican Church unfortunately had to close its doors.

mon Prayer exclusively,[2] but there will be slight variations not used in other Anglican churches.

As indicated in the body of this work, all that we did was predicated on the idea that heaven is the place to begin. Through the development of tabernacle, temple, and then synagogue liturgy, we arrive where we are. This means that worship (as we have very specifically defined it) is a communal, collective, *common* practice. By *common*,[3] we simply mean that what occurs in worship is a structured, organized service with the majority of the service being prewritten so everyone knows and understands what is happening and can intelligently offer their "amen"[4] to their worship. As we unpacked all that, we arrived at the church building itself. Though it was alluded to in the main work, it was not fully developed, one of the drawbacks of restricting oneself to a particular forum. Theologically and architecturally, the Church, borrowing her mindset from Jewish tabernacle and temple, saw each of these structures—tabernacle, temple, and eventually church buildings—as micro-representations of the cosmos. The Church at first worshiped in the Temple and then, post-Temple destruction in AD 70, kept this in mind when developing structures for worship moving forward. However, due to the growing animosity and division among Jewish-Christians and Gentile Christians, especially within the synagogue, these Christians left and did not begin to implement and reintroduce this cosmic architectural concept until the fourth century. This was facilitated by the ascendency of Constantine the Great to the Roman throne and the Edict of Milan, essentially protecting Christians from persecutions from the state. It was with Constantine the Great, and his attempt to "apologize" to Christians and make amends for Rome's persecution of them, who gave basilicas to Christians to use as churches. At any rate, churches began to present the theology of

---

2   There are Anglican churches that are very heavily influenced by Roman theology and, in addition to the Book of Common Prayer (referred to as *The Altar Service Book* or *ASB* when it is used during communion), they use what is known as the *Anglican Missal*, essentially the Roman liturgical missal with the Book of Common Prayer inserted among its pages.

3   See chapter 12, *Why Use the Book of Common Prayer?*

4   You might notice a difference in some of the "amens" in the text. When the *amen* is italicized, it means the congregation is responding as hearers of what has been said; when it is in standard font, it usually means they have been participants and offer their "amen" as such.

the particular era but with the idea of the church structure representing the cosmos.

This is seen, if you have ever visited a Roman Catholic cathedral, when first you enter the church. As you entered the church, you stepped into a very dark, somber, dimly lit area called the narthex.[5] This area was to represent the fallen, dark world—hence, the lack of bright lights. From the narthex, one leaves the fallen darkness of a sinful world and enters the sanctuary. We now move into the dwelling place of the holy, into the very presence of the Triune, Sovereign God of the universe.

---

5   The narthex is the area just after you enter a church and before you move into the sanctuary. Evangelicals refer to it as the lobby.

We begin where all traditional liturgy begins, the Processional. In a similar fashion, in the Procession, the clergy party, entering the Holy dwelling of God, approaching His divine presence, leads the congregation, the people of God, as their representatives in approaching the very throne of God in the sanctuary. As the clergy arrive at the throne of God, they stop at the rail to reverence the God of the universe, and they bow before approaching His throne.

In ancient Israel, while the nation was encamped around the tabernacle, each tribe had its own banner or flag identifying who they were. If you will recall, when Yahweh instructed the nation to strike camp and travel, the Levitical priests would disassemble the Holy Tabernacle and carry all the items as they led the nation, the Ark of the Covenant being the very first item as it was Yahweh Himself leading His people.

All the tribes of Israel would lift high their banners as God was in their presence leading them, and they obediently followed, all eyes transfixed upon Him. Devotion to Yahweh and the remembrance of redemption was paramount in their lives.

We do this because, quite simply, we are commanded by God to meet with Him, at a specified day and time. This is not a personal preference like, "Oh, I can worship in my living room, or among nature, and so on" While those may be individual expressions of personal piety, they do not meet the command of God; see all the Old Testament and Hebrews 10:24–25. The Processional party will enter with a hymn; hymn singing will be included at various points throughout the service. Depending upon the time of the liturgical season, they might be joyous, sorrowful, penitential, and so on. The point is that the service is a total incorporation of the whole person, physically, from standing, kneeling, sitting, and bowing to singing, hearing, responding. It is not a lecture, concert, Bible study, or a minister's personal devotions.

It is important to be clear at this juncture that there is no worshiping of a corporeal or physical Jesus taking place at this time or at any time during the service. Jesus is seated at the right hand of the Father. Here, God is the spectator, and we are the actors.

The next act of the priest is preparing the people for worship. The priest takes the thurible,[6] with the incense, and censes the altar.[7] Incense, as I instructed my people at St. Patrick's, was a symbol and reminder of our prayers being lifted up, before the throne of God, as a "sweet savor," and, also, the image of the smoke of the incense filling the sanctuary was a reminder that we, even though there is no thunder, lighting, or fire descending from a mountain, are still in the very presence of the Holy One of the universe.

Once this has been completed, and we have begun participating in the remembering[8] of the drama of the redemptive life and work of the Savior, Jesus Christ, the priest turns to face the altar. This movement symbolizes that at this point, he is a part of the congregation worshiping before God and not some mystical personage with magical powers. He

---

6   This a containerlike object at the end of a chain that holds incense.

7   As a reminder, in the Bible, "altar" and (communion) "table" are used interchangeably. See Malachi 1:7: "*You* offer defiled food on My altar. But say, ' In what way have we defiled You?' By saying, ' The table of the LORD is contemptible'" (NKJ) and Hebrews 13:10: "We have an altar from which those who serve the tabernacle have no right to eat" (NKJ).

8   Liturgical theologians refer to this as *anamnesis,* remembering something profoundly significant.

stands as a part of the congregation called by God to minister before God on behalf of God's people.

Here the priest may offer up a private recitation of the Lord's Prayer:

OUR Father, who art in heaven, Hallowed be thy Name. Thy kingdom come. Thy will be done on earth, As it is in heaven. Give us this day our daily bread. And forgive us our trespasses, As we forgive those who trespass against us. And lead us not into temptation; But deliver us from evil. Amen.

Or the priest, if having offered personal prayers prior to ascending to the foot of God's throne, will begin the worship service by offering to God, on behalf of himself and the congregation, this collect or Prayer for Purity. We must never take for granted that simply because the grace of God has reached down and saved us, we are never perfectly able to stand (or sit or kneel, for that matter) before the presence of God. We must always remember to approach God with a pure, humble, and contrite heart. Here, with the priest as our leader, we ask God to purify our

ever-sinful hearts in order to approach Him. Here begins the Ministry of
the Word or the Liturgy of the Word.

The Collect

A LMIGHTY God, unto whom all hearts are open, all
desires known, and from whom no secrets are hid;
Cleanse the thoughts of our hearts by the inspiration of thy
Holy Spirit, that we may perfectly love thee, and worthily
magnify thy holy Name; through Christ our Lord. Amen.

Yet, if we are honest with ourselves, we know full well that we are,
as were our Jewish brethren in the Old Testament, a stiff-necked, rebellious people, even at our best, and in order to be worthy to be in God's
presence, standing in the complete righteousness of Jesus, we still need
to mortify the flesh and sanctify our lives. We are commanded "to be
Holy" as our "Father who is in Heaven is Holy." How is this done? It is
done by constantly being exposed to the holiness of God's transcendent
nature and character. This comes to us via his commandments. So we
hear God's Ten Commandments or Jesus's Summary of the Law read to
us, and we respond, consciously aware of our shortcomings in attaining
such holiness. And now the priest, who began as a representative of the
people, with his back toward them as a part of the congregation, turns
toward the congregation and, facing the people with God's word in his
hand, is God's representative and spokesman.

The Ten Commandments or The Decalogue

1st Commandment: GOD spake these words, and said:
I am the LORD thy God; Thou shalt have none other gods
but me.
*Lord, have mercy upon us, and incline our hearts to keep
this law.*
2nd Commandment: Thou shalt not make to thyself any
graven image, nor the likeness of anything that is in heaven

above, or in the earth beneath, or in the water under the earth; thou shalt not bow down to them, nor worship them: for I the Lord thy God am a jealous God, and visit the sins of the fathers upon the children, unto the third and fourth generation of them that hate me; and show mercy unto thousands in them that love me and keep my commandments.

Lord, have mercy upon us, and incline our hearts to keep this law.

3rd Commandment: Thou shalt not take the Name of the Lord thy God in vain; for the Lord will not hold him guiltless, that taketh his Name in vain.

Lord, have mercy upon us, and incline our hearts to keep this law.

4th Commandment: Remember that thou keep holy the Sabbath-day.

Six days shalt thou labour, and do all that thou hast to do; but the seventh day is the Sabbath of the Lord thy God. In it thou shalt do no manner of work; thou, and thy son, and thy daughter, thy man-servant, and thy maid-servant, thy cattle, and the stranger that is within thy gates. For in six days the Lord made heaven and earth, the sea, and all that in them is, and rested the seventh day: wherefore the Lord blessed the seventh day, and hallowed it.

Lord, have mercy upon us, and incline our hearts to keep this law.

5th Commandment: Honour thy father and thy mother; that thy days may be long in the land which the Lord thy God giveth thee.

Lord, have mercy upon us, and incline our' hearts to keep this law.

6th Commandment: Thou shalt do no murder.

Lord, have mercy upon us, and incline our hearts to keep this law.

7th Commandment: Thou shalt not commit adultery.

Lord, have mercy upon us, and incline our hearts to keep this law.

8th Commandment: Thou shalt not steal.

Lord, have mercy upon us, and incline our hearts to keep this law.

9th Commandment: Thou shalt not bear false witness against thy neighbor.

Lord, have mercy upon us, and incline our hearts to keep this law.

10th Commandment: Thou shalt not covet thy neighbor's house, thou shalt not covet thy neighbour's wife, nor his servant, nor his maid, nor his ox, nor his ass, nor any thing that is his.

Lord, have mercy upon us, and write all these thy laws in our hearts, we beseech thee.

Then may the **Priest** say,
the Summary of the Law,
Hear what our Lord Jesus Christ saith.

THOU shalt love the Lord thy God with all thy heart, and with all thy soul, and with all thy mind. This is the first and great commandment. And the second is like unto it; Thou shalt love thy neighbor as thyself. On these two commandments hang all the Law and the Prophets.

Having now been confronted by the uncompromising power of God's Word as it cuts us to the quick, identifying our sinfulness and inability to even feign an approximation of the Holiness God's character demands, we cry out for God's mercy.

> Here, if the Ten Commandments or Decalogue hath been
> omitted, shall be said,
> Lord, have mercy upon us.
> *Christ, have mercy upon us.*
> Lord, have mercy upon us.

Then the Priest may say, Abp. Cranmer's prayer for providential care and sanctification.

Once again, the priest, recognizing his failure to achieve the required Holiness demanded by God, turns back to the altar and joins the congregation in offering a petition, pleading to God that He providentially guide us to sanctification.

O ALMIGHTY Lord, and everlasting God, vouchsafe, we beseech thee, to direct, sanctify, and govern, both our hearts and bodies, in the ways of thy laws, and in the works of thy commandments; that, through thy most mighty protection, both here and ever, we may be preserved in body and soul; through our Lord and Saviour Jesus Christ. *Amen.*

Minister.	The Lord be with you.
Answer.	And with thy spirit.
Minister.	Let us pray.

After offering the previous prayer to the Lord on behalf of all, we still must recognize and acknowledge how short of God's Holiness we fall and the continued need for instruction in righteousness to strive for the holiness demanded. So, as was customary in the first century, particularly in the synagogue, scripture reading would take place after a collect, a prayer for the particular Sunday being celebrated. Because, as we inherited our liturgy (work of the people in our worship of God) from the early Church, as she inherited her liturgy from Judaism, we find that the importance of recognizing God's presence in every aspect of life became paramount in the early Church. Therefore, they borrowed the principle of a repeating cycle of three-and-a-half-year scripture readings, dividing up the calendar year to teach various elements of the life of Jesus, beginning not in January, according to the secular calendar, but in December with Advent.

On Sundays, there were actually five different scripture readings in total; that is because in traditional Anglican services, there would be (morning) prayer, in which one Old Testament passage would be read, then one New Testament passage, and a selection from the Psalms. Then during communion, we have a New Testament epistle reading and a gospel. God's word was and is of the utmost import as it teaches us and corrects us and overwhelms us with the person of the Triune Godhead.

So, once more, we are presented with God's Holy Word because it is through His word that we are sanctified. After the epistle lesson is read, the priest and clergy move out from the altar and bring the gospel into the first few rows of the congregation, symbolizing the presentation and the giving of the gospel to the people. Just before the gospel is read, the people proclaim:

Here shall be said,
Glory be to thee, O Lord.

After the reading of the gospel is complete, the people, in adulation that God has condescended to bless us with His saving gospel, proclaim:

And after the Gospel may be said,
Praise be to thee, O Christ.

The priest, once finished with the gospel, turns again to face the altar and become a part of the congregation of God's people for the next part of the Ministry or Liturgy of the Word.

Now, having been confronted with the character of God in the *Decalogue*, and driven to recognize our total unworthiness, save for Christ, to approach God due to our sinfulness; having been lifted up before the throne of God in prayers to petition sanctification; and hearing His word to guide us to that sanctification, resulting in being blessed with His gospel, we are further humbled and privileged to recite one of the ancient Church creeds. Unless one recited these creeds, men and women could not be a part of the Church; these are creeds for which men and women were tortured and martyred. The most common is the Nicene Creed. At St. Patrick's, our parish's particular tradition was, once a month, usually the third Sunday, to recite the third of the great ancient creeds of the Church, the Athanasian Creed. However, it is most common to exclusively recite the Nicene Creed.[9]

Then shall be said the creed,

I BELIEVE in one God the Father Almighty, Maker of heaven and earth, And of all things visible and invisible:

And in one Lord Jesus Christ, the only-begotten Son of God; Begotten of his Father before all worlds, God of God, Light of Light, Very God of very God; Begotten, not made; Being of one substance with the Father; By whom all things were made: Who for us men and for our salvation came down from heaven, And was incarnate by the Holy Ghost of the Virgin Mary, And was made man: And was crucified also for us under Pontius Pilate; He suffered and was buried: And the third day he rose again according to the Scriptures: And ascended into heaven, And sitteth on the right hand of the Father: And he

---

9   The three great creeds, the Apostles Creed, Nicene Creed, and Athanasian Creed, were foundational doctrinal affirmations of the early Church. They each held an important function in the early Church. The Apostles Creed was essentially the baptismal statement of faith of the convert—one had to affirm this to be baptized; the Nicene Creed was the confirmation statement of faith of the catechumen—one had to affirm this to receive holy communion; the Athanasian Creed was the statement of orthodoxy as it defines who Jesus Christ was—one could not be considered a Christian if one did not affirm all contained within this majestic creed.

shall come again, with glory, to judge both the quick and the dead; Whose kingdom shall have no end.

And I believe in the Holy Ghost, The Lord, and Giver of Life, Who proceedeth from the Father and the Son; Who with the Father and the Son together is worshipped and glorified; Who spake by the Prophets: And I believe one Catholic and Apostolic Church: I acknowledge one Baptism for the remission of sins: And I look for the Resurrection of the dead: And the Life of the world to come. Amen.

Once we completed the glorious experience of, with one voice, uniting with our ancient Christian brothers and sisters in reciting this creed of our historic faith, we enter the culmination of the Ministry or Liturgy of the Word, the sermon. The acknowledgment of the importance of God's word was so overpowering for the Church that, early on, to symbolize that this was indeed the Word of God that comes from the mouth of our God of heaven, pulpits were raised and elevated usually around six to eight feet (measured from the bottom of the pulpit) and thrust outward toward the congregation as if it were God Himself communicating to His people directly from heaven.

The purpose of the sermon is to interpret the readings and apply them to the life of the congregation. It is not a pep talk, lecture, or piece of performance art; rather, it is a breaking open of the Word of God we have heard so that we can feed on it and Him. We have been confronted by God's Holiness in His word. We have been taught how to strive for God's Holiness in His Word. It is God's written Word, His Gospel, that we will now visibly encounter as we prepare to leave the Ministry or Liturgy of the Word and move to the Liturgy of the Sacrament, where we are blessed and humbled to receive, in holy communion, the Lord's Supper, the grace of the whole person of Christ in the bread and wine. However, before that happens, those not yet confirmed in their faith, the catechumens,[10] were ushered out of the sanctuary, and the "doors" were closed behind them, only to listen to the preparation of the congregation to receive the holy mysteries of the bread and the wine, the Body and Blood of the risen Christ, in anticipation of the marvelous day when they, too, could receive Christ's grace with their brethren in this sacrament.

Once the Liturgy of the Word has concluded, preparation begins for one of the most profound and greatest mysteries of Christianity, the reception of the person of Jesus Christ in holy communion. It isn't that there suddenly is no longer any scripture presented in the service; on the contrary, the entire service is comprised of 70% direct scripture citations and the remainder allusions to scripture—no, the worship service is bathed, immersed if you will, in Holy Writ.

Here with the Word of God and the statement of the faith of the Church resounding in our hearts and minds, we have the glorious, magnificent, humbling blessing to show God our love, adoration, and appreciation for all His gifts to us by giving back to Him what is ultimately His anyway in the offering.

In the early Church, the practice was for each member of the congregation to bring to Church with them, whatever it is they had to give to God. Some would bring bread, some wine, some money, and so on. The wealthy brought excess to provide for those who were not as blessed; those with less brought what they could. All of these gifts, then, were given to one of the clergy, usually a deacon, and at this juncture in the service they would process, if you will, with the congregation's gifts to

---

10   Those new to Christianity being trained in the essentials of the Christian faith.

God, and the deacon would present them to the priest, who would then place them on the altar.

However, even though the visible presentation is of material offerings, the true meaning of the offering is found in Romans 12:1, where we are giving ourselves to the service of God. As these physical gifts will be used for God's work, so will we by giving up ourselves.

The priest would say one or more of the following sentences to signal the beginning of the move into the Liturgy of the Sacrament. Word and sacrament form the core of all worship.

REMEMBER the words of the Lord Jesus, how he said, It is more blessed to give than to receive. Acts xx. 35.

Let your light so shine before men, that they may see your good works, and glorify your Father which is in heaven. St. Matt. v. 16.

Lay not up for yourselves treasures upon earth, where moth and rust doth corrupt, and where thieves break through and steal: but lay up for yourselves treasures in heaven, where neither moth nor rust doth corrupt, and where thieves do not break through nor steal. St. Matt. vi. 19, 20.

Not every one that saith unto me, Lord, Lord, shall enter into the kingdom of heaven; but he that doeth the will of my Father which is in heaven. St. Matt. vii. 21.

He that soweth little shall reap little; and he that soweth plenteously shall reap plenteously. Let every man do according as he is disposed in his heart, not grudgingly, or of necessity; for God loveth a cheerful giver. 2 Cor. ix. 6, 7. While we have time, let us do good unto all men; and especially unto them that are of the household of faith. Gal. vi. 10.

God is not unrighteous, that he will forget your works, and labour that proceedeth of love; which love ye have showed for his Name's sake, who have ministered unto the saints, and yet do minister. Heb. vi. 10.

To do good, and to distribute, forget not; for with such sacrifices God is well pleased. Heb. xiii. 16.

Whoso hath this world's goods, and seeth his brother have

need, and shutteth up his compassion from him, how dwelleth the love of God in him? 1 St. John iii. 17.

Be merciful after thy power. If thou hast much, give plenteously; if thou hast little, do thy diligence gladly to give of that little: for so gatherest thou thyself a good reward in the day of necessity. Tobit iv. 8, 9.

And the King shall answer and say unto them, Verily I say unto you, Inasmuch as ye have done it unto one of the least of these my brethren, ye have done it unto me. St. Matt. xxv. 40.

How then shall they call on him in whom they have not believed? and how shall they believe in him of whom they have not heard? and how shall they hear without a preacher? and how shall they preach, except they be sent? Rom. x. 14, 15.

Jesus said unto them, The harvest truly is plenteous, but the labourers are few; pray ye therefore the Lord of the harvest, that he would send forth labourers into his harvest. St. Luke x. 2.

Ye shall not appear before the LORD empty; every man shall give as he is able, according to the blessing of the LORD thy God which he hath given thee. Deut. xvi. 16, 17.

Thine, O LORD, is the greatness, and the power, and the glory, and the victory, and the majesty: for all that is in the heaven and in the earth is thine; thine is the kingdom, O LORD, and thou art exalted as head above all. 1 Chron. xxix. 11.

All things come of thee, O LORD, and of thine own have we given thee. 1 Chron. xxix. 14.

With the presentation of our sacrificial offering, in thanksgiving to God, we are blessed to lift up, before the throne of Grace, in prayer, the entire Body of Christ, all of Christianity. The priest will face the congregation, for God is now inviting His people to "tell Him" their needs, wants, pains, sorrows, to express their personal joys, victories, and accomplishments and bring them to the foot of the throne. From the beginning of the service, since we first entered the church and stood in God's presence, we entered the realm of Christianity that is transcendent. Now, we will be brought directly into this transcendent mystery as we come to that great mystery of holy communion. We are specifically involved with the Church of Our Lord through all of time. In the Prayer for the Church, we are participating in intercessory prayer for the Church throughout not only the world but the heavens. Read the words carefully; see the six categories of the prayer identified in the bubbles on the side; watch the movement of the prayer, to heaven, back to earth, and back to heaven again. It is our glorious opportunity to be a part of what Hebrews calls "so great a cloud of witnesses." Here is a pointed reminder that the Church is a living community. The priest, after inviting the congregation to share their petitions before God, turns back to face the altar as a part of the people of God, to include his requests, and states the following:

Let us pray for the whole state of Christ's Church.

[Gifts] ALMIGHTY and everliving God, who by thy holy Apostle hast taught us to make prayers, and supplications, and to give thanks for all men; We humbly beseech thee most mercifully to accept our [alms and] oblations, and to receive these our prayers, which we offer unto thy Divine Majesty; beseeching thee to inspire continually the Universal Church with the spirit of truth, unity, and concord: And grant that all those who do confess thy holy Name may agree in the truth of thy holy Word, and live in unity and godly love.

[*Rulers*] We beseech thee also, so to direct and dispose the hearts of all Christian Rulers, that they may truly and impartially administer justice, to the punishment of wickedness and vice, and to the maintenance of thy true religion, and virtue.

[*Clergy*] Give grace, O heavenly Father, to all Bishops and other Ministers, that they may, both by their life and doctrine, set forth thy true and lively Word, and rightly and duly administer thy holy Sacraments.

[*Laity*] And to all thy People give thy heavenly grace; and especially to this congregation here present; that, with meek heart and due reverence, they may hear, and receive thy holy Word; truly serving thee in holiness and righteousness all the days of their life.

[*Sick and Afflicted*] And we most humbly beseech thee, of thy goodness, O Lord, to comfort and succour all those who, in this transitory life, are in trouble, sorrow, need, sickness, or any other adversity.

[*Faithful Departed*] And we also bless thy holy Name for all thy servants departed this life in thy faith and fear; beseeching thee to grant them continual growth in thy love and service, and to give us grace so to follow their good examples, that with them we may be partakers of thy heavenly kingdom. Grant this, O Father, for Jesus Christ's sake, our only Mediator and Advocate. *Amen.*

We have participated in a wonderful, transcendent moment of prayer for the entire Church of God, prayer for the unity of the Church of God. We have given our offering, including ourselves, to God, and we stand on the precipice of engaging in that great mystery of communion, receiving Christ in the bread and wine. But we must continually acknowledge, as we begin the glorious sequence of moments leading up to communion, that we are still fallen, sinful, unholy people in the presence of a Holy, Transcendent, Almighty God, about to receive the most precious gift He has given mankind, His Son, through the instruments of bread and wine. Therefore, it is incumbent upon us to *ensure* we are as ready and prepared as possible to receive Him. That we do not partake "unworthily" (read I Corinthians 11:27–30), we must know what we are doing; hence, we are instructed as such via the sermon. Sometimes that feeding may refresh us. Sometimes it may give us spiritual indigestion. Whatever the case may be, it should provoke a response in us, a response that will take shape in the remainder of the liturgy and overflow into our daily lives, where we bear witness to the good news we have heard for the sake of the world and not simply our own edification. We are instructed by the priest as he turns to face us, before we commence to engage the transcendent mystery of communion, to look into our hearts and confess and repent of whatever sins might be in our lives, known and unknown, before the Throne of Grace as we are called by God to confess and repent.

YE who do truly and earnestly repent you of your sins, and are in love and charity with your neighbours, and intend to lead a new life, following the commandments of God, and walking from henceforth in his holy ways; Draw near with faith, and take this holy Sacrament to your comfort; and make your humble confession to Almighty God, devoutly kneeling.

After the call to repentance, the priest turns back to the altar and kneels before the throne of God and leads us in confession now as a member of the congregation, one of us. There is no priestly privilege here; we are all sinners before our God.

Then shall this general confession be made, by the Priest and all those who are minded to receive the holy communion, humbly kneeling.

ALMIGHTY God, Father of our Lord Jesus Christ, Maker of all things, Judge of all men; We acknowledge and bewail our manifold sins and wickedness, Which we, from time to time, most grievously have committed, By thought, word, and deed, Against thy Divine Majesty, Provoking most justly thy wrath and indignation against us. We do earnestly repent, And are heartily sorry for these our misdoings; The remembrance of them is grievous unto us; The burden of them is intolerable. Have mercy upon us, Have mercy upon us, most merciful Father; For thy Son our Lord Jesus Christ's sake, Forgive us all that is past; And grant that we may ever hereafter Serve and please thee In newness of life, To the honour and glory of thy Name; Through Jesus Christ our Lord. Amen.

After the corporate confession and repentance of the entire congregation, priest and people, the priest stands and turns to face the people in what is the most reassuring, comforting, blessed gift of God, His absolution of our sin through Jesus Christ. Pay close attention to the words; understand what has been communicated all throughout concerning the position of the priest—he is not forgiving anyone's sins. As the priest faces the people, he is pronouncing to the congregation that it is God who is forgiving the truly repentant through the Lord Jesus Christ. Read the final clause of the absolution.

> Then shall the **P**riest (the **B**ishop, if he be present) stand up and, turning to the people, say God's absolution,

A LMIGHTY God, our heavenly Father, who of his great mercy hath promised forgiveness of sins to all those who with hearty repentance and true faith turn unto him; Have mercy upon you; pardon and deliver you from all your sins; confirm and strengthen you in all goodness; and bring you to everlasting life; through Jesus Christ our Lord. *Amen.*

The sovereign, holy, majestic God of the universe, to those with a pure heart, pure intentions, and no deceit, used His spokesman, the priest, to reassure you that you are indeed and genuinely forgiven of your sins by God Himself. Yet we all know that we have doubts sometimes, uneasiness, insecurities; so, because our God is a loving God, He reinforces His forgiveness in the work of Christ by adding words of reassurance and comfort to our tender hearts and minds.

> Then shall the **P**riest say,

Hear what comfortable words our Saviour Christ saith unto all who truly turn to him.

C OME unto me, all ye that travail and are heavy laden, and I will refresh you. St. Matt. xi. 28.
　　So God loved the world, that he gave his only-begotten

Son, to the end that all that believe in him should not perish, but have everlasting life. St. John iii. 16.

Hear also what Saint Paul saith.

This is a true saying, and worthy of all men to be received, That Christ Jesus came into the world to save sinners. 1 Tim. i. 15.

Hear also what Saint John saith.

If any man sin, we have an Advocate with the Father, Jesus Christ the righteous; and he is the Propitiation for our sins. 1 St. John ii. 1, 2.

Not only has the God of all creation forgiven us, but He has also made sure we know we are forgiven in His comfortable words. We are at peace with God. We are forgiven by God. We are comforted by God. Our hearts should be overflowing with joy and praise and thanksgiving. And the priest, still facing the people, speaking for God Almighty, says to the congregation, "Lift up your hearts" (the implication is to heaven, I might add), the *Sursum Corda*. God the Father is now calling us to spiritually join Him. Join Him. Before His eternal throne. Contemplate that glorious privilege for a moment. How amazingly far we have come from the processional, the acknowledgement of our sin before God, hearing the Decalogue, His Word, and so on, to be brought to this point, to be spiritually invited by God Himself, to kneel before His heavenly throne and worship Him. Following this transcendent moment of spiritual joy, we hear one of the Proper Prefaces (prayers) appointed for the specific time in the liturgical year.

After which the Priest shall proceed,
saying he Sursum Corda,

Lift up your hearts.

Answer.	*We lift them up unto the Lord.*
Priest.	Let us give thanks unto our Lord God.
Answer.	*It is meet and right so to do.*

Then shall the Priest turn to the Holy Table and say,

I T is very meet, right, and our bounden duty, that we should at all times, and in all places, give thanks unto thee, O Lord, Holy Father, Almighty, Everlasting God.

Here shall follow the Proper Preface, according to the time, if there be any specialty appointed; or else immediately shall be said or sung by the Priest,

T HEREFORE with Angels and Archangels, and with all the company of heaven, we laud and magnify thy glorious Name; evermore praising thee, and saying, HOLY, HOLY, HOLY, Lord God of, hosts, Heaven and earth are full of thy glory: Glory be to thee, O Lord Most High. Amen.

PROPER PREFACES
CHRISTMAS
Upon Christmas Day, and seven days after.

B ECAUSE thou didst give Jesus Christ, thine only Son, to be born as at this time for us; who, by the operation of the Holy Ghost, was made very man, of the substance of the Virgin Mary his mother; and that without spot of sin, to make us clean from all sin. Therefore with Angels, etc.

EPIPHANY
Upon the Epiphany, and seven days after.

T HROUGH Jesus Christ our Lord, who, in substance of our mortal flesh, manifested forth his glory; that he might bring us out of darkness into his own glorious light.
Therefore with Angels, etc.

PURIFICATION, ANNUNCIATION, AND TRANSFIGURATION
Upon the **Feasts of** Purification, Annunciation, and Transfiguration.

B ECAUSE in the Mystery of the Word made flesh, thou hast caused a new light to shine in our hearts, to give the knowledge of thy glory in the face of thy Son, Jesus Christ our Lord.

Therefore with Angels, etc.

EASTER.
Upon Easter day, and seven days after.

B UT chiefly are we bound to praise thee for the glorious Resurrection of thy Son Jesus Christ our Lord: for he is the very Paschal Lamb, which was offered for us, and hath taken away the sin of the world; who by his death hath destroyed death, and by his rising to life again hath restored to us everlasting life.

Therefore with Angels, etc.

ASCENSION
Upon Ascension day, and seven days after.

T HROUGH thy most dearly beloved Son Jesus Christ our Lord; who, after his most glorious Resurrection, manifestly appeared to all his Apostles, and in their sight ascended up into heaven, to prepare a place for us; that where he is, thither we might also ascend, and reign with him in glory.

Therefore with Angels, etc.

WHITSUNTIDE
Upon the Feast of Whitsunday, and six days after.

T HROUGH Jesus Christ our Lord; according to whose most true promise, the Holy Ghost came down as at this time from heaven, lighting upon the Apostles, to teach them, and to lead them into all truth; giving them boldness with fervent zeal constantly to preach the Gospel unto all nations; whereby we have been brought out of darkness and error into the clear light and true knowledge of thee, and of thy Son Jesus Christ.

Therefore with Angels, etc.

TRINITY SUNDAY
Upon the Feast of Trinity only.

WHO, with thine only-begotten Son, and the Holy Ghost, art one God, one Lord, in Trinity of Persons and in Unity of Substance. For that which we believe of thy glory, O Father, the same we believe of the Son, and of the Holy Ghost, without any difference of inequality.

Therefore with Angels, etc.

Or this:

FOR the precious death and merits of thy Son Jesus Christ our Lord, and for the sending to us of the Holy Ghost, the Comforter; who are one with thee in thy Eternal Godhead.

Therefore with Angels, etc.

ALL SAINTS.
Upon All Saints' day, and seven days after.

WHO, in the multitude of thy saints, hast compassed us about with so great a cloud of witnesses that we, rejoicing in their fellowship, may run with patience the race that is set before us, and together with them may receive the crown of glory that fadeth not away.

Therefore with Angels and Archangels, and with all the company of heaven, we laud and magnify thy glorious Name; evermore praising thee, and saying,

Now, with our hearts lifted up to the heavenlies, we join the heavenly throng in reciting Isaiah 6 and Revelation 4:

HOLY, HOLY, HOLY, Lord God of, hosts, Heaven and earth are full of thy glory: Glory be to thee, O Lord Most High. Amen.

Then, during the *trishagion* (holy, three times), one of the clergy party will ring bells. It is important to understand what the bells actually mean. Remember, historically, the catechumens are not in the church and have not been since the end of the sermon. They have not seen or been a part of all that transpired in the ensuing time. In many churches, there were limited to no lines of sight for them to peer into the sanctuary. Some might have been able to stand on a stone bench and look over the wall, but most could not and did not know where they were in service or what was taking place. Further consider that this was the moment they were all anticipating. It is this special blessing, receiving the most precious Body and Blood of our Lord Jesus Christ in the bread and wine. They longed for this, as should we all. Therefore, to bring them back, so to speak, to draw their attention that, "Hey, the great mystery is now upon us," the church would ring bells to draw their attention to this holy moment. This is also the meaning during the elevation of the bread; there is no worshiping of the bread taking place. Over the years, especially during the Medieval period, it has taken on other—incorrect, I might add—meanings. But this is what the *sanctus* bells are doing in the service.

From here, the priest immediately begins the Prayer of Consecration; he is setting apart these particular elements, on this day, "these creatures" of bread and wine. Remember, we are dealing with the whole Christ, divine/human, the God/Man, the Incarnation, in the Eucharist. These are not bare, empty pieces of bread and a cup of wine (yes, Jesus drank wine, not Welch's grape juice); this is the entire person of Jesus we are receiving, human and divine nature, through the means of bread and wine. Just as they are not empty of content, and they are merely bread and wine, they also are not the physical body of Christ. There is no physical sacrifice about to be performed; there is no corpse on the altar; what we are experiencing is a divine mystery in the same way that Jesus is both God and Man is a mystery (which is exactly what we receive in communion), in the same way there are three persons of the Triune Godhead, yet only *one God* is a mystery. Mystery should not be a shocking, scary, awful, heretical taboo concept for Christians; it is an essential element of what Christianity is: heavenly and earthly, word and sacrament, mind and body.

So, as we are grafted into Him, His Body, at baptism (see John 15), it is here that, via the means of bread and wine, He feeds us, by the Holy Spirit, who is uniting us to His Head, to Christ; the same Holy Spirit who is indwelling us, indwelling Christ's Church, unites His Body and Head in communion because the Head of the Holy Spirit, the Head of the Church, Jesus, is never separated from His Body. In this spiritual union, through the ministry of the Holy Spirit, we, the Body of Christ, connected to our Head, Jesus, receive His Body and Blood; we receive His Grace. Now do you see? Now do you understand why it is imperative we do not partake unworthily?

In this prayer, we see how Jesus reenacted the core elements of the Passover: took bread, blessed bread, broke bread; took the cup, blessed the cup, distributed the cup. Yes, it was one cup He offered. This was His implementation of the New Covenant, not using the four cups as in Jewish tradition. The apostles all partook of one cup, a common cup. We are reliving right before our eyes and ears, as one unified congregation, one unified body, the drama of redemption, Christ's redemptive sacrifice on our behalf, in our place.

No multiple, mini cups isolating us from the full participation in

Christ's Body and Blood, together as the Body of Christ. No "individual Christians," partaking of their individual pieces of the Body of Christ. The priest, after himself having participated in receiving the bread and wine, the Body and Blood of the whole Christ, as a member of the congregation, turns now, worthy by God's gift to stand as God's representative and offer the bread and wine, Body and Blood of Christ, to each and every member of the congregation, together, jointly as they kneel at the rail before God's throne! Not sitting in our seats, disconnected from everyone else, but together before God as a family.

We sometimes overlook the fact that what we are doing is not only repeating the Lord Jesus's celebration of His final meal with His disciples but also the enactment of a New Covenant! Covenants in scripture involve a sacrifice and a meal. Read Genesis 31:46, Exodus 24:11, and Matthew 26:28. We are participating in a covenantal meal with God (see footnote below).[11] A meal that, later, could only be eaten by priests. We are living as the "priesthood of all believers" right here in this celebratory act. And while we are not re-sacrificing Jesus, for that was a once-for-all time act, we get to share in, receive, be blessed by the grace that He gives us as we do this in remembrance of Him.

One final point: read the Prayer of Consecration closely. No matter how bad my sermons were, no matter how terribly any priest or deacon preached, no matter how tragically we might have obscured the gospel, if you paid attention to the liturgy up to this point—and especially in the upcoming Prayer of Consecration—you will have noticed that the gospel has been presented the entire time. Our liturgy protects our congregation from us clergy, from our pastoral failures.

God has so gloriously, graciously, lovingly cared for us that He ensured, if we worshiped Him in this way, properly, as He commanded, we will always hear His gospel.

When the Priest, standing before the table, hath so ordered the Bread

---

11   Exod. 24:9–11: [9]"Then Moses went up, also Aaron, Nadab, and Abihu, and seventy of the elders of Israel, [10]and they saw the God of Israel. And there was under His feet as it were a paved work of sapphire stone, and it was like the very heavens in its clarity. [11]But on the nobles of the children of Israel He did not lay His hand. So they saw God, and they ate and drank" (NKJ).

and Wine, that he may with the more readiness and decency break the
    Bread before the people, and take the Cup into his hands,
        he shall say the Prayer of Consecration, as followeth:

ALL glory be to thee, Almighty God, our heavenly Father, for that thou, of thy tender mercy, didst give thine
only Son Jesus Christ to suffer death upon the Cross for our
redemption; who made there (by his one oblation of himself
once offered) a full, perfect, and sufficient sacrifice, oblation, and satisfaction, for the sins of the whole world; and
did institute, and in his holy Gospel command us to continue, a perpetual memory of that his precious death and
sacrifice, until his coming again: For in the night in which
he was betrayed, (a) he took Bread; and when he had given
thanks, (b) he brake it, and gave it to his disciples, saying,
Take, eat, (c) this is my Body, which is given for you; Do this
in remembrance of me. Likewise, after supper, (d) he took
the Cup; and when he had given thanks, he gave it to them,
saying, Drink ye all of this; for

(e) this is my Blood of the New Testament, which is shed
for you, and for many, for the remission of sins; Do this, as oft
as ye shall drink it, in remembrance of me.

WHEREFORE O Lord and heavenly Father, according to
the institution of thy dearly beloved Son our Saviour Jesus
Christ, we, thy humble servants, do celebrate and make here
before thy Divine Majesty, with these thy holy gifts, which we
now offer unto thee, the memorial thy Son hath commanded
us to make; having in remembrance his blessed passion and
precious death, his mighty resurrection and glorious ascension;
rendering unto thee most hearty thanks for the innumerable
benefits procured unto us by the same.

AND we most humbly beseech thee, O merciful Father,
to hear us; and, of thy almighty goodness, vouchsafe to bless
and sanctify, with thy Word and Holy Spirit, these thy gifts and
creatures of bread and wine; that we, receiving them according
to thy Son our Saviour Jesus Christ's holy institution, in remem-

brance of his death and passion, may be partakers of his most blessed Body and Blood.

AND we earnestly desire thy fatherly goodness, mercifully to accept this our sacrifice of praise and thanksgiving; most humbly beseeching thee to grant that, by the merits and death of thy Son Jesus Christ, and through faith in his blood, we, and all thy whole Church, may obtain remission of our sins, and all other benefits of his passion. And here we offer and present unto thee, O Lord, our selves, our souls and bodies, to be a reasonable, holy, and living sacrifice unto thee; humbly beseeching thee, that we, and all others who shall be partakers of this Holy Communion, may worthily receive the most precious Body and Blood of thy Son Jesus Christ, be filled with thy grace and heavenly benediction, and made one body with him, that he may dwell in us, and we in him. And although we are unworthy, through our manifold sins, to offer unto thee any sacrifice; yet we beseech thee to accept this our bounden duty and service; not weighing our merits, but pardoning our offences, through Jesus Christ our Lord; by whom, and with whom, in the unity of the Holy Ghost, all honour and glory be unto thee, O Father Almighty, world without end. Amen.

The moment is almost upon us; we have heard the word consecrating the bread and wine as special creatures to be distributed for God's mysterious use. We have, as the ancient Church did, requested the spiritual presence of the Holy Spirit to ensure and guarantee our union with our Head that we might, as members of His Body, receive the blessing of His grace through the bread and wine in His Body and Blood. And, as He gave Himself for us on that horrible tree, which He turned into a glorious, triumphant icon of grace, we give ourselves to Him as offerings of praise and sacrifice, not physical martyrs, as if our human sacrifice could add anything to His "once for all sacrifice, oblation, and satisfaction" for all of sin, but for the purpose of receiving anything and everything else He might deign to give us.

We take the first of the remaining two steps of preparation before receiving our Savior by praying as He prayed, for the things He taught us to request; we acknowledge His realm in heaven, which is all of the universe; we hallow His name, recognize it as holy; we plead for His Kingdom of heaven to come to earth; we ask that His will, not our will, be done here on earth as His will is done in heaven; we ask for our daily bread (how powerfully poignant given what we are about to receive); we emulate His forgiveness to us in others; we pray for His protection from the evil one because everything is His: the Kingdom, power, and, of course, glory, for all time.

And now, as our Saviour Christ hath taught us, we are bold to say,

O UR Father, who art in heaven, Hallowed be thy Name. Thy kingdom come. Thy will be done, on earth, As it is in heaven. Give us this day our daily bread. And forgive us our trespasses, As we forgive those who trespass against us. And lead us not into temptation, But deliver us from the evil one. For thine is the kingdom, and the power, and the glory, for ever and ever. Amen.

If the recitation of the Lord's Prayer was the first step of final preparation, the following Prayer of Humble Access is the second, taken from the synoptic gospels (Matt 15:27, Mark 7:28, Luke 16:21). We once more acknowledge that this heavenly grace, this glorious gift, undeserved blessing, to be able to receive our Savior in this way, drives us to our knees in humility to recognize that even though it is only through the grace of Jesus that we are able even to kneel before God's throne, no less receive God's Son, we are unworthy, in ourselves, to partake of this Eucharist, to partake of this blessing. That it is only in Him, and through Him, and because of Him that we are so blessed.

Then shall the **Priest**, kneeling down at the Lord's table, say, in the name of all those who shall receive the **Communion**, this **Prayer** following
the Prayer of Humble Access.

W E do not presume to come to this thy Table, O merciful Lord, trusting in our own righteousness, but in thy manifold and great mercies. We are not worthy so much as to gather up the crumbs under thy Table. But thou art the same Lord, whose property is always to have mercy: Grant us therefore, gracious Lord, so to eat the flesh of thy dear Son Jesus Christ, and to drink his blood, that our sinful bodies may be made clean by his Body, and our souls washed through his most precious Blood, and that we may evermore dwell in him, and he in us. Amen.

Here may be sung a hymn.

A hymn is usually sung as the clergy party receives the Eucharist. After they are finished, the priest, assisted by a deacon if one is present, will turn to the congregation and announce that all who desire may come forward to receive "the Lamb of God, who takes away the sin of the world," and he shall say,

THE Body of our Lord Jesus Christ, which was given for thee, preserve thy body and soul unto everlasting life. Take and eat this in remembrance that Christ died for thee, and feed on him in thy heart by faith, with thanksgiving.

THE Blood of our Lord Jesus Christ, which was shed for thee, preserve thy body and soul unto everlasting life. Drink this in remembrance that Christ's Blood was shed for thee, and be thankful.

Those who have communed have just received the greatest blessing a human could imagine; they have received, via bread and wine, the Body and Blood of the Second Person of the Triune Godhead. Pause for a moment and reflect on that sentence: *we just received, via bread and wine, the very Body and Blood, the whole person, of Christ, the Second Person of the Triune Godhead.* Is there a more wonderous, mind-shattering experience in which a human could partake? He, the Second Person of the Triune Godhead, has taken the place of His people on that hideous cross; He, the Second Person of the Triune Godhead, has borne our punishment; He, the Second Person of the Triune Godhead, has been judged for our sin, for He was without sin; He, the Second Person of the Triune Godhead, has tasted death for all His people so they will never have to taste death. "O death, indeed, where is thy sting?"

The God of the universe literally moved heaven and earth to save His people in order to bring them to this moment while they remain on earth. And we are blessed enough, privileged enough, to revel in it. What a glorious moment of adoration, joy, thanksgiving, praise, and adulation. We then, as the priest calls us to pray, give thanks for all of what we have experienced and received that day.

Let us pray.

A LMIGHTY and everliving God, we most heartily thank thee, for that thou dost vouchsafe to feed us who have duly received these holy mysteries with the spiritual food of the most precious Body and Blood of thy Son our Saviour Jesus Christ; and dost assure us thereby of thy favour and goodness towards us; and that we are very members incorporate in the mystical body of thy Son, which is the blessed company of all faithful people; and are also heirs through hope of thy everlasting kingdom, by the merits of his most precious death and passion. And we humbly beseech thee, O heavenly Father, so to assist us with thy grace, that we may continue in that holy fellowship, and do all such good works as thou hast prepared for us to walk in; through Jesus Christ our Lord, to whom, with thee and the Holy Ghost, be all honour and glory, world without end. Amen.

Having given God thanks, we now, with one voice as the people of God, give Him the glory to which He is entitled, which He deserves.

Then shall be said *Gloria in Excelsis*, all standing, or some proper **Hymn.**

GLORY be to God on high, and on earth peace, good will towards men. We praise thee, we bless thee, we worship thee, we glorify thee, we give thanks to thee for thy great glory, O Lord God, heavenly King, God the Father Almighty.

O Lord, the only-begotten Son, Jesus Christ; O Lord God, Lamb of God, Son of the Father, that takest away the sins of the world, have mercy upon us. Thou that takest away the sins of the world, receive our prayer. Thou that sittest at the right hand of God the Father, have mercy upon us.

For thou only art holy; thou only art the Lord; thou only, O Christ, with the Holy Ghost, art most high in the glory of God the Father. Amen.

With the triumphant voice of praise, the congregation kneels to receive the blessing handed down from Aaron to us today, another unfathomable reminder of our incredible religious heritage.

Then, the **People** are kneeling, the **Priest** (the **Bishop**, if he is present) shall let them depart with this **Blessing**.

The Peace of God, which passeth all understanding, keep your hearts and minds in the knowledge and love of God, and of his Son Jesus Christ our Lord: And the Blessing of God Almighty, the Father, the Son, and the Holy Ghost, be amongst you, and remain with you always. *Amen.*

The priest then leads everyone in saying a post-communion prayer, followed by a hymn and a closing recession. The final act of our common worship is the dismissal, which formally closes the worship with a call for us to go out as Christ's servants, as a kingdom of priests, bringing the good news, the gospel, to a fallen, sinful, and rebellious world. It reminds us that the purpose of worship is not simply to encourage and build ourselves up, but for all of us to be empowered and sent forth as ministers of Christ. I recall visiting one church, and as I left the parking lot, I looked up, and there was a sign suspended from the top of a gate that read, "You are now entering the mission field."

I pray, if nothing else, you found this a useful explanation of the theological reasons one parish of Anglicans worshiped this way. May our sovereign Lord richly bless you as you worship Him in spirit and truth.

Appendix C

Why Use the Book of Common Prayer?

And they devoted themselves to the apostles' teaching and the fellowship, to the breaking of bread and the prayers (Acts 2:42, ESV).

Introduction

Before getting into the meat of a discussion on the Book of Common Prayer itself, it will benefit all involved to understand the mindset as to why written or precomposed prayers are used in traditional worship. The following are just some of the general reasons the Church, for so many centuries, has used written prayers in liturgy or worship.

Among Evangelical and Charismatic Christians, and most nonliturgical Churches, reactions to liturgical aspects of worship[1] and prayer vary greatly from intrigue, to delight, to bewilderment, to straight-up scoffing. When someone who worships from these backgrounds attends a traditional liturgical worship service, where precomposed prayers are utilized, the general reaction is "Why? We have the Bible; we have the Spirit. Why do you need prewritten prayers? That's kind of an old, outdated way to worship God." The assumption is that only extemporaneous or spontaneous prayers are truly spiritual or genuinely from the heart.

It is important to consider a few points at the outset. First, the Bible

---

1   The following twelve points were taken from an online post years ago that has either been taken down or cannot be located. The name of that post was *Why Use Written Prayers?* Unfortunately, due to a computer crash, the author's name and specific location were lost to me. However, I must state at the outset that I am merely borrowing this material from that unnamed author and in no way claim to be the source.

itself is written and is old and cannot be altered via an extemporaneous or spontaneous urge or so-called spiritual impulse.[2] Second, the hymns we use in Church, which invariably have deep spiritual and emotional significance for individuals, are prewritten and not composed immediately during a worship service.[3] Third, churches will weekly distribute a bulletin that indicates what people will be doing at specific points during the service; this is essentially a prewritten order of worship.[4] Spontaneity or extemporaneous involvement would create a chaotic scene. Regardless as to whether a particular church hands out a bulletin or not, the order of worship is going to be the same each week.[5]

What one can see, then, is all Christians in all churches use prewritten, non-extemporaneous elements in their order of worship.[6] As a matter of fact, if one is attentive while attending these nonliturgical churches that do not use prewritten material, one will notice much of the so-called spontaneous involvement is quite similar, identical in fact, from week to week.[7]

The following will attempt to explain some of the reasons behind liturgical prayer aimed at people with little or no (positive) experience with it, though ideally it will also be an encouragement to those already versed in such tradition. I will give lists of reasons for various aspects with (hopefully) brief explanations. We will look first at written prayers or, that is, prewritten prayers. Many people have a hard time seeing why someone would ever want to repeat prewritten prayers as a significant part or any part of one's devotional life. Here are a few thoughts, though by no means exhaustive:

1. *They teach us how to pray:*[8] Most people learned to write by copying letters printed in a book or even tracing over them. We learned math by repeating times tables over and over until they were automatic. Using written prayers works in the same way.

---

2   From David Bennett, *Why Do You Use Written Prayers?* Ancient-Future.Net. Online blog.
3   Ibid.
4   Ibid.
5   Ibid.
6   Ibid.
7   Ibid.
8   *Op. Cit., "Why Use Written Prayers?"*

We "trace over" the prayers of the Saints, and over time, they become a part of us.

2. *They prime the pump:*[9] Written prayers solve the dilemma of what to say while praying. Instead of staring off into space or daydreaming during our prayer time, we can prime the pump using written prayers to get us started.

3. *They remind us what we ought to pray:*[10] When left to our own devices, we could easily pray only for that which immediately concerns us, kind of like a tyranny of the urgent, only in prayer. As C. S. Lewis says, "The crisis of the present moment will always loom largest. Isn't there a danger that our great, permanent, objective necessities, often more important, may get crowded out?"

4. *They infuse our prayer life with rich biblical and theological content:*[11] My own spontaneous prayer can only possibly be filled with whatever biblical content I have in retrievable memory and am able to string together into coherent sentences on the fly. Praying on my own is then dependent upon the reservoir of the biblical knowledge I am able to recall, which is rather limited and, as C. S. Lewis remarked, in danger of quickly dispersing into "wide and shallow puddles." Written prayers make instantly accessible a rich depth of content in prayer without requiring the least bit of ingenuity on my part.

5. *They connect us to the wider church, both geographically and historically:*[12] I can pray in unity with believers all over the world and throughout history by praying the same words with them.

6. *They are time tested:*[13] Of course, not all are, but many written prayers in historic liturgies are over a thousand years old.

---

9   Ibid.
10   Ibid.
11   Ibid.
12   Ibid.
13   Ibid.

These have stuck around for reasons that are well worth exploring.

7. *They are short and stay focused:*[14] Precomposed prayers help people engage the mind with those prayers compared to the rambling or stream-of-consciousness extemporaneous praying that so often occurs when one person prays for a long time. So many topics are covered in no organized or coherent fashion that it is nearly impossible to stay connected. The other people attempting to pray often zone out because they cannot keep track of what is going on. Written prayers are shorter and to the point. They are unified around a coherent theme and with a specific objective. This helps either an individual or a group connect and agree with them.

8. *They spare us from narcissism*[15] (i.e., idolatrous idiosyncrasy): We naturally gravitate around our pet doctrines, ideas, passions, and concerns. We are certainly entitled to them. However, when we only entertain and accept our own premises, we are moving onto dangerous ground. If prayer only bears the mark of my uniqueness, it may keep me locked up in the bubble of that same uniqueness. Written prayers call us out beyond the confines of our limited understanding and perspective to a participation in the thoughts, issues, and concerns of the wider Church.

9. *They are easy and accessible:*[16] No spiritual acumen is needed, no special experience, talents, gifts, anointings, or education—simply the ability to read. You can be a complete novice in prayer or a veteran believer who is overwhelmed with frustration concerning their prayer life and instantly access an incredibly rich prayer life. Written prayers are for everyone and accessible immediately.

---

14   Ibid.
15   Ibid.
16   Ibid.

10. *They are unifying:*[17] Because they are so easy and accessible, they can be immediately unifying for people of all different levels in experience of prayer. Everyone is on an equal playing field. There are no prayer experts who must lead the way as the novices sit in befuddled silence. All engage, all participate, all are one.

11. *They help us relax:*[18] It is remarkable how much anxiety people have about what and how they pray and worship, especially in public. With written prayers, all you must do is say the words that are already given to you, with no other expectations. In other words, you can spend less time worrying about what you are going to say, what other people are going to think about it, how to have a really good prayer, and so on and focus your energy on actually praying and connecting with God.

12. *They teach us grace:*[19] This is ironic considering the frequent accusations of written prayers being stiff and too formally religious. Written prayers teach us that prayer is about God and not about our effort. Many people try so hard to have a prayer life and feel so defeated. The Church's treasury of written and liturgical prayer is one of God's greatest gifts to us. It is sheer grace that we can have such an easy entry point into prayer of unspeakable wealth and depth. Thus, prayer is not so much about how disciplined, spiritual, discerning, passionate, or contemplative we are; it is about God's grace freely given to us, who are in such desperate need.

If that is not compelling enough, specifically prewritten prayers:[20]

a. *(Pre-) Written Prayers Provide a Solid Structure for Worship*

Originally, the purpose of using written prayers was to create a basic

---

17 Ibid.
18 Ibid.
19 Ibid.
20 *Op. Cit.* The following seven points are taken from Mr. Bennett's blog article.

order for worship and prayer. This can be seen as far back as the early Church, and the very terms and phraseology of the majority of written prayers and the liturgies of which they are a part are, for all intents and purposes, taken verbatim from the Bible. The traditional core elements of the order of worship, which are deemed spiritually essential, were confession, thanksgiving, communion, and so forth. Some contemporary Christians use the acronym CATS, which stands for confession, adoration, thanksgiving, and supplication.

b.   *(Pre-) Written Prayers Allow for Common Prayer*[21]

The close-knit relationship of Christians in the early Church was predicated upon the concept of corporate unity or solidarity. Unfortunately, our Western culture is so fractured that religion in general and Christianity in particular are viewed as being highly personal and private matters. The early Church knew nothing of this mindset. In many instances, there were numerous prayers prayed collectively, together, and as the minister presiding would end the prayers specifically or the service as a whole, the congregation would jointly offer a resounding "amen." To participate in a worship service where one would come to sing a few hymns or songs, sit for thirty to sixty minutes to listen to a sermon, and offer up their own individual "spontaneous" private prayers without including the entire congregation is completely and totally unknown in the early Church conception of worship.[22] This understanding of worship was not accepted, for the most part, until the latter part of the twentieth century.

c.   *(Pre-) Written Prayers Allow for Real Freedom of Worship*[23]

Often, one preparing for a worship service or even personal, private devotions will struggle to develop or create an appropriate prayer spontaneously. There is difficulty in knowing where or even how to begin,

---

21   Ibid.
22   Refer back to the previous chapter and look at how the "Prayer for the Whole State of Christ's Church" proceeds.
23   *Op. Cit.* Bennett.

how to focus on specific cares or concerns, or how to even express what is in one's heart. Prewritten prayers eliminate that lack of structure in one's thinking. In practice, having this type of structure prevents aimless wandering and constant repetition of certain words or phrases because one has no idea what to truly say and provides more, not less, freedom. If you are a parent, I am certain you have heard that children need structure. Structure sets guidelines and boundaries and allows the child the freedom to explore their individuality while knowing their limits. Or, if you prefer, think of a football game. You have rules, sidelines, the back of the end zone, yard and hash marks, yet look at all that takes place within those boundaries. What would happen if the teams simply showed up for a game on Sunday and spontaneously did whatever they felt like doing? Other than the comedic value of watching such a keystone cop routine, there would not be much real excitement or fun, if we happen to be on one of the teams.

This is what liturgical, prewritten, established patterns allow. Within these confines, worship is, if one is truly worshiping from a heart-based faith and not merely going through the motions, incredibly meaningful, profoundly biblical, and deeply moving spiritually.

d. *(Pre-) Written Prayers Connect Us to the Past and to the Wider Church*[24]

Traditional churches experience something that more contemporary devotees of nonliturgical worship experience, and that is transcendent connection through time and space. When we invoke prewritten prayers, and together, as a congregation, when we participate in these prewritten prayers, we are not only joining with our brethren in the pews around us, not only Christians all around the world (connection), not only with the historical Church throughout the centuries (time and space) who recited the very same prayers, but we are joining with the "cloud of witnesses" (transcendent) all around us in heaven. Imagine, you can pray the very same prayer that one of the early Church martyrs

---

24   Ibid.

prayed when he worshiped, to say nothing of praying exactly what Jesus prayed.

When praying prewritten prayers, we are not being "lone ranger" Christians or spiritually isolating ourselves in our own private religious experience in the pew. We are enjoying the true fellowship that Christians have, in Christ, exceeding our own specific time and place. We connect back and up and anticipate the forward connection that Christians will have with us in the future when they participate in these same rewritten prayers.

And if that does not take your breath away, when you pray prewritten prayers, you are joining Christians in Africa, Asia, South America, Russia, and so on. You are joining billions of Christians reciting the Lord's Prayer, *Agnus Dei*,[25] or the *Sanctus*—Christians of all races and social classes.[26]

e. *(Pre-) Written Prayers Are Time Tested*[27]

This almost falls under the category of 'really, Captain Obvious?' One of the reasons prewritten prayers are with us today is because their theology has stood the scrutiny of theological rigor. They are theologically orthodox. They succinctly present the theology of the Bible. How many times has one been to a nontraditional church that doesn't use prewritten prayers and listened to someone go on and on and on and on with virtually no substantive theological content, repeating the same few phrases over and over, "Dear Lord, we, dear Lord, love You so much, dear Lord. Father God, you cannot, Father God, be contained in all the universe, Father God." Well, you get the point. That is not meant to hurt anyone's feelings as they attempt to sincerely express their devotion to the Triune God of the universe. It is simply to point out what many have experienced and one of the pitfalls of eschewing prewritten prayer.

---

25 "Lamb of God, who takes away the sins of the world, have mercy upon us."
26 "Holy, Holy, Holy, Lord God of Hosts, heaven and earth are full of Thy Glory. Glory be to Thee O Lord Most High."
27 *Op. Cit.* Bennett.

f. *Jesus Gave Us a Set Form for Prayer*[28]

Jesus Himself gave us a prayer to pray. It came directly from the Temple/synagogue worship service (see below) when His disciples asked Him how they should pray. Notice Jesus did not say, "Hey, all that old, formal praying stuff is old hat. God is your copilot; He's your friend, your buddy, ole pal. Just say whatever comes to your mind from your heart when you're in a worship service." Jesus's model for prayer is a form, showing the value of this type of prayer, and though critically important for the devotional life of a Christian and the intent of the Christian in worship, spontaneous prayer from the heart is limited in its function in a worship service.

g. *(Pre-) Written Prayers Are Scriptural*[29]

Though last on the list, this point is probably the most crucial; after all, who cares whether a prayer is spontaneous or prewritten if it is unbiblical or theologically in error? Prewritten prayer, as mentioned previously in point "e," is time tested and comes to us, in the majority of instances, from centuries of the combination of use privately and in liturgical worship. The liturgy of the Jewish community, the heritage of all Christianity, is steeped in a mixture of prewritten prayer tested, as it were, in liturgical worship. Jewish ritual was heavily dependent on prewritten prayers. The Aaronic Benediction (not to mention the Psalms) is said by many nonliturgical ministers:

The LORD bless you and keep you;

[25] The LORD make His face shine upon you, And be gracious to you;

[26] The LORD lift up His countenance upon you, And give you peace. (Num. 6:24–26, NKJ)

This benediction was to be recited verbatim as the blessing the priests were to give, a prewritten prayer directly from God.

This is the pattern Christian worship follows for the reasons men-

---

28   Ibid.
29   Ibid.

tioned earlier in the book. These prayers, taken directly from the Bible, allow the Christian to directly pray the Bible. And even when they are not taken directly from the Bible, they are based on biblical themes with biblical symbolism.

Once again, this is not to dismiss spontaneous prayer out of hand. Having experience with prewritten prayers, one will begin to think with a certain structure and cadence so that even when one prays spontaneously, it will sound as if it were prewritten. This gives rise to true spontaneity and freedom.

As stated, anything can be misused, spontaneous prayers or prewritten prayers, but the misuse of something does not negate the truth or original benefit of it. It is not the fault of prewritten prayers that they can and have been misused.

Use of the Book of Common Prayer

The general purpose of this section is not an exhaustive defense of the Anglican Church's use of the Book of Common Prayer. The main reason is to provide a short introduction to non-Anglicans and a refresher for cradle Anglicans.

One of the most striking elements of the Book of Common Prayer is its connection with the ancient Church and her liturgies. When one begins to assess the merits of using a prayer book *per se* and the Book of Common Prayer in particular, one finds a deep, reverent identification with the ancient primitive Church. The liturgies of St. James, St. Mark, St. Ignatius, St. Hipploytus, St. Clement, and St. John Chrysostom and the sacramentaries and the brevaries used in the ancient primitive Church all point to the roots of our Book of Common Prayer.

This dependence upon those ancient documents gives us a comfort that we are not only connected with the ancient Church but worshiping in essentially the same fashion she did: the way the primitive Church was taught to worship by the disciples of the apostles, the apostles themselves, and the way they understood how Our Lord and Savior wanted them to worship. Except for the Roman Church and the Greek Orthodox Church, no other body in Christianity can claim such a rich historical and liturgical connection.

I. Historical Context[30]

A: *The Jewish Church*

The very first common form of devotion that we find in the Bible is a hymn composed by Moses to celebrate the deliverance of the Israelites out of Egypt, and it is worth noting that this hymn was to be sung responsively by the men and women. Precomposed forms of prayer will be found in Deuteronomy. 21: 7–8; Numbers 6:22; 10:35–36; and Deuteronomy 26:3–15. Many of the psalms, as appears both from their titles and their internal structure, were intended for the common use of the temple congregations. See Psalm 4; 5; 6; 42; 44; 92. The Jews had not only fixed forms but also a fixed order in their public worship, both in the temple and in their synagogues: the temple worship consisting of prayers, psalms, lections from holy scripture, sacrifices, and incense and the synagogue worship of prayers, psalms, lections, and exhortations only (Lk 4:16; Acts 13:15).

B: *Our Lord's Example[31]*

We have abundant evidence that our Lord took part in the services of the Jewish Church, whether celebrated in the temple or the synagogue. These services, as we have seen, were conducted according to precomposed forms. The Lord Jesus even complied with traditions and ceremonies not prescribed by the law of Moses but legalized by the Jewish Church at various periods in its history. He was present, for instance, at the Feast of the Dedication (Hanukkah). And again, at the celebration of His last Passover, He complied with established usage in various particulars, such as the dipping of the sop and the singing of a hymn, of which no mention is made in the Pentateuch.

Except for the clause "as we forgive those that trespass

---

30   This section and the section on "Practical Advantages" are taken from Evan Daniel, *The Prayer-Book: Its History, Language, and Contents*. London: Wells Gardner, Darton & Co., 1913: 1–6.

31   Ibid., 2.

against us," every petition in the Lord's Prayer had been found somewhere in the ancient liturgies of the Jews. "Our Father which art in heaven" is in their *Seder Tephilloth*, or form of prayers; "let Thy great Name be sanctified and Thy kingdom reign" in their form called *Kaddish*; "let Thy memory be glorified in heaven above and in earth beneath" once again in their *Seder Tephilloth*; "forgive us our sins" in the sixth of their eighteen daily prayers; "deliver us not into the hand of temptations" and "deliver us from the evil figment" in that and the book *Musar*; "for Thine is the owner and the kingdom for ever and ever" is, saith Drusius, their usual doxology (cp. Matthew 6:9–13 with Luke 11:2., where the word used in Matthew is often used in the Septuagint in places where a fixed form is undoubtedly prescribed [Numbers 6:23; 23:5, 16]).

Moreover, the disciples expressly asked our Lord to teach them to pray "as John also taught his disciples," and there can be little doubt that in doing so, John had simply conformed to the common practice observed by Jewish teachers of giving their disciples a form of prayer from which they were not to depart. That the primitive Church understood our Lord's words as enjoining a permanent, fixed form of prayer is clear from the testimony of Tertullian: for he speaks of it as "the ordinary prayer which is to be said before our other prayers, and upon which, as a foundation, our other prayers are to be built" and tells us that "the use of it was ordained by Christ." Saints Cyprian, Cyril, Chrysostom, Augustine, and many other fathers bear similar testimony.[32]

C: *The Usage of the Primitive Church*[33]

That the apostles used precomposed forms of prayer is clear from the Acts of the Apostles, where we read: "And they continued steadfastly . . . in the breaking of bread and *the prayers*" (Acts 2:42–*pais proseuxais*). We also read how on one occasion the apostles "lifted" their voice to God "with one ac-

---

32 Ibid., 2–3.
33 Ibid., 3.

cord," and the very words used are recorded (Acts 4:24–30). The expression "with one accord" (*homothumadon*)[34] proves conclusively that the prayer was common and, of necessity, either precomposed or communicated to all at the time by the Holy Spirit.

That common forms of devotion were used in the Apostolic Church appears also from the apostle Paul's censure of the Corinthians (I Cor. 14:26) for departing from these common forms.

In an injunction of the apostle Paul to Timothy, bishop of Ephesus, we find unmistakable traces of an orderly system of divine service (I Tim 2:1). We seem to have here an expansion of what are called "the prayers" in Acts 2:42. Similarly we find an enumeration of the various forms of thanksgiving in Ephesians 5:19 and again in Colossians 3:16. Corresponding to this threefold division of forms of praise, we have in our own service selections from the psalter, liturgical hymns like the *Gloria in Excelsis*, and metrical songs.

It seems in the highest degree improbable that the apostles left the churches that they founded without any instructions as to the conduct of public worship of the ministration of the sacraments. Paul expressly enjoins the Corinthians to "keep the ordinances" (traditions—*paradoseis*) as he had delivered them to them (I Cor. 11:2).[35]

To leave apostolic times and come to the age immediately following, Justin Martyr speaks expressly of "common prayer," Origen of "appointed prayers," and Cyprian of "*preces solennes*" (i.e., solemn prayers). Liturgies are still extant that have been used in various parts of Christendom from sub-apostolic times. That ascribed to St. James, which was the Liturgy of Jerusalem, was certainly used in the third century, for Cyril wrote a comment on it early in the fourth century. He would not be likely to

---

34 This word is especially intriguing when considering its etymology. It is a composite word, linking *homo,* meaning "same," and *thumos,* meaning "passionate or passionately," so essentially the apostles lifted up their voices with "the same passion" or "with the same passionate voice."
35 *Op. Cit.,* 3–4.

comment on a book that was not of some standing. We also have the Liturgy of St. Mark, which was used in the Church of Alexandria. St. John Chrysostom's liturgy was used in the Church of Constantinople. St. Basil's was used in the churches of Cappadocia. The Clementine (St. Clement of Rome), the Ethiopian, the Malabar, the Mozarabic all were used in Spain.

It will be observed that these liturgies belong to churches widely separated, and this is strong evidence that the practice of having precomposed forms of prayer must have originated in one common source.

If further evidence must be sought for the antiquity of precomposed prayers, what can be more decisive than the decree of the Council of Laodicea, which provided "that the same Liturgy or form of prayer should be always used, both at the 9th hour and in the evening." This canon was subsequently adopted by the Council of Chalcedon (451 AD) and made obligatory to the whole Church.

II. Scriptural Authority

The Book of Common Prayer[36] is composed of more than 70% direct selections from scripture and the rest allusions to it.[37] This is because God has commanded that worship must be according to how He has revealed it to us in His word (II Timothy 3:16–17).[38]

The Book of Common Prayer, often simply called the Prayer Book, essentially structures the biblical text in a specific order suitable for worship.[39] We then can be confident that the manner in which we worship is acceptable to God because our worship utilizes the very words that He has given us in scripture, modeled upon the very structure He has given us in scripture.[40] God has given us historically, in the nascent

---

36 Specifically, the 1662 and 1928 American editions are referenced. All of the more so-called modern revisions are theologically suspect in one form or another.
37 Refer to Henry Ives Bailey, *The Liturgy Compared with the Bible*. Whitefish, Montana: Kessinger Legacy Reprints, original edition 1835.
38 *Op. Cit.* 1.
39 Ibid., 1.
40 Ibid., 1.

form of temple worship, then in the synagogue, and finally in the early churches, the application of the historical assimilation of that worship.

III.   Worthy Worship[41]

God commands us to "worship in spirit and truth" (John 4:24). We are commanded to approach in holiness (Lev. 11:44) and must be aware of approaching God correctly, not only internally but externally, the way He demands us to (Lev. 19:1–13; Heb. 10:22, Heb. 12:28–29).

God's word is truth (John 17:17). God has spoken with a repeated emphasis that we ignore at our peril. As has been stated, only worship specifically commanded by God, as clearly revealed by Him in scripture, is worthy of Almighty God,[42] as well as constituting a proper understanding of how the Church has worshiped in history. Imaginative dramas, carnival-like celebrations, or afternoon sessions on a grassy hill with folk songs, praise music, and personal testimonies may be offered to God with the best intentions, but they fall far short of that worship that God Himself commands.[43]

IV.   An Orderly Framework

If you noticed in the previous appendix, the example of an Anglican worship service, the Prayer Book presents to us and leads us in a dignified, orderly framework by which the Holy Spirit takes God's word and applies it to the congregation.[44] If one follows closely what is happening during a Prayer Book communion service, we see that God calls us to worship Him. To worship Him properly, biblically, we must both know who He is and what He requires. He requires holiness to approach Him. So we are presented with the written encapsulation of God's holy character, the law or Jesus's summary of the law. Since we are incapable of keeping even one word of the law, we beg God's mercy in the Kyrie

---

41   Sections 2–6 and "Some Objections" (with minor additions by Fr. P. A. F. Castellano) are derived from a pamphlet produced by the Reformed Episcopal Church entitled "Worthy Worship in the Book of Common Prayer." None of the following material is original with me.

42   Ibid., 1.

43   Ibid., 1.

44   Ibid., 2.

Eleison, "Lord have Mercy, Christ have Mercy, Lord have Mercy." It is here where we are led into instructions as to grow in grace and holiness to worthily approach God and the throne of Grace. We hear Cranmer's prayer for God's providence in sanctifying us. Then we are called to listen to and be instructed by the collect (composed prayer for the particular day). God's word is then presented to us in the epistle and gospel. After hearing God's word read to us, we are privileged to recite the Nicene Creed, linking and unifying us with the faithful through all generations on earth and that great cloud of witness in heaven. We then hear God's word preached to us as one additional instructive lesson in grace and sanctification.

After the sermon, we receive the honor to present our offerings, both physical and spiritual. Once again, this connects us with the ancient Church as its members would give out of their abundance to help those who had less, and those who had little gave what they could. This connection is continued by the priest offering a Prayer for the Whole State of Christ's Church, where we offer our voice to God to receive our prayers for our gifts, government officials, clergy, laity, the sick and afflicted, and the faithful departed.[45] Next, as we prepare to receive the grace of Christ in His Body and Blood, we are called to repentance; then with one unified voice we publicly confess our sins to God the Father Almighty, after which He gives us absolution of our sins as we hear these words of forgiveness uttered by the priest. It is not the priest forgiving anyone. He is extending God's forgiveness to those listening.

Once we are absolved of our sins by God, we are further assured of this forgiveness in the Comfortable Words, where we are presented with Jesus's words of comfort and forgiveness directly from scripture. There is then a series of additional prayers preparing us to move into one of the most solemn aspects of the service, the consecration of the bread and wine. We are immersed in the profound mystery of what is about to happen; we pray for the Holy Ghost's continued, direct, and constant ministry to us as He unites us with Christ seated on His throne at the right

---

45   It is important to note at this point that we are not praying for the salvation of the dead or their release from a purgatorial region. It is a prayer of gratitude for their faithfulness in serving Christ, and as living members of the heavenly Kingdom, they will continue more and more (as we know they will be in heaven) in the grace God has for them.

hand of God in the heavenlies. We ask that God's will be done on earth as it is in heaven when we recite the Lord's Prayer. There is then one final reminder of who we are before God and how truly unworthy we are to even be here if not for Jesus's sacrifice for us. We hear the Prayer of Humble Access, where we come before the throne to receive the grace of God in the Body and Blood of Christ. We partake of the bread and wine, not as if they have become the physical body and blood of Jesus but as the means whereby the Holy Ghost (who dwells in the Church and is never separated from the Head of the Church, Christ), via the means of the bread and wine, unites us to the whole Christ, human and divine, who is in heaven.

Then, having our hearts filled with joy at the great mystery presented to us in and by the Triune Godhead, Father, Son, and Spirit, we desire to praise God with psalms and hymns in a spirit of wonder and gratitude. There is a prayer of exuberant praise and thanksgiving, and finally the entire congregation stands in a shout of acclamation to sing to the glory of God for all He has done for us, for all we have experienced in our service, and we sing the *Gloria in Excelsis*. From here, we are dismissed with the ancient benediction to go out into the world and be priests and prophets, proclaiming the truth of God's word and work to a fallen world.

V.   An Accurate Picture of God

In that the entire Book of Common Prayer employs scripture, we are not only presented but confronted with a most accurate and complete picture of the full character of God as He has revealed Himself through the scriptures.[46] God is Triune, Father, Son, and Holy Spirit, inseparably One, eternal, holy, and sovereign.[47] Our worship must declare His perfect nature as revealed to us in His word; our worship must declare by our practice that this is who our God is and how He is to be approached; our worship must be based on His objective revelation and not our personal, subjective feelings, desires, or so-called felt needs. The heart will follow what the mind presents to it. "The Prayer Book also depicts us as we truly are, unworthy sinners in need of forgiveness and

---

46   Ibid., 2.
47   Ibid., 2.

grace. We do not address God in casual or familiar terms, for we are not His equal in Holiness."[48]

VI.   Objective, Thoughtful Participation[49]

The Book of Common Prayer fosters the objective engagement of mind and the interaction of every member of the congregation without discrimination. The focus is not on our subjective feelings but on God's objective word that comprises the Book of Common Prayer. It matters not how old one is, one's background, how long one has been a Christian, and so forth. All participate intelligently regardless of age, background, or spiritual maturity. The service is responsive and corporate and involves everyone present. One does not attend a prayer book service and allow the clergy to do everything. All collectively respond, sing, or pray at various points in the service.

The fact that the worship is common to all means that there are no individual, personal prayers of which no one is aware and incapable of giving their "amen." The prayers are common for all believers, to be shared.[50] There is, then, less influence of the personal, subjective viewpoints or biases of the minister. God's revelation remains central.[51]

VII.   Practical Advantages[52]

Written or precomposed prayers that are established as permanent forms of prayer are a crucial condition of common prayer; how else would we be able to join with one accord in presenting our supplications before the throne of God, especially if we have to pause to hear every word coming out of the minister's mouth because we have no idea what he's going to say? If we do not know prior to his utterance, how can we ever, in good conscience and firm confidence, say "amen"? Many often forget that to say "amen" is to assert that we are agreeing with what

---

48   Ibid., 2.
49   Ibid., 3.
50   Ibid., 3.
51   Ibid., 3.
52   Ibid., 3–4. This section is taken directly from Evan Daniels.

was just prayed or said. How can we say "amen" or "so be it" or "let it be so" if we do not know what is going to be said beforehand? It becomes a risky proposition, to be in the house of God, praying before the throne of God, and say "amen" to something that might be a problem. To have fixed prayers allows us, with full knowledge, confidence, and heartfelt conviction, to say "amen." There is also a certain superiority, too, for worshipers, lifting up their prayers, not to rely on the memory, or ease of presentation, or individual quirks, or personal attitude of the minister who conducts the service.[53] Regardless of the exemplary Christian character the minister might have, no matter his level of spiritual devotion and holiness, there is always the possibility he might fail to mention numerous things that are critical and should never be left out in common prayer.[54] He might overemphasize a particular doctrine due to having an axe to grind or inordinately focus on personal pet issues, or even, especially in today's climate, concentrate on visceral and provocative political topics that are in themselves fleeting and already a matter of excessive focus of the congregation and miss the centrality of the gospel message presented in the Book of Common Prayer.[55] There might be tiresome repetition as well.[56] Additionally, he might separate prayer from principal doctrines of redemption, forgiveness, mercy, and holiness, doctrines upon which prayer rests.[57] There is the danger of personal wrongs or slights subtly inserted into his prayers, which are totally inappropriate for common worship.[58] Finally, when exercising extemporaneous, unscripted prayer, the minister might pause and lose his place or get confused, causing the congregation to be distracted and have their concentration wander in the middle of their devotions.[59]

Alternatively, the employment of precomposed prayers as used in the Anglican Church frees the congregation from all the above concerns and ensures they are unimpeded by the minister as they offer

---

53   Ibid., 4–5.
54   Ibid., 5.
55   Ibid., 5.
56   Ibid., 5.
57   Ibid., 5.
58   Ibid., 5.
59   Ibid., 5.

their petitions to God.[60] For, whatever issues the minister himself might have, the security of having prayer written down and in front of them in the Book of Common Prayer guarantees the ability to, in an unfettered manner, offer their "amen" without hesitation because they can read what is being requested of God.[61] They can then attach their total, knowledgeable devotion to said prayer. What a joy to be able to read prayers written via the benefit of centuries of the Church's wisdom, holiness, piety, devotion, and theological reflection.[62] Not the product of one mind but many great minds over the centuries. Plus, they get to join with the voice of the Church throughout history participating in the prayers of the one universal body of Christ. Spontaneous, off-the-cuff prayers are no competition for such Christian piety.[63]

Evan Daniels offers an excellent summation of the practical advantages of using the Book of Common Prayer. I end this section with his words:

> That prayers often repeated are liable to be mechanically repeated is perfectly true; but the framers of the Prayer-Book met this tendency with great wisdom, by making the service responsive, by constantly blending prayer and praise, and by frequently varying the attitude of the worshipper. People may indeed, listen more intently to the novelties of extemporaneous prayer than to prayers with which they have been familiar from infancy; but to listen is not necessarily to pray! They who have no consciousness of spiritual needs will not necessarily acquire that consciousness by listening to prayers of another person. Surely it is better to trust to the power of a well-ordered variety of fixed forms to sustain attention than to the capricious novelties of extemporized prayer. Attention is dearly bought when

---

60   Ibid., 5.
61   Ibid., 5
62   Ibid., 5.
63   Ibid., 5.

it is purchased, as it often is in extemporaneous prayer, at the expense of order, proportion, coherency and pertinence.[64]

In concluding this chapter, it is important to address, a bit more generally, the various objections to the use of the (or a) Book of Common Prayer. Though there might be some overlap or repetition from previous chapters, I think it will be helpful to marshal, as it were, responses to the most prevalent criticisms as a list. Again, with some minor additions on my part, all of these are found in *Worthy Worship in the Book of Common Prayer*, published by the Reformed Episcopal Church.[65]

VIII. Some Objections

- *"It is mechanical, vain repetition."*

Not all repetition is vain.

As young children, we learn language, the alphabet, mathematical equations, and our family's values by repetition. We learn courtesy, "please," "thank you," "I'm sorry," by repeating these over and over. So, too, by repeating scripture in prayers and creeds, we learn the language and values of our spiritual family. The teaching value of repetition is apparent in scripture (e.g., Ps. 118 and 136 remind us over and over that God's mercy endures forever). We are told that knowledge comes through repetition (Is. 28:9–10).

- *"Why have these special seasons such as Advent, Epiphany, and so on?"*

---

64 Ibid., 6.

65 Unfortunately, it seems that this work is no longer published by the Reformed Episcopal Church in this format. It is, however, available for download for free off the internet in two versions. Here is the one used in this work: http://www.trecus.net/downloads/Worthy-Worship.pdf. And here is the newer version: https://static1.squarespace.com/static/57646b-c515d5db3461521573/t/58092636b3db2b7e782a6b63/1476994615433/worship_in_rec.pdf. Both are brief and useful with slightly different emphases. I leave it up to the reader to choose.

This is not a violation of Colossians.

These seasons remind us of all that Christ has done for us. Thus, we fix our attention on the major events in the life of Christ and essential doctrines of our Christian faith.

In addition, what is called the liturgical calendar teaches us that all of creation, every moment of our existence, is dependent upon God, set within the boundaries of His universe. We see that this understanding of God's absolute sovereignty was impressed upon the Nation of Israel with her various feasts, festivals, and even the sacrificial system (i.e., Yom Kippur was celebrated on a special, particular day only once a year). The early Church, from her Jewish roots, continued the practice, simply applying New Covenant Christology into the meaning of the days and seasons while adding unique days (unique to the Christian expression of the Church) that highlight the life and ministry of our Lord.

Therefore, our focus should be on what Jesus has done for us and that His life is also set in the context of what God has created for us. We live our lives in sacred time and sacred space, not only in church but everywhere.

- *"Precomposed prayers are just not as sincere as spontaneous prayers."*

This is blatantly false.

We unite in precomposed hymns for praise and adoration without feeling insincere. In fact, just the opposite is the case; many of us have favorite hymns that express our thoughts better than we could ourselves. They evoke strong emotions even though we hear them frequently and know them by heart. Can't the same be said for spoken prayers of confession, petition, and/or adoration? Scripture, again and again, gives us examples (i.e., Ps. 51 and David's cry to God for confession and plea for mercy). And Jesus Himself gave us the Lord's Prayer. They also allow us to voice our "amen" without reservations and concern for the subjectivism or doctrinal error of the individual praying.

For, if I hear another pray and know not beforehand what he will say, I must first listen to what he will say next; then I am to consider whether what he saith be agreeable to sound doctrine, and whether it be proper and lawful for me to join with him in the petitions he put up to God Almighty: and if I think it is so, then I am to do it. But before I can well do that, he is got to another thing; by which it is very difficult, if not impossible, to join with him in everything so regularly as I ought to do. But by a set form of prayer all this trouble is prevented; for having the form continually in my mind, being thoroughly acquainted with it, fully approving of everything in it, and always knowing beforehand what will come next, I have nothing else to do, whilst the words are sounding in mine ears, but to move my heart and affections suitably to them, to raise up my desires of those good things which are prayed for, to fix my mind wholly upon God whilst I am praising Him, and so to employ, quicken, and lift up my soul in performing my devotions to Him. (William Beveridge)

These words were written four hundred years ago! They could have been written yesterday. The difficulty is that most Christians do not even pay attention to what is being prayed by the minister; they just blindly contribute their "amen." They probably do not even know what their amen is doing.

- *"Fixed forms of prayers cramp or inhibit genuine devotion."*

This is similar to the above complaint.

If the Prayer Book were intended to supersede all spontaneous utterance of the soul's needs, then it might be reasonably charged with cramping devotion, for no book can meet all our spiritual necessities. But it is not so intended. It is a manual of public prayer, and considered from that point of view, its fixed order and fixed language are helps, not hindrances. In our closets and by our family hearths, we may, if we so desire, pour forth our hearts freely in the language that our hearts suggest, but even there our devotions will often be assisted by the use of precomposed forms. Our minds will be kept from wandering by the words before us, which keeps our true, real, deepest heartfelt needs foremost in our thoughts, protecting us from losing sight of them in the urgency of the need of the moment.

It is an exaggeration to say that our Prayer Book does meet particular exigencies, for not only are all its prayers large in expression and wisely comprehensive in structure, but in the litany, the collects, and Prayers upon Several Occasions will be found special petitions suitable for almost every conceivable occasion calling for common prayer.

Common prayer does not exclude simultaneous individual prayer, and every thoughtful worshiper will mentally refer the general petitions of the liturgy to the particular needs, whether public or private, that are uppermost in his or her mind.

All of this moves us into a complete worship experience, mind, body, and heart, which we now share with, in common with, each and every member of the congregation (and the entire Church militant and triumphant: past, present, and future) without losing our individual participation and involvement in said worship or devotion. What could be more glorious to the soul and faith of any believer than to worship in the manner in which the historic Church has always worshiped, to worship according to the same pattern as the Lord Jesus worshiped?

I think, in conclusion, it is more than appropriate to end with a collect from the Book of Common Prayer:

> Almighty God, who pours out on all who desire it the spirit of grace and of supplication: Deliver us, when we draw near to you, from coldness of heart and wanderings of mind, that with steadfast thoughts and kindled affections we may worship you in spirit and in truth; through Jesus Christ our Lord. *Amen.*

Printed in the USA
CPSIA information can be obtained
at www.ICGtesting.com
LVHW040232271123
765001LV00008B/73